The Art of Reciting the Qurʾan

T0323967

Modern Middle East Series, No. 11
Sponsored by the Center for Middle Eastern Studies
The University of Texas at Austin

KRISTINA NELSON

The Art of Reciting the Qurʾan

UNIVERSITY OF TEXAS PRESS AUSTIN

Copyright © 1985 by the University of Texas Press
All rights reserved

First Edition, 1985

Requests for permission to reproduce material from this work should be sent to Permissions, University of Texas Press, Box 7819, Austin, Texas 78713.

This publication has been supported by the National Endowment for the Humanities, a federal agency which supports study of such fields as history, philosophy, literature, and languages.

Library of Congress Cataloging in Publication Data
Nelson, Kristina, 1945–
The art of reciting the Qur'an.
(Modern Middle East series ; no. 11)
Bibliography: p.
Includes index.
1. Koran—Recitation. I. Title. II. Series: Modern Middle East series (Austin, Tex.) ; no. 11.
BP131.6.N44 1985 297'.122 84-17383

ISBN 978-1-4773-0620-8

www.utpress.utexas.edu/index.php/rp-form

First University of Texas Press paperback printing, 2015

Contents

Transcription Tables

Several conventions are applied: 1. omission of the word-initial glottal stop (e.g., *al-ṣawt* for *ʾal-ṣawt*, *Abū* for *ʾAbū*) except in the context of recited Qurʾanic Arabic; 2. indication of the elision of the glottal stop of the definite article (e.g., *fī l-bayt* for *fī al-bayt*); 3. in titles, proper names, and uncontextualized phrases the definite article is transcribed *al* (e.g., *ṣifāt al-ḥuruf* for *ṣifātu l-ḥurūf* and Labīb al-Saʿīd for Labību l-Saʿīd; 4. the *tāʾ marbūṭah* (at) in construct is transcribed *at*: otherwise it is transcribed *ah* (e.g., *sūrat al-Baqarah* for *sūrah al-Baqarah, al-majallah al-mūsīqiyyah* for *al-majallatu l-mūsīqiyyah*); 5. in spoken Egyptian Arabic the *ah* of the *tāʾ marbūṭah* is transcribed *a* (e.g., *naġama* for *naġamah*).

Words that have a certain frequency in English (Qurʾan, Ramadan, al-Azhar, Mohammad) are not given diacritics except in the context of quotations transcribed from Arabic. Further, the names of Arab authors published in Western languages are spelled as they appear in their respective publications.

Table 1 applies to all literary references and to proper names. Tables 1 and 2 reflect the sound of recited Qurʾanic Arabic. Tables 1 and 3 reflect spoken Egyptian Arabic. The transcription of interviews and comments often reflects the speaker's mixing of literary and colloquial pronunciations. Also, transcriptions of both recited Qurʾanic Arabic and spoken Egyptian Arabic show the elision of the /l/ of the definite article (e.g., *aṣ-ṣawt* and *iṣ-ṣōt*, respectively).

Table 1. Transliteration of Literary References and Proper Names

ʾ	ء	z	ز	q	ق	i	ـِ
b	ب	s	س	k	ك	u	ـُ
t	ت	š	ش	l	ل	ā	ـَا
ṯ	ث	ṣ	ص	m	م	ī	ـِي
j	ج	ḍ	ض	n	ن	ū	ـُو
ḥ	ح	ṭ	ط	h	ه	ay	ـَي
x	خ	ḏ̣	ظ	w	و	aw	ـَو
d	د	ʿ	ع	y	ى	ʾā	آ
ḏ	ذ	ġ	غ	ah/at	ة		
r	ر	f	ف	a	ـَ		

Table 2. Transliteration of Recited Qurʾanic Arabic

Table 1 plus the following:

ṛ	single tap /r/, unrolled /r/	̃	nasalization (*ghunnah*)
ž	voiced, dorso-alveolar spirant	ə	schwa
ạ	low, back, slightly rounded vowel	( )	partial assimilation
ḷ	pharyngealized /l/		
ē	medium high, medium front vowel		

Table 3. Transliteration of Spoken Egyptian Arabic

Table 1 plus the following:

ē	medium high, medium front vowel
ō	middle, moderately rounded, back vowel
g	voiced palative stop
ẓ	pharyngealized /z/
ḷ	pharyngealized /l/

Acknowledgments

This book is based on my dissertation at the University of California at Berkeley. I conceived the desire and intent to study the recitation of the Qurʾan some years ago, and I am extremely grateful to everyone in Berkeley and in Egypt who helped me to actualize the project. In particular, I thank Professor Mounah Khouri, who started me on the path of Arabic studies. I am also indebted to Professor Bonnie Wade for opening to me the new scholarly vistas of ethnomusicology and the social sciences in general and for helping me to form and sharpen the concept of this dissertation into a viable piece of research.

The research could never have been accomplished without the generous financial support of the Social Science Research Council and the HEW Office of Education Fulbright-Hays Research Abroad Program and the letters of encouragement and support I received from their administrators.

In Egypt the list is long: everyone I met in the course of my research was extremely helpful and generous with time, information, and hospitality. I would particularly like to thank the professional reciters I interviewed (who are listed by name in Appendix A). They are all prominent and busy men who, without exception, were gracious and generous in sharing their knowledge, experience, talent, and enthusiasm, inviting me into their homes and to their performances.

The administrators and staff of the religious radio station Iḏāʿat al-Qurʾān al-Karīm also showed great interest in the research: not only were they helpful and cooperative in interviews and requests for information on schedules, performances, and the like, but they often anticipated my requests, initiating some introductions and facilitating my attending some otherwise inaccessible performances. My great thanks to the director, Dr. Kāmil al-Būhī; the general secretary, Šayx ʿAbd al-Hāfiḍ; Mr. Aḥmad of the technical staff; Mr. ʿAbd al-Xālia ʿAbd al-Wahhāb; and Mr. ʿAbd al-Badīʿ al-Qamḥāwī.

I would like to thank the members of the Lajnat al-Qurrāʾ for allowing me to sit in on their sessions, for their patience in answering my questions, and for their general guidance in directing me to bibliographic sources and to research contexts I might otherwise have missed. I thank the late Šayx Saʿīd al-Saḥḥār (d. 1983) for introducing me to Šayx ʿAbd al-Fattāḥ al-Qāḍī, and to the activities of the Administration of Qurʾanic Affairs, where he was serving as a judge for the children's Qurʾan competition and the Friday prayer auditions. I thank Šayx Muḥammad Mursī ʿĀmir for his generous help in obtaining bibliographic material, including his gift of a recently published text, and for his interest and hospitality. I thank Šayx Rizq Ḥabbah and Šayx ʿAfīfī l-Sākit for their interest and helpful comments. I am grateful to Dr. Maḥmūd Kāmil, professor of music and author, for sharing his expertise with me and for introducing me to activities in the musical world of Cairo. I thank Mr. Aḥmad Ṣidqī, prominent composer, for his interest and support.

I am particularly grateful to engineer Maḥmūd Muṣṭafā for welcoming me to his weekly listening session and introducing me to valuable contacts, and for his generous donation of his collection of the recorded performances of Šayx Kāmil Yūsuf al-Bahtīmī, Šayx Muḥammad Ṣiddīq al-Minšāwī, and Šayx Muḥammad Salāmah to the University of California library. Over a period of several weeks Mr. Maḥmūd spent all of his free time copying the tapes with the help of his colleague, Mr. Ḥasan Šarārah. Both Mr. Maḥmūd and Mr. Ḥasan were generous in sharing their information and time with me, escorting me to performances, and answering my queries with patience, good humor, and enthusiasm. I thank them both.

I thank Ḥājj Ḥusayn Faraj, the hospitable host of another listening session, and patron of reciters, for opening his home to me and including me in the recitation activities he sponsored. I am very appreciative of his gift of recordings from his collection. I am particularly grateful for the faithful correspondence of Ḥājj Ḥusayn and his colleague, Mr. ʿAbd al-ʿAzīz ʿAlī ʿAbd al-Laṭīf, in the seven years since I left Egypt. I thank them for their continued interest and their efforts to keep me up to date with news of particular interest to this research.

I thank all of the participants of these two listening sessions for their interest and comments.

I am indebted to Dr. Maḥmūd Ġurāb, pharmacist, patron and friend of a great number of Egypt's professional reciters, and tutor to many of their children. Dr. Maḥmūd introduced me to many of these reciters and took me to many performances, freely sharing his comprehensive knowledge with me, and communicating it with an irresistible enthusiasm.

I am grateful to my teachers: I thank Šayx ʿĀmir al-Saʿīd ʿUṯmān for allowing me to participate in the recitation class and for his demanding and challenging guidance of my efforts to master the rules of recitation. I thank Šayx ʿAbd al-Mutaʿāl Manṣūr ʿArafah for his skilled and patient teaching. My study with him was, perhaps, the key which unlocked this dissertation, and his support and vigilance over my progress was, and continues to be, invaluable. I thank Mr. Mansī Amīn Fahmī for helping me to understand the musical aspects of recitation and to appreciate the skill and talent of the reciters. His lessons were always a delight.

I thank the administrative staff of the Institute of Qirāʾāt for their active interest in the project.

I am grateful to Mr. Aḥmad Muṣṭafā Kāmil for sharing with me his time, his insights, and his comprehensive collection of the recordings of Šayx Muṣṭafā Ismāʿīl. I thank Mr. Ḥusayn Rifʿat for sharing with me memories and private recordings of his father, Šayx Muḥammad Rifʿat.

I thank Mr. Muḥsin al-Širbīnī, director of the Office of Administration of Qurʾanic Affairs (in the Ministry of Religious Endowments) for all his help. I thank Šayx ʿAbd al-Fattāḥ al-Qāḍī for his interest and for sharing with me the benefits of his scholarship. I am appreciative of the help given me by Dr. Hamāsah, professor at the American University in Cairo and Dār al-ʿUlūm, who introduced me to Šayx Maḥmūd al-Ṭablāwī. I thank Mr. Suleiman Gamil, Egyptian music critic and composer, presently the cultural attaché at the Egyptian Embassy in Brussels, for sharing with me his insights and expertise. I thank Dr. Ḥasan al-Šāfiʿī, scholar and teacher at Dār al-ʿUlūm, for his support, comments, and careful consideration of my material. I also thank Dr. Saʿīd al-Maṣrī for sharing his knowledge with me and for making his extensive collection of recordings of Egyptian music and recitation available to me. I thank Mme. Bruxanne Aḥmad Amīn for her cooperation in letting me copy material from the library of the Egyptian Puppet Theater. I also owe thanks to the personnel of the audio-visual department of the American University in Cairo for allowing me to use the tape-copying service.

My special thanks to those who helped turn the dissertation into the book. I value the experience and unflagging encouragement of my editor, Daniel Goodwin, and the support and advice of Richard Martin and Ira Lapidus. For help on linguistic terminology, I thank John McCarthy and Anthony Woodbury. I am especially grateful for the careful reading and insights of Humphrey Davies, Pamela Swing, and Tom Turino.

Finally, to all those, too numerous to name or single out, who offered their help, opinions, and insights with sincere interest and warm support, I offer my grateful appreciation.

Introduction

Night falls as small groups of people make their way toward a large tent straddling a Cairo street. As they draw near, a clear ribbon of sound begins to separate itself from the dense fabric of street noise all around. The sound is that of the recited Qur'an; a public performance has begun.

At the tent's entrance, the men of the host family greet arriving guests. Inside, bright globe lights illuminate rows of high-backed gilt chairs and colored arabesques on the tent walls. Members of the audience are dressed variously in Western business suits, shirt sleeves, or traditional robes, and the waiters pass among them, carrying trays with small glasses of tea and coffee. There are no women visible.

The emotion of the crowd is diffused—here and there small groups chat quietly; other conversations are animated with extravagant gestures; some people silently sip tea, while others are concentrating on the reciter seated alone in a raised chair against a far wall. He recites with his eyes closed, one hand tensely shaping the sound. This reciter is unknown to most of the crowd—the reciter they have come to hear will appear later in the evening. But as he begins a high passage he catches their attention. Suddenly the power of the phrase seizes the scattered sensibility of the crowd, focusing it, and carrying it forward like a great wave, setting the listeners down gently after one phrase and lifting them up in the rising of the next. The recitation proceeds, the intensity grows. A man hides his face in his hands, another weeps quietly. Some listeners tense themselves as if in pain, while, in the pauses between phrases, other shout appreciative responses to the reciter. Time passes unnoticed . . .

The public recitation of the Qur'an is a familiar event in Egyptian daily life; the performance just described is only one of many contexts in which it occurs. The prominence of Qur'anic recitation can be explained by the importance of the Qur'an to Islamic society: according to Muslim belief, the Qur'an is the word of God as it was revealed in Arabic, and this revelation is the central reality in the life of Islamic society. As the divine articulation of God's plan for humanity, it serves both as the generator of Islamic civilization and as its highest authority—on the one hand, the primary source of law, on the other, the attributed, if not actual, referent of custom.

The recitation of the Qur'an is not unique to Egypt: it is significant in any Islamic context. But the characteristically Egyptian tradition of Qur'anic recitation enjoys unequaled popularity, prestige, and authority throughout the Muslim world. Such is its status that the Egyptian style is generally considered to be the model of Qur'anic recitation. Not only do reciters from other traditions come to Egypt to master the style of a favorite reciter, but during Ramadān, the month of fasting, Egypt exports its most prominent reciters all over the world as well, at the invitation of Muslim communities.

The transmission of the Qur'an and its social existence are essentially oral. Qur'anic rhythm and assonance alone confirm that it is meant to be heard. But the oral nature of the Qur'an goes beyond euphony: the significance of the revelation is carried as much by the sound as by its semantic information. In other words, the Qur'an is not the Qur'an unless it is heard. The familiar sound of recitation is the Muslim's predominant and most immediate means of contact with the word of God. The first formal Qur'an learning for young boys and girls is oral, and even when they have acquired knowledge of the written text and read from it in private, they usually read aloud. For many Muslims, recitation remains their only access to the Qur'an.

To the casual listener the most accessible sound of the Qur'anic recitation is the elaborately melodic style variously classified by those outside the tradition as a form of "religious" or "Islamic" music. However, Muslim religious authority insists that, by definition, the tradition of Qur'anic recitation must be kept distinct from music, and, indeed, Muslim perception of the melodic recitation of the Qur'an makes it a unique phenomenon.

This perception is based on the divine nature of the text. The parameters of rhythm, timbre, and phonetics are all perceived as having a divine source and organization in that they preserve the sound of the revelation as it was transmitted to the Prophet Muhammad. Moreover, the divine identity of the text gives it an inherent perfection and makes of it a model of beauty, while imbuing it with an authority and prestige that distinguish it from music. To label Qurʾanic recitation as music undermines the perfection and uniqueness of the text, trivializing its effect on listeners and reducing it to the status of entertainment. The Islamic tradition itself classifies religious and secular music as one art and Qurʾanic recitation as another, separate art. This classification is supported by the ramifications of the *samāʿ* polemic, a centuries-old debate concerning both the appropriateness of associating music with the Qurʾan and the appropriateness of music per se in the Islamic community.

Specific guidelines maintain an actual separation between the art of recitation and the art of music in terms of intent of performance, priority of text, and the characteristic and unique way in which musical material is used. These guidelines are articulated in scholarly discussions of the ideal recitation. It is in reference to this ideal that we confront the Islamic belief that, in sharp contrast to Western assumptions, melody and vocal artistry do not necessarily involve music.

However, listener response to a melodic recitation may not correlate with theoretical perception of it as a unique art, separate from music. This circumstance is most visible in listener behavior and media treatment of professional reciters. Several factors are responsible. First, the melodic recitation shares a number of aspects with music in addition to pitch organization, such as ornamentation, a body of descriptive terminology, emotional and physical responses, and aesthetic and economic standards. Second, although the ideal recitation may not be called music, a certain musicality, such as use of melody and vocal artistry, is not only accepted but required to fulfill the intent of the ideal. This requirement is based on the recognition of the power of music in general to engage the emotions and thus involve the listener more totally in the recitation.

The traditional classification of recitation that distinguishes it from music thus results in an apparent contradiction between the theoretical understanding of recitation as a unique art and the response to it as music. Or, more accurately, a dual perception allows for this contradiction. The creative tension between perception and response is central to the modern Cairene tradition and shapes every aspect of it—from the characteristic sound of the recitation, its contexts, and its performance practice conventions to the behavior and attitudes of its patrons and listeners. In other words, this tradition derives its characteristic identity from the interaction of the perception of the divine nature of the Qurʾan with the popularity of the melodic style, and from the resulting scholarly discussion. It is not a simple dichotomy of perception versus response, or model versus practice, for each part affects, and is in turn affected by, the other.

Accordingly, a primary aim of this study is to examine the implications of a particular perception within its tradition: given that recitation is the product of both divine and human ordering, how does this juxtaposition work in the mind of the performer and in the expectations of the listeners to shape the recitation of the Qurʾan in Egypt today?

In other words, this study is ultimately concerned with meaning: What does the recitation of the Qurʾan mean within the tradition? How is meaning communicated? How has it come to mean what it does? What is the effect of the meaning on the tradition? Given the multiplicity of approaches and levels of analysis required of a study of meaning, I cannot hope to answer all of these questions comprehensively; however, by examining Qurʾanic recitation as a phenomenon of behavior, and as a phenomenon of organized sound informing and informed by the perceptions of its listeners and performers, I hope to point the way to an understanding of Qurʾanic recitation as an expression of the totality of the cultural system of which it is a part.

The centrality of the Qurʾan in the Islamic community is unquestioned, yet scholars have tended to ignore the dynamics of its most obvious manifestation: recitation. Muslim scholars have not studied recitation as melodic sound or as human behavior or as any sort of dynamic event because the study of recitation as melodic sound risks a violation of the perception which makes it unique and separate from music. Except for pitch, all aspects of recitation may be discussed in terms consistent with its divine nature. As pitch is not regulated by religious authority, it would have to be discussed in terms of theoretical and practical music (*mūsīqā* and *ġinā'*). These carry connotations unacceptable to religious subjects and have traditionally been excluded from Qur'anic scholarship in spite of the reality of the melodic practice. The study of recitation as human behavior also risks violating the divine nature of recitation, because such a study would associate the Qur'an with the human-centered disciplines of anthropology, sociology, and folklore, and thus might color what is considered fixed and immutable with the transience of the human condition. Moreover, as the scope of the Qur'anic disciplines has been firmly and authoritatively established and that body of knowledge has traditionally been considered fixed and given,[1] there has been a reluctance to look at the Qur'an in new ways.

That this prejudice against nontraditional study can be overcome is demonstrated in recent works such as Dr. Labīb al-Saʿīd's *Al-Taġannī bi-l-Qur'ān* (1970), which not only treats the well-documented polemic over the acceptability of melodic recitation, but describes something of actual practice. Further evidence is the enthusiastic response and the cooperation I received from Egyptian religious scholars in the course of my research for this book.

Muslim studies of recitation (and of the Qur'an in general, since the text is essentially indivisible from its oral rendering) focus primarily on the three disciplines of *tajwīd*, *qirā'āt*, and *tafsīr*, and secondarily on Arabic grammar, rhetoric, and orthography. *Tajwīd* is the system which codifies the divine language and accent of Qur'anic recitation in terms of rhythm, timbre, sectioning of the text, and phonetics. It is the very basis and identifying mark of the recited Qur'an. *Qirā'āt* characterizes the different text-systems in use and codifies the variant applications of the rules of *tajwīd*. *Tafsīr* is concerned with the meanings of the text, that is, exegesis. Essentially a scholarly pursuit, *tafsīr* is based on the written text of the Qur'an, supplemented by generations of interpretive texts, rather than on the actual sound of recitation. However, the importance of *tafsīr* to recitation is obvious: the reciter's understanding of the text affects the style and structuring of the recitation. More importantly, however, the clearer and more sensitive the reciter's understanding of the text, the more skillful the evocation of its meanings in the hearts of the listeners.

Tajwīd and *qirā'āt*, both essentially oral in their transmission, are central to Qur'anic studies in Egypt. The numerous texts dealing with *tajwīd* are manuals intended to supplement oral transmission of the material and differ from each other only in format. *Qirā'āt*, like *tafsīr*, exists as a field of study independent of actual performance practice. For example, the majority of doctoral dissertations on *qirā'āt* are concerned with demonstrating the absolute unity of the text (which the phonemic and, especially, the morphemic variations of the text-systems may call into question). Many professional reciters master the *qirā'āt* and find that their knowledge is rewarded with greater skill and prestige; however, the minimum requirements for a professional reciter are only those demanded of all Muslims: mastery of the rules of *tajwīd* according to the prevailing text-system (in Egypt, *ʿĀṣim* as transmitted by *Ḥafṣ*, *Ḥafṣ ʿan ʿĀṣim*).

I emphasize the significance of *tajwīd* and *qirā'āt* for Qur'anic studies in Egypt because they are largely ignored by Western scholars, except as they apply to the written text of the Qur'an. To most Muslims the Qur'an is equally the written text and its oral rendering, and many have more intimate knowledge of the latter than of the former, whereas to Western Qur'anic scholars the Qur'an has been largely defined by its written tradition. This scholarship has been shaped not only by the prestige of literacy, but by the fact that the Qur'an has been so much more accessible in the West as a written document. Consequently, the emphasis in Western scholarship has been on those aspects of the Qur'an which manifest a written tradition, such as *tafsīr*, *luġah* (philology), *balāġah* (rhetoric), *rasm* (orthography), and so forth.

The classic works of Western Qur'anic scholarship may be summarized as follows: Goldziher reviews the main issues and schools of *tafsīr*. Bergsträsser, Pretzl, and Jeffrey deal variously with the history of the written text and a comprehensive exposition of the classic Islamic textual studies of the Qur'anic disciplines. Blachère and Watt present general introductions to the Qur'an, focusing on the circumstances of revelation, the collection of the written text, and descriptions of its form, style, and content. In the same tradition, the more recent scholars John Wansbrough and John Burton reinterpret the history of the written text, and Gätje updates Goldziher's work on exegesis.

These contributions to Qur'anic scholarship are of monumental and undeniable importance in that they have evaluated this material and made it known and accessible to the wider scholarly community. That some of the assumptions and conclusions of these scholars contribute little to our understanding of the Qur'an as a dynamic force in the lives of believers or even negate Muslim tradition and thus cannot be accepted by their Muslim counterparts is not of concern here. What is significant is that, although the Qur'an has been subjected to Western scholarship in a multitude of its aspects, almost all such studies deal with the written rather than the recited Qur'an.

There are also some musicological studies which approach the Qur'an as a recitation, such as those of Cantineau and Barbès, Bergsträsser, Pacholczyk, and Touma. But these remain within the tradition of the textual studies in that the sound is described as a system of pitches and durations (although Bergsträsser does give some indications of timbre) without reference to the melodic and aesthetic principles of Arabic music, let alone the interlocking of social and cultural patterns which ultimately determines the sound in performance.[2]

Exceptions to this one-dimensional textual or formalistic approach are the recent studies of some scholars in the field of religious studies and anthropology such as Geertz, Eickelman, and Martin. Although none of these scholars deals specifically with Qur'anic recitation, they all share a perspective central to the present study in that they acknowledge that Islam is defined by the dynamics of practice as much as by unchanging precepts, and they look at the Qur'an in contemporary contexts, exploiting both fieldwork and interdisciplinary approaches.[3] So varied are the issues raised when the Qur'an is considered, so many are the points at which it touches Islamic societies, so broad is its significance, that only a multidisciplinary approach will do it justice.

My own interest in Qur'anic recitation was caught and held by the power of the sound itself. I wanted to understand how it worked and to explain its effect. One of my first discoveries, which has remained central to this study, was that while the rules governing pronunciation, timbre, and meter have been carefully delineated, actual melodic practices and reciting conventions remain unregulated and generally even undocumented. This imbalance was my first indication of the fundamental dynamic of perception and response in the Egyptian recitation tradition, a dynamic which has led to the elaboration of a highly developed model of the ideal recitation. The effort required to maintain the separation of recitation and music in the perceptions of both audience and reciter accounts for this model's complex elaboration and for its prominence.

It should be made clear at the outset that the ideal does not exist in a direct relationship to the actual experience of recitation. Like the meaning it expresses, the model is multilayered and constantly shifting in emphasis, with single elements of the sound able to invoke several of its dimensions simultaneously. The approach I have taken here is thus necessarily multidisciplinary, correlating extended scholarly and religious debates with the thought and practice of contemporary exponents of the reciter's art.

What distinguishes this approach from others mentioned above is not only the equal consideration given to the theory and practice of recitation and the analysis of their interactions, but my own direct participation in the tradition as student and performer.

This study falls into two parts—the first examines the ideal and draws primarily on written sources. The first four chapters present material about the Qur'an itself; the rules regulating its correct recitation (*tajwīd*); the issues and implications of the *samā*ʿ polemic; and the terminology and issues which define the ideal recitation according to the meaning of the Qur'an and the nature of its role in the Muslim community. The next three chapters present the current practice of Qur'anic recitation in Egypt through information drawn from fieldwork activities, such as interviews and my own participation/observation. These chapters deal with the ways in which the sound incorporates the ideals and realities of Qur'anic recitation, and the rules regulating its beautiful recitation (aesthetics); how the ideal is maintained in practice; and the dynamics of perception and response so characteristic of the Egyptian tradition. Although each part of the study emphasizes different topics and kinds of source material, the whole is integrated by the constant dialogue and reference between ideal and practice.

Most of the source material for this study comes from a year's fieldwork conducted in Cairo, Egypt (1977–78). Because of the many different kinds of contexts in which the Qur'an is recited, and because of the different roles I fulfilled in the course of my research, I was involved in a variety of activities. In all these roles I was received with enthusiasm and support. I mention this because I am inevitably asked how, as a non-Muslim, non-Egyptian woman, I was able to conduct the research. Being an outsider freed me from the burden of expectations placed on an Egyptian woman, and people were flattered by the extent of my interest and intrigued by the novelty. But primarily, I was accepted on the basis of the sincerity of my intentions toward Qur'anic recitation, my respect for the religious ideals underlying that tradition, and my emotional appreciation of the sound itself. The interest taken in the project was evidenced in how quickly and positively news of it spread by word of mouth and by the media. Media exposure brought me offers of help from all over Egypt.

My choice of Egypt as the place to conduct the research was initially made for three reasons: my knowledge of the language; my three years' experience living and working there; and the fact that my familiarity with the sound of the recited Qur'an came mostly from commercially available recordings, all of them Egyptian. Only later did I become aware of the particular prestige and influence of the Egyptian tradition in Qur'anic recitation, which make it an obvious starting place for one wishing to understand the recitation of the Qur'an.

A number of factors contribute to the unique status of Egyptian recitation. First, Egypt's long-established tradition of religious scholarship, centered at al-Azhar University and its network of affiliated institutes, attracts students from all over the world. Scholars and teachers trained in the Azhari tradition enjoy high status both at home and abroad. This tradition figures prominently in the training of most professional Qur'anic reciters in Egypt. The reciter's access to a prestigious and rigorous training in Qur'anic studies gives him a religious authority beyond the emotional and aesthetic appeal of his art.[4] Second, the image of the Egyptian reciter as artist is enhanced by Egypt's lively musical tradition, which is also well known beyond its borders through films, recordings, broadcasts, and personal appearances of its stars. The unique aspects of the Egyptian recitation tradition include not only the characteristic melodic style, but the high standard of musicality expected of the reciter both by the general public and by the religious establishment.

The extent to which the media are involved in the dissemination and popularization of the tradition is a third factor which defines the characteristic image and status of Egyptian recitation. Egypt's well-developed communication industry has been linked to the recitation tradition since the 1930s, and Egyptian reciters are broadcast all over the Middle East on radio and television. A number of reciters have further expanded their audience and reputation through government, commercial, or private issues of recordings of their reciting. These cassettes and phonograph records are distributed worldwide.

The media thus contribute to another aspect of Egypt's unique tradition of Qur'anic recitation, namely, the professional status of the reciter. Recitation traditions in other countries may be melodic and authoritative, but only in Egypt are male reciters so widely accepted into the social and religious fabric of society as a professional and artistic elite. The Egyptian recitation tradition is known for the personal styles and personalities of individual reciters, and it is the individual reciter's art, as much as the experience of the recited Qur'an, which draws listeners. The reciter is thus responsible not only to the ideal of the larger tradition of Qur'anic recitation but, as a performer, to the immediate expectations of his audience.

Finally, the factor of the *samāʿ* polemic, the ongoing debate concerning the appropriateness of associating the Qur'an with music, assumes a crucial status in Egypt, given the popularity of the elaborately melodic style and the integration of the recitation into the world of music and show business.

The network of people involved in recitation in Cairo is such that I had access to almost every kind of activity touching recitation. In addition to the primary research activities described below, I had meetings with scholars, administrators, and technicians involved in the various aspects of recitation. The Acknowledgments and Appendix A list my primary consultants.

The sound of recitation is by no means restricted to the more obviously religious contexts of human activity, for it also occurs in many situations non-Muslims would label secular. The two basic styles, *murattal* and *mujawwad*, are heard in these contexts, and my research indicates that these styles mark the two basic intents and uses of Qur'anic recitation according to which its contexts may be classified as either public or private.

The contexts with which the *murattal* style is associated tend to be those of a private nature in the sense that the reciter directs his recitation only to God. Thus, *murattal* is generally heard in private devotions, and in the five daily ritual prayers (*ṣalāt*).[5] It is also the teaching style for learning correct recitation in the schools, universities, and approximately 500 public classes (*maqra'ah*) sponsored by the government. In these contexts the transmission and preservation of the oral text is most important, and the sound of *murattal* reflects this intent: emphasis is on clarity of the text, and the limited pitch variation and vocal artistry make for a relaxed and speech-bound style accessible to all.[6]

So essentially private is the nature of *murattal* that it is given little emphasis in the media. Short presentations of *murattal* are heard only on the religious radio station, and these are devotional or pedagogical in intent and effect. There are no commercial recordings in this style. The only *murattal* recording generally available to the consumer is the official government issue, which is intended for the preservation of the oral Qur'an and the establishment of an authoritative pedagogical model.

My own knowledge of the *murattal* style arises from a year of lessons with Šayx ʿAbd al-Mutaʿāl Manṣūr 'Arafah, former dean of the Institute of Qirā'āt in Šubrā (Maʿhad al-Qirā'āt).[7] I studied *tajwīd*, memorization, and exegesis. The lessons followed a standard and traditional procedure: I would recite the verses I had memorized and prepared and Šayx ʿAbd al-Mutaʿāl would comment or correct my recitation. Then he would recite a new text and have me repeat it after him line by line, after which I would read aloud the complete passage. Then he would dictate to me the rules for correct reciting, giving examples from the text in general, and from the passages I had learned. From time to time he would test me, asking me to explain the rules governing the recitation of a particular phrase.

The lessons were time-consuming—three hours, three times a week, but they were the most important part of all my fieldwork activities. Since this learning process is shared by performers and listeners alike, systematic learning within the system was necessary for me to understand and participate in any discussion or evaluation of recitations. The learning process is oral, and I could not have learned the technical terminology without access to oral example. The lessons, and my resulting ability to recite, also allowed me to prove my seriousness as a researcher. In addition, the more I learned and was able to participate actively in recitation, the more I realized that my questions were based on an awareness of aspects that I would otherwise have ignored. My position as a student also facilitated contact with the Institute, and observation of classes, so that I was able to obtain a fairly complete picture of the Institute in regard to its aims, students, and curriculum.

My fieldwork also included a second recitation class, in the *murattal* style, held in the mosque of the Egyptian Petrol Company. The class was open to the public and was attended by children and adults, among them businessmen, clerks, housewives, and students. Lessons followed the traditional format in which each student recites what he or she has prepared for the teacher (in this case Šayx ʿĀmir al-Saʿīd ʿUṯmān), who makes corrections where necessary. The ability and experience of the students ranged from elementary to advanced levels, some of the students preparing recitations of *qirāʾāt* other than the prevailing one. Thus I had the advantage of observing a learning situation not set up especially for my benefit. I was also exposed to the *qirāʾāt* in a fairly detailed and systematic way.

In contrast to the private and devotional nature of the *murattal* style, the *mujawwad* recitation is reserved for public occasions. It is directed to, and largely dependent upon, an audience, for the *mujawwad* reciter seeks to involve the listeners. *Mujawwad* recitation is identified with male professionals who, if not highly trained, are at least highly conscious of the aesthetic effect of their performance. The dramatic use of register and sectioning of the text and a conscious use of vocal artistry and melody heighten the listener's emotional involvement. The use of microphone and loudspeakers to transmit the sound both signals and underlines the more public and performative nature of this style.

I conducted interviews with a number of professional reciters. They were very accessible (even the "superstars"), and subsequent contact with them and the members of their families allowed me to evaluate the material elicited from the first and more structured interview. The reciters, without exception, took great pride in the demands and skills of their calling, and hence they were eager to talk about the nature of their art and training. All of them had thought about, and were able to articulate, both the role of music and the value of their musical training to their profession.

To further my appreciation and understanding of the specific musicality of the *mujawwad* style I had weekly lessons with Mr. Mansī Amīn Fahmī, an Arabic lute (*ʿūd*) player and teacher, and an admirer of the art of Qurʾanic recitation. He has taught reciters the melodic parameters of the art, and he taught me the musical material from which reciters draw. We would listen to recordings together, and he would explain what was happening melodically in the specific performance. I would imitate and memorize parts of recordings, and sing along with him to get the melodic patterns in my ears. Gradually, I learned to sing and recognize the various melodic modes (*maqāmāt*),[8] and to understand and appreciate the effects of modulation and transposition. It was only when I began to try to improvise melodies onto the exacting phonetic and rhythmic systems of *tajwīd* that I realized the difficulty and complexity of the art and could appreciate the artistic challenge that makes the professional reciter a member of a skilled elite. I also began to sense what was musically acceptable in recitation, the general conventions, and elements of personal style.

I classify the many different public contexts in which *mujawwad* is heard as liturgical, rites of passage, ceremonial, media, and nonoccasional.[9] The most widespread liturgical context of recitation in the *mujawwad* style is the communal Friday noon prayer in the mosque (*ṣalāt al-jumʿah*). Half an hour of recitation characteristically precedes this prayer session. The corporateness of the prayer is signaled by the *mujawwad* style of recitation, and by the fact that it is the only one of the ritual prayers which is regularly amplified and transmitted into the surrounding neighborhood, and regularly broadcast over the media as well.

As a component of rites of passage, recitation plays its most prominent role in ceremonies honoring the dead. When a Muslim dies, the family hires the services of a professional reciter. If the family cannot afford the elaborately decorated tent set up to house the reciter and listeners, a microphone and loudspeakers may be hired to project the reciter's voice beyond the room in which he recites into the streets to a wider audience. Where there is a tent, the listeners are made up of friends and members of the family who have come to offer condolences and to honor the memory of the deceased, as well as strangers, generally male, who have come to listen to a favorite performer or to enjoy the sound in general.[10]

Ceremonial contexts can be divided into those linked to religious events and those not so specifically religion-bound. An example of the first is the *mawlid* (celebration of the birth of the Prophet Muhammad, a member of his family, or a popular saint). Another is Ramadan, the month of fasting and a period special to the Qur'an, during which there are many celebrations. Recitations held during these celebrations, whether sponsored publicly or privately, are open to the general public and may be held in tents or mosques. Examples of ceremonial contexts not linked to specific religious observance are the inaugurations of new buildings, schools, and private businesses. Official government functions often begin with Qur'anic recitation as well.

Before discussing the media and nonoccasional contexts, I would like to point out examples that incorporate several contexts and are thus more difficult to classify. Events held to honor an official or distinguished visitor, to celebrate the opening of a mosque or school, or to celebrate the birthday of a venerated, historical religious figure are integrated into the "religious evening gathering," the *sahrah dīniyyah*. In this context the evening prayer ritual is extended with a performance of religious song and Qur'anic recitation.

I attended a number of these performances in each of these contexts (including memorial services, *saharāt dīniyyah*, and the inauguration of an export business) in which I was able to observe the various kinds of interaction between listeners and performers. Due to the size of the crowds, and the intense excitement which large public performances usually generate, I was afforded a certain degree of invisibility in spite of my being the only woman present.

The media context both expands the audience of live performances and initiates its own performances of Qur'anic recitation. The religious radio station, Iḏāʿat al-Qur'ān al-Karīm, in conjunction with two other stations, broadcasts the Friday noon prayer from a different mosque in Egypt each week. The *sahrah dīniyyah* is a frequent part of evening programming. Many of the memorials for prominent Qur'anic reciters are not only broadcast, but sponsored by the media. An example of the way in which the media may be establishing new contexts for recitation is the broadcasting of *mujawwad* recitation preceding the dawn prayer (*ṣalāt al-fajr*) from the mosque of Sayyidunā l-Ḥusayn, a style of recitation otherwise never heard at this time.

All Arabic-language radio stations open and close with recitation in the *mujawwad* style, and many feature regular daily recitation programs which vary in length from five minutes (*murattal* style) to several hours (*mujawwad* style). Ramadan and other religious holidays are observed by the media with specially prepared programs of recitation.

All broadcasts of recitation are screened by an official committee, Lajnat al-Qurrā' (the Reciters' Committee). It also auditions all candidates for employment as radio reciters. Every Sunday I sat in on these audition and evaluation sessions, which last three hours and follow a set procedure. From the discussions I was able to observe how a recitation is classified for evaluation, and I also learned the terminology and aesthetic standards applied officially to Qur'anic recitation in Egypt.

Although the *murattal* and *mujawwad* styles of recitation are available to the public on phonograph records and cassette tapes, the *mujawwad* style is more widely recorded and disseminated. Cassette recorders are very popular in Cairo, and many people who attend the public recitations do so armed with a recorder. In fact, most professional reciters are now accustomed to reciting before a battery of microphones. The tapes from these recitations are passed around, copied, and traded among private collectors.

The final classification of the different public contexts in which *mujawwad* is heard is that which I have termed nonoccasional. This is the *nadwah*, or salon, which is devoted to listening to recitation (live or, more often, recorded). In this context recitation is presented and discussed critically as a unique art in its own right and not as part of a larger event or occasion. The host of a listening session is usually a collector, less often a patron, and once a week he opens his home and shares his collection of taped peformances with aficionados, professional reciters, other collectors, students, or anyone interested in serious listening. I attended two such sessions every week. The others who attended were men who, through their love for recitation, have become extremely knowledgeable, sophisticated critics, either concentrating on the performances of one reciter or giving their attention to the whole range of performances and performers. They all have a deep commitment to the highest standards of recitation and to the preservation of the heritage of this art, and their comments provided me with a more informal and unofficial evaluation of recitation. Although evaluation in this context tends to be more subjective than that of the radio committee, the same guidelines of correct *tajwīd*, melodic inventiveness, and voice quality govern the justification of personal preference. Fiercely defended personal biases on the part of the participants made for lively discussions, and I obtained much material in the form of anecdotes, reminiscences, and the gossiplike information unavailable in other contexts.

The sound of Qur'anic recitation, heard day and night, on the street, in taxis, in shops, in mosques, and in homes, is thus much more than the pervasive background music of daily life in Cairo. It is the core of much of the liturgy, the sanctioning spirit of official and social life. It is also an art in its own right that attracts an audience which is extremely demanding and vocal in its articulation of high standards—an art which fosters a conscious response and active listening on the part of the populace. Recitation draws its support from the whole of Egyptian society, uniting the elite and the masses, the traditional and the Westernized. It counts among its supporters Christians, Jews, and even nonbelievers who are drawn by, and acknowledge, the miraculous power and beauty of the sound.

That the Qur'an is central to Islamic society, that its significance is communicated by the sound as well as by the meaning and history of the revelation, and that most access to the Qur'an is through the oral tradition explains to a great degree the suffusion of the sound throughout the fabric of society and the prestige and respect accorded it.

The Art of Reciting the Qur'an

1. The Text: The Qur'an

History of the Revelation and Compilation of the Written Text

To Muslims the Qur'an is the word of God in Arabic. It is the last of God's revelations to humanity, correcting the distortions to which his previous revelations, the Torah and the Gospels, were subjected. God revealed this message to the Prophet Muhammad through the intermediation of the Angel Gabriel. One of the earliest revelations was in the form of a command: "Recite, in the name of thy Lord" (*iqra' bi smi rabbik*, Qur. 96/1).[1]

Over the next twenty years, until Muhammad's death in A.D. 632, the Angel Gabriel transmitted the message to Muhammad, who in turn transmitted it to his followers. Tradition says that the revelation was given to Muhammad in seven *aḥruf* (generally interpreted here to mean "dialects") in order to accommodate the various tribes living in the Arabian peninsula.[2] A community of believers formed around this message and its deliverer which took its guidance in both spiritual and temporal matters from the revelation. This was the first Muslim community, a body consciously participating in God's revealed destiny for humanity.

There are accounts of Muhammad dictating the revelations to his scribes, but the writings were not compiled into a book during his lifetime. The idea of the revelation as a discrete book was present; there are references in the Qur'an to its existence in the heavenly dimension, preserved on tablets (Qur. 85/21–22), and presumably having a beginning and end, its material divinely ordered in a particular way. Tradition says that the whole Qur'an was sent down to the first heaven on a night in Ramadan, from whence it was given to Muhammad in parts.

The order of the parts given to Muhammad reflects the circumstances of his dealings with the Arabs, as he was called to warn them against their disbelief, encourage the believers, and legislate for the new community. Muhammad himself is said to have dictated the sectioning and ordering of the parts of the revealed material, but it was obviously open-ended as long as he was alive to receive new material or to abrogate older material. Tradition also says that before his death Muhammad was given a final review (*al-ʿarḍ al-axīr*) of the revealed material during the month of Ramadan.

Some months after the Prophet's death, his successor as leader of the community, Abū Bakr, had a written text compiled, but it was not intended to supersede any of the privately existing versions. Rather, it was intended to assure the existence of one complete text. This in itself was without precedence in the Prophet's lifetime, and, therefore, without his sanction, but it was felt to be crucial to the survival of the revelation. Abū Bakr's text was incorporated into the text we have today.

The present written text was not compiled until the reign of the third successor, Caliph ʿUṯmān (644–56). After the time of Abū Bakr a number of versions of the text were in existence, and factions argued over the question of which was the true Qur'an. In response to this possible crisis of unity in the Muslim community, Caliph ʿUṯmān directed that a single standard and authoritative text be established. He felt that the dialectal differences accommodated by the variant Qur'anic readings had merged into one language in the army camps to a degree which would permit the use of one standard vulgate. Given the divine sanction of the presence of different versions (see below), the denial or ranking of existing versions was an act of blasphemy. But Muslims are careful to point out that the existence of one authorized Qur'an does not deny the existence of its other true manifestations. The following parable by Ibn Qayyim al-Jawziyyah (1292–1350) explains the proper relationship:

> A house may have a number of roads leading to it. If it is the ruler's judgment that allowing people to use all the roads causes conflict and confusion, then he may decide to permit the use of one road only, forbidding the others. He does not thereby abolish the roads as such, as they could still lead to the house; he merely forbids their use.
>
> (translated in Weiss, Berger, and Rauf 1975: 25)

Nature of the Text

It is necessary to understand references to "versions," "variants," and "readings" of the Qur'an in order to understand the relationship of the oral nature of the revelation to the written text. For if the Qur'an is revered as the word of God to be preserved against the change which compromises the divine nature of the previous revelations, it cannot be subjected to the versions and variants of oral tradition and the laws of folklore like a fairy tale. The Heavenly Book exists not as a single linearly ordered original from which subsequent versions emanate, but as one transcendent phenomenon embracing a number of manifestations, oral and written. I have already mentioned the Qur'an preserved on heavenly tablets and the seven parallel revelations of the *aḥruf.* The latter demonstrate that variation is seen as part of the original transmission of the Qur'an.

A further manifestation of variance is in the seven (some say ten or fourteen) text-systems known as the *qirā'āt.* These represent readings drawn from the basic phonetic pool of the seven *aḥruf* and associated with prominent reciters of the eighth century and their students.[3] These particular readings were fixed into written form, codified, and canonized in the tenth century. One criterion of their acceptance was that they conform to the consonantal skeleton of the text compiled by Caliph ʿUṯmān. But even this fixed system does not violate the fluid nature of the Qur'an or its transcendence over linear, fixed text-systems, for certain orthographic conventions and the absence of diacritical marks in the ʿUṯmānī text accommodate the phonetic variances of the *qirā'āt.*[4]

The written text does not exist to preserve against change; it is taken for granted that oral tradition does that. Nor is the written text the ultimate referent of the oral. Oral tradition has served as the final arbitrator of the written traditions; only those fragments written down in the presence of the Prophet were accepted as material for the written text, and any differences in the fragments were settled by oral tradition. Muhammad spread the message by sending out reciters, not texts, and Caliph ʿUṯmān sent with each copy of the standard text a reciter who could teach its recitation.[5]

Further evidence of the recognition given to the orality of the revelation lies in the name itself. Although the revelation is referred to with a number of terms (*al-kitāb, al-furqān, al-tanzīl,* for example), the one most widely used and most revealing of this nature is *al-qur'ān*. The noun is formed from the consonantal root cluster Q R ', which conveys the sense of reciting. *Qur'ān* appears in the text as a synonym for *qirā'ah*, the noun from this root, meaning "reciting"/"recitation": "And when we recite it, heed its recitation" (*fa 'iḏā qara'nāhu fa ttabiʿ qur'ānahu*, Qur. 75/18). *Qur'ān*, may refer to the reciting of a single passage or to the revelation as a whole. Scholars point to a second sense of the same root, that of gathering together, collecting, and explain the application of this sense as a reaping of the fruits of the previous revelations (Kafāfī 1972: 3). This sense, however, is little known generally: it is the idea of "reciting" which is universally associated with the term *qur'ān*.

External Form of the Text

The external form of the written text is marked by its division into 114 chapters called *suwar* (singular *sūrah*) arranged roughly by order of length (the longest to the shortest, 286 to 3 verses), with the exception of the opening prayer, *al-Fātiḥah*, which has only 7 verses. The *suwar* are set off from each other by self-contained headings giving the title of the chapter (this is usually a single word, drawn from the body of the text), its date in terms of the location of its revelation (in fact, many *suwar* are composite, and contain material from both locations, Mecca and Medina), and the number of verses (*āyāt*, singular *āyaḥ*). The headings may also contain information such as the number of the *sūrah*, and more specific dating relative to the other *suwar* (e.g., "it was revealed after *sūrat* . . ."). The *suwar* (except for *al-Tawbah*, no. 9) are further set off from each other by the invocation "In the name of God, the Compassionate, the Merciful" (*bi smi llāhi r-raḥmāni r-raḥīm*). The pronouncing of this phrase (the *basmalah*) is also a feature of the recited text.

Like the chapters, the verses vary in length (ca. 60 to 3 words) and manifest both an external division, in that they are numbered, and an internal division, in that they are marked by end-rhyme or assonance.

For purposes of memorizing and reciting, the text is divided into 30 approximately equal parts corresponding to the 30 days of Ramadan, the month of fasting. The 30 parts are called *ajzā'* (singular *juz'*). Each *juz'* is divided into two *aḥzāb* (singular *ḥizb*), and each *ḥizb* into four *rubʿāt* (singular *rubʿ*). These divisions are usually marked in the margin of the text. A further sectioning, the *ʿašr*, is not marked. The *ʿašr* designates a recitation of ten lines or so of text.

Superimposed on this structure are the notations which guide the reader in the correct recitation according to the rules of *tajwīd*. These include signs indicating such details of performed recitation as places of stopping and beginning, points of extended duration, and elision of consonants.

The text may be further marked in the margin in 14 places by the term *sajdah*, which indicates where the reciter and listener are required to perform a prostration (e.g., Qur. 84/21).

Content, Language, and Style

What is the Qur'an about?[6] What information does it convey? The Qur'an is a testimony to the power and glory of God, a clear statement of His will and of the recompense awaiting both those who submit to it and those who reject it. It is a history of humanity vis-à-vis the reality of God. As such, it contains stories of prophets and peoples of the Judeo-Christian tradition, such as Noah, Abraham, Mary, and Jesus, as well as others unknown to that tradition, such as the Prophet Ṣāliḥ and the people of ʿĀd and Ṯamūd. These narratives serve to illustrate the nature of God's dealings with humanity and to reinforce the lesson of submission to His will. Finally, as a guide to those who would actively participate in the fulfillment of the divine will, the revelation contains the prescribed law and the code of conduct which constitute the path of righteousness. To Muslims, the set of legal, metaphysical, and eschatological doctrines of the Qur'an conveys the structure of reality and explains the nature of humanity's relationship to it.

The surface logic of the content of the Qur'an is not readily apparent at first reading. The themes and subject matter are not systematically developed; rather, aspects, repetitions, or varied images of the same theme are woven throughout the whole. The effect, on superficial reading, is one of abrupt and bewildering shifts in subject, mood, and speaker, of "human language crushed by the power of the Divine Word . . . human language . . . scattered into a thousand fragments like a wave scattered into drops against the rocks at sea" (Naṣr 1966: 47).

Some Muslim scholars attempt to explain the underlying unity of the text, but the clue to the perception of that unity lies in the Muslim's participation in a society founded on revelation. Islamic revelation abolishes the atomism of tense: there is no past, no present, no future, but one absolute present. The revelation is the past in that it is the beginning and source of knowledge and action. It is the present in its continuousness, and the future in that it is the complete and final message. The moment of revelation is eternal.[7] This transcendence of linear time is manifested in various ways in the text. There is no systematic treatment of the material, whether it be law or history. For example, a single narrative may be episodically scattered throughout the text (the story of Joseph, *sūrah* 12, is an exception), and not necessarily in chronological order. The story of Moses, for example, can be traced as follows: Moses' childhood (Qur. 20/38–40, 28/7–13); Moses called by God (19/51–53, 2/9–56, 28/29–35); Moses and Pharaoh (7/103–137, 10/75–92, 11/96–99), and so forth. Moreover, each part of the text refers to other parts, by means of association and repetition of image, phrase, and rhythm, so that the whole is constantly present.

This particular feature is especially noticeable in the *mutašābihāt*, phrases of varying length which recur throughout the text with little or no variation. As such, they function as cadential formulae or refrains. For example, the phrase "gardens of Eden under which rivers flow" (*jannātu ʿadnin tajrī min taḥtihā l-anhār*) is found with slight variation in over twenty different passages of the text: Qur. 9/72, 89; 14/23; 16/31; 20/76; 22/14; and so forth. The most commonly cited example of the *mutašābihāt* is: *qāla āmantum bihi qabla an aḏana lakum*, and *qāla āmantum lahu qabla an āḏana lakum* (Pharaoh said "believe ye in him before I give you permission!") (Qur. 20/71; 26/49). This is often cited as an example of why it is difficult to memorize the Qur'anic text.[8]

I mention this quality of the Qur'an in particular because it seems to be reinforced in the performance structure of recitation by the reciter's use of melodic pattern to refer to other parts of the text, other recitations, and other reciters. As far as I know, this technique is not consciously employed to evoke the effect of timelessness, nor am I able to claim that any of my informants volunteered such an interpretation of the experience of recitation. Still, there seems to be at least a superficial correlation of nonlinear continuity between the reality of the revelation, the structure of the Qur'anic text, and the performance structure of its recitation. That recitation evokes the moment of revelation, that is, the sound of the revelation as Muhammad learned it, that the various manifestations of the Qur'an are at the same time the whole, reinforces this continuity.

The beauty of the Qur'anic language and style is itself considered a proof of the divine origin of the text. This idea, expressed in the concept of *iʿjāz* (inimitability), thus adds an aesthetic dimension to the Qur'an—not only is it an expression of the nature of the divine, and of the human in relation to the divine, it is a model of beauty to which human expression can only aspire. In that regard, the language of the Qur'an has served for 1,400 years as the exalted standard for Classical Literary Arabic in matters of syntax, vocabulary, rhetoric, and, to a large extent, phonetics.[9]

The Qur'an is revealed through a variety of modes, such as narrative prose, poetic imagery, and oratory. A respected scholarly tradition exists which identifies and analyzes the literary devices used in the poetic and rhetorical expression of the Qur'an. These devices, such as rhyme, metaphor, simile, paronomasia, anaphorism, and concision, are often referred to as the "music" of the Qur'an.[10]

The aspects of the Qur'anic style which are most obvious in recitation are the rhyme, assonance, and rhythm, all of which serve to unify the various speech modes of the text. The types of rhyme are simple and multisyllabic end-rhyme and internal rhyme.

The structure of the Arabic language is conducive to rhyme, both multisyllabic and simple, in that all morphemes fit into one of a number of syllabic patterns. These mark such aspects of meaning as passive voice, plurality, gender, case, intent or desire, reciprocity, and so forth. To a large extent, the rhyme and rhythmic patterns inherent in the language account for the untranslatability of the sound of the text. Compare, for example, the alternating rhyme and the parallel rhythms in the following Qur'anic texts with the English versions (here, as in other extended passages of

Qur'anic quotation, the transcription is an attempt to show all details of pronunciation peculiar to the recited Qur'an so as to provide the most accurate rendering of its sound): [11]

> – ˘ – – ˘ – ˘ – – ˘
> al-xạbīṭ**ātu** li l-xạbīṭ**īna**
> – ˘ – – ˘ – ˘ – –
> wa l-xạbīṭ**ūna** li l-xạbīṭ**āt**
> – – ˘ – ˘ – – ˘ – ˘
> 'aṭ-ṭạyyib**ātu** li ṭ-ṭạyyib**īna**
> – – ˘ – ˘ – ˘ –
> wa ṭ-ṭạyyib**ūna** li ṭ-ṭạyyib**āt**
>
> Impure women are for impure men
> and impure men are for impure women.
> Women of purity are for men of purity
> and men of purity are for women of purity.
>
> (Qur. 24/26)
>
> – – ˘ – ˘ – – ˘ – ˘
> 'aṣ-ṣạbir**īna** wa ṣ-ṣạdiq**īna**
> – – ˘ – ˘ – ˘ – –
> wa l-qạniṭ**īna** wa l-mu͂(n͂)fiq**īna**
> – – ˘ – ˘ – ˘ – –
> wa l-mustaġfir**īna** bi l-aṣḥāṛ
>
> Those who show patience, who are true,
> who worship devoutly, who spend [in the way of God]
> and who pray for forgiveness in the early hours of the morning.
>
> (Qur. 3/17)
>
> wa l-laḏīna yaṛmūna
> – – ˘ – – – ˘ – – ˘ – ˘
> l-muḥs**ināti** l-ġạf**ilāti** l-mu'm**ināti**
> lu'inū fi d-dunyā wa l-'āxiṛati
> wa lahum 'aḏābun 'aḏīm
>
> Those who slander
> chaste, indiscreet, but believing
> women are cursed in this life and in the hereafter, for
> them is a grievous penalty.
>
> (Qur. 24/23)

Rhyme serves to mark the verse line, which may be short:

ʾiḏa š-šamsu kuwwi**ṛạt**
wa ʾiḏa n͠-nujūmū(n͠) kada**ṛạt**
wa ʾiḏa jibālu suy͠yi**ṛạt**
wa ʾiḏa lʿišāṛu ʿuṭṭi**lat**

(Qur. 81/1–4)

ʾiqəṛạʾ wa ṛạbbuka l-ʾak**ṛạm**
ʾallaḏī ʿallama bi l-q**ạlam**
ʿallama l-ʾĩ(n͠)sāna mā lam yaʿ**lam**

(Qur. 96/3–5)

The unifying role of the rhyme in recitation is more evident in the longer verse line, which is not otherwise marked:

wa'āyatul lahumu l-aṛḍu l-maytatu ʾaḥyaynāhā wa ʾaxṛạjənā minhā ḥabbã(n) fa minhu **ya'kulūn**.

wa jaʿalnā fīhā jan͠nātim͠ min͠ naxīliw͠ wa ʾaʿnābiw͠ wa fajjaṛnā fīhā min **al-ʿuyūn**.

li yaʾkulū mĩ(n͠) ṯamarihī wa mā ʿamilathu ʾaydīhim ʾa fa lā **yaškurūn**.

(Qur. 36/33–35)

wa la qadə ṣạṛṛafnā fī hāḏa l-qurʾāni lin͠nasi mĩ(n) kulli maṯali w͠wa kāna l-ʾĩ(n͠) sānu ʾakṯaṛạ šayʾĩ(n͠) **jadalā**.

wa mā manaʿa n͠-nāsa ʾay͠ yuʾmina iḏ jāʾahumu l-hudā wa yastaġfiṛu ṛạbbahum ʾillā ʾã(n͠) taʾtiyahum sun͠natu l-ʾaww͠alīna ʾaw yaʾtiyahumu l-ʿaḏābu **qubulā**.

wa mā nuṛsilu l-muṛsalīna ʾillā mubašširīna wa mũ(n͠)ḏirīnā wa yujādilu l-laḏīna kafaṛū bi l-bạṭili li-yudəhidū bihi l-ḥaqqạ wa ttaxạḏū ʾāyātī wa mā ʾũ(n͠)ḏiṛu **huzuwā**.

(Qur. 18/54–56)

Assonance has an effect similar to that of rhyme:

sum͠mũ(m͠) bukmun ʿumyũ(n͠) fahum lā yarjiʿūn. (Qur. 2/18)

li ʾilāfi **quṛạyš**
ʾīlāfihim riḥlata š-šitāʾi wa **ṣ-ṣạyf**
fa lyaʿbudū ṛạbba hāḏa **l-bayt** . . .

(Qur. 106/1–3)

Although some of the lines of the Qurʾan may be scanned according to the Classical Arabic meters,[12] these are not as characteristic of Qurʾanic syllabic rhythmic patterns as are the abrupt or progressive shifts in rhythmic patterns and length of line, and the shifts between regular and irregular patterns:

ʾa ṛa ʾay tal la ḏī yu kaḏ ḏi bu bid dīn
fa ḏā li kal la ḏī ya duʿ ʿul ya tīm
wa lā ya ḥuḍ ḍu ʿa lā ṭạ ʿā mil mis kin
fa way lul lil mu ṣạl līn
ʾal la ḏī na hum ʿa(n) ṣạ lā ti him sā hūn
ʾal la ḏī na hum yu ṛā ʾūn
wa yam na ʿū nal mā ʿūn

(Qur. 107/1–7)

wal fa jər
wa la yā lin ʿašr
waš šaf ʿi wal watr
wal lay li ʾi ḏā yasr
hal fī ḏā li ka qạ sa mul li ḏī ḥi jər

(Qur. 89/1–5)

Rhythm and length of line may serve to highlight a particular line in the text, or to underscore a meaning. In the following example it is the sudden regularity of poetic feet and the relative shortness of the line which highlight the crucial question:

wa mā ṣā ḥi bu kũ(m) bi ma jə nūn
wa la qạ də ṛa ʾā hu bil ʾu fu qil mu bīn
wa mā hu wa ʿa lal ġạy bi bi ḍạ nīn
wa mā hu wa bi qạw li šay ṭā niṛ ṛạ jīm
fa ʾay na taḏ ha būn
ʾin hu wa ʾil la ḏik rul lil ʿā la mīn

li mā͞(n̄) šā 'a mī͡(n̄) kum ay͞yas ta qīm   _   ‿ _   ‿ _ _

wa mā ta šā 'ū nā 'il lā 'ay͞ya šā 'al la hu ṛabbul 'ā la mīn.

And your companion is not one possessed,
And without doubt he saw him in the clear horizon
Neither doth he withhold grudgingly a knowledge of the
Unseen
Nor is it the word of an evil spirit accursed.
Then whither go ye?
Verily this is no less than a Message to the Worlds
(with profit to whoever among you wills to go straight:
but ye shall not will except as God wills, the Lord of the
Worlds.

(Qur. 81/32–39)

In the following *sūrah*, one line is set off from the more lilting rhythm of the rest of the text by the equal duration of its syllables. This has the effect of slowing down the line and highlighting the gravity of what is in fact the key line in the *sūrah*:

_   ‿ _   ‿ _   ‿ _

way lul li kul li hu ma za til lumazaḥ

'al la dī ja ma 'a mā la hū wa 'ad da dah

yaḥ sa bū 'an͞na mā la hu 'ax la dah

kal lā la yū͡(n̄) ba ḍan͞na fil ḥu ṭa mah

wa mā 'a də ṛā ka mal ḥu ṭa mah

nā ṛul lā hil mū qạ dah

'al la ḏī taṭ ṭạ li 'ū 'a lal 'af 'i dah

'in͞na hā 'a lay him mu'ṣạdah

fī 'a ma dim͞mu mad da dah

Woe to every scandalmonger and backbiter,
Who pileth up wealth and layeth it by
Thinking that his wealth would make him last for ever.
By no means! He will be sure to be thrown into that which
breaks to pieces.
And what will explain to thee That which breaks to pieces?
It is the fire of the wrath of God kindled to a blaze.

Which doth mount to the hearts.
It shall be made into a vault over them,
In columns outstretched.

(Qur. 104/1–9)

Rhyme, rhythm, and syntax interact to set up expectations which may then be delayed before final resolution. In the following example, parallel syntax, rhythm, and end rhyme set a pattern, the effect of which is interrupted by the addition of extra syllables and a change in syntax, but resolved according to expectation by the end-rhyme and rhythm, *āhā*:

– – ˘ ˘ ˘ – –
waš šam si wa ḍu **hā hā**
– ˘ ˘ ˘ ˘ – ˘ – –
wal qa ma ri ʾi ḏā ta **lā hā**
– ˘ – ˘ ˘ – – – –
wan͠na ha ri ʾi ḏā jal **lā lā**
– – ˘ ˘ – – – –
wal lay li ʾi ḏā yaġ **šā hā**
– ˘ – ˘ ˘ – ˘ – –
was sa mā ʾi wa ma ba **nā hā**
– – ˘ ˘ – ˘ – –
wal ʾaṛ ḍi wa ma ṭa **hā hā**
˘ – – ˘ – – – –
wa naf siw͠wa mā saw **wā hā**
˘ – ˘ ˘ – ˘ – ˘ – ˘ ˘ ˘ – –
fa ʾal ha ma hā fu ju ṛa hā wa ta qə **wā hā**

(Qur. 91/1–8)

Another device is to delay the resolution of each line by making it longer than the previous one:

wa lʿaṣṛ
ʾin͠na lʾī(n)sāna la fī xusr
ʾillā llaḏīna ʾāmanū wa ʿamilu ṣ-ṣāliḥati
wa ta wā ṣaw bi l-ḥaqqi wa ta wā ṣaw bi ṣ-ṣabər

(Qur. 103)

The end-rhyme with its resolution of tensions set up by variations in rhythmic and syntactic patterns serves to emphasize the end of the line. This effect is paralleled in the aesthetics of Arabic music, in which tension is heightened or resolved in the melodic cadence and the pause which follows (see chapter 5). The use of the melodic cadence is a characteristic feature of the melodic style of recitation, and it serves to emphasize the qualities of the Qur'anic text.

Ultimately, scholars and listeners recognize that the ideal beauty and inimitability of the Qur'an lie not in the content and order of the message, on the one hand, and in the elegance of the language, on the other, but in the use of the very sound of the language to convey specific meaning. This amounts to an almost onomatopoeic use of language, so that not only the image of the metaphor but also the sound of the words which express that image are perceived to converge with the meaning.

The implications of the form, its oral nature, and the significance of the revelation for its recitation are many. Both the prominence of the recitation and its characteristic sound may be explained by three widely recognized concepts of the Qur'an: 1. it is meant to be heard—therefore the most common means of transmission is oral; 2. it is of divine and inimitable beauty—therefore listeners approach it with expectations of heightened experience; 3. it is the last of God's revelations—therefore it must be preserved, and high value is placed on its accurate transmission. The discipline which regulates the correct oral rendering of the Qur'an is *tajwīd*, the basis of all recitation.

2. *Tajwīd*

Introduction

Tajwīd is the system of rules regulating the correct oral rendering of the Qur'an. The importance of *tajwīd* to any study of the Qur'an cannot be overestimated: *tajwīd* preserves the nature of a revelation whose meaning is expressed as much by its sound as by its content and expression, and guards it from distortion by a comprehensive set of regulations which govern many of the parameters of the sound production, such as duration of syllable, vocal timbre, and pronunciation. Furthermore, *tajwīd* links these parameters to the meaning and expression, and indicates the appropriate attitude to the Qur'anic recitation as a whole.

Tajwīd is believed to be the codification of the sound of the revelation as it was revealed to the Prophet Muhammad, and as he subsequently rehearsed it with the Angel Gabriel.[1] Thus, the sound itself has a divine source and significance, and, according to Muslim tradition, is significant to the meaning.

Reciting according to the rules of *tajwīd* also fulfills a divine command: Muslims interpret the Qur'anic verse "Recite the Qur'an with *tartīl*" (*wa rattil il-qur'āna tartīlā*, Qur. 74/4) as meaning "Recite the Qur'an according to the rules of *tajwīd*."[2] The following is taken from the introduction to one of the more basic and widely used manuals in Cairo: "The Prophet said, Grace be upon him who learns and teaches the Qur'an. . . . In the name of God the Merciful and Compassionate, praise is His who created humanity and taught it what is clear [*al-mubīn*] . . . and prayers and peace upon the Messenger of God to whom it was revealed: 'Recite the Qur'an with *tartīl*.' . . . *Tajwīd*, in the technical sense, is articulating each letter from its point of articulation, giving it its full value. The intent of *tajwīd* is the recitation of the Qur'an as God Most High sent it down, and the authorization for it is that knowledge of it is a collective duty and the practice of it is a duty prescribed for all who wish to recite something from the Holy Qur'an" (Muḥaysin 1970: 2, 3).

Thus, learning to recite according to the rules of *tajwīd* is authorized by divine command, the acknowledged duty of every Muslim, and, logically, the foundation of Qur'anic studies in Egypt. Learning the Qur'an means learning the correct sound of the Qur'an. The science of *tajwīd* is itself transmitted orally, the student imitating and practicing the sounds produced by the teacher. Since many of the rules for pronunciation are uniquely applied to the Qur'an and are not applicable to the literary language or to the colloquial dialect, they are incomprehensible without oral example. This is why the many texts which set out the rules of *tajwīd* are considered supplementary to the oral transmission. The written rules function only as an aid to help the student identify and remember what he or she has heard.

For example, one of the principles governing pronunciation of a syllable-final /n/ or /m/ before certain letters is *ixfā'*. This is defined in the written sources as "the pronunciation of a letter between full pronunciation [*iḏhār*] and assimilation [*idġām*], free of doubling [*tašdīd*], and with nasality [*ġunnah*] of the letter" (Muḥaysin 1970: 809), or "a state between full pronunciation and full assimilation" (al-Qāri' 1948: 44). Another definition reads, "The /n/ governed by *ixfā'* has two points of articulation, its own, and that of nasality" (Ibn al-Jazarī 1908: 54). In a manual for non-native speakers of Arabic we read that *ixfā'* "is the sound between *nūn ġunnah* (nasalized n) and the ordinary sharp sound of nun. This can only be learned under the guidance of a teacher. The beginner however, should not pronounce n very sharp in such cases" (Tufayl 1974: 85). Bergsträsser (1932–33) defines *ixfā'* as "reduction," a type of "incomplete assimilation," marked by the absence of doubling (*tašdīd*), "as in mi(n) taḥtiha . . . rabbahu (m)bihim," and in contrast to "incomplete assimilation in the real sense . . . as in majjaqulu . . . miwwalin" (Bergsträsser 1932–33: 8), with no mention of nasality. Such definitions do not guide the student to producing the intended sound; rather, they identify a sound which the student has heard and learned by imitation (see below for a more prescriptive definition of *ixfāʾ*).

Most Western studies of *tajwīd* have overlooked both the significance of the sound of recitation and the importance of *tajwīd* as the system which shapes that sound. Two related factors may account for this oversight: the Western scholarly tradition, with its emphasis on the Qurʾan as written scripture, has been text-bound. Therefore, in addition to being less accessible to the Western scholar, the oral tradition has been accorded a low priority in Islamic studies. The rare exposition of *tajwīd* (and I know of no complete and systematic exposition in Western scholarship) presents it as a written code of rules to be applied to the reciting of the Qurʾan, but there is little effort to make the standard definitions comprehensible in terms of the actual sound.

The problem lies first in grasping the significance of *tajwīd*, and then in translating from written texts what can only, ultimately, be understood by ear. The text-oriented scholar may too easily miss the significance of *tajwīd* and consider the written translation adequate to convey its material and sense.[3] This has often led to the type of article on *tajwīd* found in the *Shorter Encyclopedia of Islam* (ben Cheneb 1961: 557–58). *Tajwīd* is presented there as a confusing string of arbitrarily selected rules, which ignores both the comprehensiveness of the science (no mention is made of durations) and the significance of *tajwīd* to the oral nature of the Qurʾan. Another work (Semaan 1968) presents it as a contribution to the study of Arabic phonetics and falls into the trap of confusing the science of *tajwīd* with the use of the term *tajwīd* meaning "melodic recitation," so that, in his glossary, the author defines *tajwīd* merely as "cantillation of the scripture" (Semaan 1968: 67). Elsewhere, he elaborates:

> The attempt to do this ["adorn the Qurʾan with recitation and ornament it by the finest chanting," his translation of *jawwadu l-Qurʾān wa zayyinuhu bi-aḥsan il-aṣwāt*] produced tajwīd. The details of this art as set forth in the numerous little manuals of tajwīd are outside the range of this study. What concerns us is the phonetic interest involved in tajwīd.
>
> (Semaan 1968: 35)

Semaan accounts for the "arbitrary" and "strange" effects of *tajwīd* as "some experimenting in its effort to 'ornament' Arabic for more attractive cantillation and to produce effects pleasing to the hearers. At times this ornamentation seems somewhat artificial to the modern phonetician, and more so to the grammarian" (Semaan 1968: 35–36), presumably because all of this "is alien to the working mechanisms of classical Arabic" (Semaan 1968: 36).[4]

Of these scholars who have attempted to describe the sound of recitation, a few are aware of the importance of accounting for that sound, and some do attempt to link the science of *tajwīd* to practice.[5] Most of these works, however, neglect to include *tajwīd* as a major factor in shaping the sound they study. Cantineau (Cantineau and Barbès 1942–47), for example, describes the sound of the reciting of two informants, without relating it to the principles of *tajwīd*. Thus, although the durations of individual syllables are carefully noted (pp. 68ff.), the reader is unable to determine whether the regulating principles are the rules of *tajwīd*, incomplete mastery of these rules, or conscious personal style. The same applies to Cantineau's observations of sectioning (p. 75) and the frequency of nasalization (p. 74). K. Huber's musical transcription (Bergsträsser 1932–33: 113–125) of Qur'anic recitation accounts not only for durations, but for nasalized durations (see his footnote, p. 124), but is separated from the material on *tajwīd*, which is itself dealt with in terms of the official written text. Alone among ethnomusicologists, H. H. Touma has recognized the importance of *tajwīd* to the "organization of the melodic line" (1975*a*: 90). The implications of this importance, however, remain to be dealt with. This is unfortunate, for if one ignores the role of *tajwīd* in shaping the recited text, one can only describe the sound, not explain it.

The following, then, is a general survey of the material of *tajwīd*. It is not intended as a manual of the rules of *tajwīd*, but rather as a background for the more detailed discussion of those aspects of *tajwīd* which most clearly account for the characteristic sound of Qur'anic recitation. As regards the rules of *tajwīd*, there is no standard system of classification: every manual presents them differently. I have defined the material according to three main areas: articulation, duration, and sectioning. The opening and closing formulae and the general styles of reciting are secondary, in that they are not consistently included in the *tajwīd* manuals.

Material of *Tajwīd*

Production of Phonemes

*Points of Articulation (*maxārij al-ḥurūf*).* These are classified according to the position in the vocal tract, starting with the larynx (*aqṣā l-ḥalq*), and proceeding forward to the lips (*šifatān*).[6]
*Manner of Articulation (*ṣifāt al-ḥurūf*).* These are classified according to "strength" or "weakness" (important for the rules of assimilation), nasality, voiced/unvoiced, retracted/unretracted, as well as by the categories of liquids, spirants, dentals, and so forth. These classifications do not wholly correspond to non-Arabic linguistic categories.
*Allophones (*al-ḥurūf al-farʿīyyah*) and Other Features Included under the Rules for Assimilation, Gemination, Nasality, and Manner of Articulation.* These include the softened glottal stop (*al-hamzah al-musahhalah*), the fronted and raised /ā/ (*imālah*), the pharyngealized /l/, the pharyngealized and the trilled /r/, the /ṣ/ tending toward /ž/ or /s/, the geminate /m/ and /n/, the /l/ of the definite article, the assimilation and partial assimilation of /n/ and /m/, the consonants /q/, /ṭ/, /b/, /j/, and /d/ with a following epenthetic schwa (*qalqalah*), and so forth. These may be selected by a specific phonetic environment (e.g., partial assimilation of /n/ before /b/), or by pause position (e.g., the barely audible or inaudible articulation of final vowels called *rawm* or *išmām*, change of accusative nunation from /an/ to /ā/), the status of which may vary from text-system to text-system.
*Assimilation (*idġām*) and Dissimilation (*iḏhār*).* This is really a subcategory of the above, but it is so extensive that it deserves independent treatment. This section can be classified into two main parts: assimilation based on point of articulation and on manner of articulation and vocalization, the latter including a hierarchical classification of consonants into "strong" and "weak." Thus, *qạlat ṭāʾif* → *qạlaṭ/ṭāʾif*, but *basaṭta* → *basaṭta*, the rule being that when two consonants sharing a point of articulation but differing

in manner of articulation (*al mutajānisān*) are in sequence, the first assimilates to the second, if it is "weaker."

*Extended Duration of Syllables (*madd*)*

Syllables are classified according to whether their duration is fixed (*aṣlī* or *ṭabīʿī*) or variably extended (*farʿī*). The durations vary from one beat (*ḥarakah*) to six, and the variation is determined by phonetic environment, text-system (*qirāʾah*), or the reciter's choice of the given options. For example C$\bar{V}$ preceding a glottal stop or a syllable-final consonant (*sukūn*) may take two to six beats, whereas C$\bar{V}$, an open syllable, takes a mandatory two beats. This subject is treated in detail below.

*Pause and Beginning (*al-waqf wa l-ibtidāʾ*)*

This treats the rules for sectioning of the text. The types of pauses are characterized by the syntactic and semantic completeness or incompleteness of the preceding phrase and determine whether the reciter is to stop, to continue with what follows, or to back up to bridge a break in meaning or syntax. This is the second parameter in which the reciter may exercise choice, and it is treated in detail below.

Pronouncing and Placing the Opening and Closing Formulae

The opening and closing formulae are the *istiʿāḏah* (*ʾaʿūḏu bi llāhi mina š-šayṭāni ṛ-ṛajīm*—"I take refuge in God from the power of evil"), the *basmalah* (*bi smi llāhi ṛ-ṛaḥmāni ṛ-ṛaḥīm*—"In the name of God the Merciful and Compassionate"), and the *ṣadaqah* (*ṣadaqa ḷḷāhu l-ʿaḏīm*—"God has spoken truly"). The *istiʿāḏah* must begin a recitation, followed by the *basmalah* (except for *sūrat/Al-Tawbah*, no. 9). The *basmalah* must preface resumption of reciting after short breaks. The *ṣadaqah* is pronounced at the conclusion of the recitation. There is some difference of opinion between the schools of law as to whether the pronunciation of these formulae needs to be audible or not.

General Styles of Reciting

Also included in many manuals of *tajwīd* is a section on the three ways of reciting the Qur'an (*ṭuruq*). These are *taḥqīq*, *ḥadr*, and *tadwīr*. These are all subject to the rules of *tajwīd*, and their differences are largely a matter of tempi and their associations with the different *qirā'āt* (i.e., the various options as regards the rules of *tajwīd*).

Taḥqīq is a very slow recitation in which the reciter takes the longest durations, the most complete articulations (e.g., the glottal stop is never elided except in accordance with the rules of Classical Arabic). This type of reciting is characteristic of the text-systems of *Ḥamzah* and *Warš*. Šayx Sa'īd al-Saḥḥār adds that this is the basis of melodic reciting in general.

Ḥadr is very quick recitation in which the reciter takes the shortest durations, as well as all options to lighten, drop, elide, or assimilate phonemes. As explained by Šayx al-Saḥḥār, this is how one recites to oneself, usually under the breath, and in a monotone.

Tadwīr is recitation of medium tempo. Again, there is a correlation with the durational options, the reciter choosing the middle range of durations.

A term in use today is *al-muṣḥaf al-mu'allim*, "the teaching Qur'anic text." This is of medium tempo and durations and is used in recorded recitation for teaching purposes. The reciter allows for a long silence between phrases so that the student may repeat what has just been rendered. Sayx al-Ḥuṣarī has recorded the whole Qur'anic text in this mode.

Tartīl, sometimes included in discussions of the *ṭuruq* of recitation, is applied to the straightforward and private (*murattal*) style of reciting, as well as to the comprehensive sense of *tartīl* as the ideal recitation (see chapter 5). As explained by Šayx al-Saḥḥār, *tartīl* has some melody, but not "complete voice." The tempo is relaxed, but not slow. According to al-Ḏānī (as quoted in Ibn al-Jazarī 1908: 7), the difference between *tartīl* and *taḥqīq* is that in *tartīl* one may choose to drop or elide the glottal stop, use the shorter durations, and so forth. In another work (Ismā'īl 1978*b*: 51) we read that the difference between *taḥqīq* and *tartīl* is that "*taḥqīq* is for practice, learning, and rehearsing, and *tartīl* is for contemplating, thinking, and discovering the profundity. Every *taḥqīq* is *tartīl*, but not every *tartīl* is *taḥqīq*."

Sound of *Tajwīd*

Rather than elaborate on the rules of *tajwīd* as a subject in itself, I will discuss only those areas of this science which account for the uniqueness of the sound of the Qur'anic language, attempting to make them comprehensible to those outside the tradition, by applying them directly to the actual sound.[7]

The effect of *tajwīd* on the sound of recitation can be described not only in terms of the constants, those rules which, in their invariability, characterize the sound and shape of recitation, such as nasality, single-breath phrase, and so forth, but in terms of the variables, the options in duration and sectioning which the individual reciter can manipulate to maximum artistic advantage, and the use of which may characterize personal style in recitation.

Ġunnah (nasality)

One of the most obvious characteristics of Qur'anic recitation is its nasal quality. This is not to be attributed to custom, aesthetics, or natural voice quality (although it may be intensified in a nasal voice), but to the rules of *tajwīd*. These regulate what phonemes and syllables are to be articulated through the nasal cavity. Nasality (*ġunnah*) governs geminate /m/ and /n/, the phonetic phenomena of *ixfā'*, *iqlāb*, and some contexts of *idġām*. An example of the geminate consonant nasality would be in such words as *in͠na*, *Muḥam͠mad*, and so forth. Although phoneticians would argue that these consonants are naturally articulated through the nasal cavity, the rules of *tajwīd* single out the geminate consonants for nasality, with the result that they are pronounced with an intensified and conscious nasality.

Ixfā' may be described as partial articulation of syllable-final /m/ or /n/ (the lips do not quite close for the /m/, and the tongue does not quite touch the alveolar ridge for the /n/), the vocal cavity holding the shape of the preceding vowel and the total sound articulated through the nasal cavity. The vowel may be given something of the quality of a subsequent emphatic consonant as well by dropping the jaw: there is a discernible difference between the ĩ(n) of *mĩ(n) tuṛāb* and *wa ʾĩ(n) ṭāʾifatan*. *Ixfāʾ* governs the conjunction of syllable-final /n/ with following consonants /s/, /ḏ/, /ṯ/, /k/, /j/, /s/, /q/, /š/, /ḍ/, /t/, /ḏ̣/, /f/, /t/, /d/, and /z/, and of syllable-final /m/ with following consonant /b/. Conjunction may occur within a word (*ʾã(n)zalnā*) or between two words (*mĩ(n) jibāl, fī yawmĩ(n) kān, kũ(n)tũ(m) bihi*).

Iqlāb. Syllable-final /n/ before the consonant /b/ is governed by *iqlāb*. This is traditionally defined as the transforming of /n/ into /m/ with incomplete assimilation and *ġunnah*. In fact, the /n/ drops out, the preceding vowel is nazalized while the lips shape the /m/ sound, but do not close until the /b/ is articulated (e.g., *mĩ(m) baʿd* from *min baʿd*, *ʿalīmũ(m) bi-ḏāti iṣ-ṣudūṛ* from *ʿalīmun bi-*). The sound is the same as that of *ixfāʾ* of syllable-final /m/.

Idġām. Full assimilation is called *idġām*, and it governs the conjunction of syllable-final /n/ with the consonants /m/, /n/, /w/, /y/ (with *ġunnah*), and /r/ and /l/ (without *ġunnah*). In *idġām* the /n/ assimilates totally to the following consonant, yielding a geminate. Since the consonants in question are voiced, they, rather than the preceding vowel, carry the nasality (e.g., *mim͠māl* from *min māl*, *qawmum͠min͠nisāʾ* from *qawmun min nisāʾ*, *lahabiw͠wa* from *lahabin waʾ*, *may͠yaqūl* from *man yaqūl*).

The effect of *ġunnah*, in the case of *ixfāʾ* and *iqlāb*, and of *ġunnah* and doubling in *idġām* and the doubled /m/ and /n/, is to prolong the duration as well as to change timbre. This duration is not regulated except by convention, which gives the syllable almost double the value of the equivalent non-nasalized syllable. In practice, the nasalized syllable may be even longer. In a single phrase the reciter must practice a quick alternation between throat timbre and nasal timbre, according to the phonetic environment of each /n/ or /m/ and adjust the durations accordingly.[8]

Qalqalah

A quality unique to recitation is *qalqalah*. This is the insertion of ə (schwa) after syllable-final /q/, /d/, /ṭ/, /b/, and /j/ and is traditionally defined as vibrating the place of articulation so that a strong tone is heard. Naṣr (1930: 62) and al-Qāriʾ (1948: 28) only describe its usage, taking for granted the production or effect of its sound. Boubakeur's definition is "consonnes bruyantes" (1968: 396). The effect is to change the familiar prosodic and stress patterns of the line. Thus,

´– – – ´⌣ –

wa sjud wa qtarib

becomes

´– ⌣ ⌣ ´⌣ ⌣ ⌣ ⌣ ⌣

wa sjudə wa qətaribə

and

⌣ – ⌣´– – – ´– ⌣ – ´– ⌣ ⌣ – ´–

la qad xalaqnā l-ʾinsāna fī ʾaḥsani taqwīm

becomes

⌣ ⌣ ⌣ ⌣´⌣ ⌣ – – ´– ⌣ – ´– ⌣ ⌣ ⌣ ⌣ ´–

la qạdə xạlaqənā l'ī(n̄)sāna fī ʾaḥsani taqəwīm

Perhaps it is because qalqalah, unlike assimilation and elision, is unique to *tajwīd* that it is often overlooked by those outside the tradition.[9]

Tafxīm

The backing and pharyngealization of the short and long vowel /a/ and /ā/ (becoming /ạ/ and /ạ̄/) and the pharyngealized quality of some consonants (/ṣ/, /ḍ/, /ṭ/, /ḍ/—the status of /ṛ/, /r/ and /ḷ/, /l/ vis-à-vis the vowel is bivalent) are familiar features in Classical Arabic. To this group the Qurʾan (like some dialects) adds /x/ and /ġ/. Thus Qurʾanic pronunciation is *ġạ̄šiyah* (versus *ġāšiyah*) and *xạyr* (versus *xayr*). These consonants are collectively called the *ḥurūf al-istiʿlaʾ*, and the phenomenon of pharyngealization, *tafxīm*. Another feature in which Qurʾanic pronunciation differs from Classical Arabic (and the dialects) with regard to pharyngealization is that the phenomenon is only immediately progressive and never regressive. In other words, the influence of pharyngeal does not extend to the whole word, but only affects an immediately following vowel. Thus the Qurʾanic pronunciation is *ʾaṣḥāb* (versus *ʾạṣḥạ̄b*), *qạmar* (versus *qạmạr*), and *ṭạʿām* (versus *ṭạʿạ̄m*).

Moreover, there are two types of /r/ in Qur'anic pronunciation, one governed by trilling (*takrīr, tarqīq,* or *taxfīf*), the other by pharyngealization (*tafxīm*).

/R/. The /r/ must be trilled in the following contexts: 1. if it is immediately followed by /i/ (*kasrah*) (e.g., *rizq*); 2. if it is syllable-final and follows an /i/ or /ī/ which is part of the stem (*kasrah* or *yā' aṣlī*), that is, not due to inflection, and is not followed by any of the pharyngeals (e.g., *xạbīr w-astaġfir, fir'awna*); 3. if a geminate /r/ is immediately followed by /i/ (e.g., *šarri*).

/Ṛ/. The /r/ is pharyngealized /ṛ/ (as is any following /a/ or /ā/: 1. if it is immediately followed by /a/ or /u/ (*fatḥah* or *ḍammah*) (e.g., *ṛạbb, ṛūh*); 2. if it is syllable-final and follows /a/ or /u/ (e.g., *baṛq, quṛb*); 3. if it is syllable-final after an /i/ which is part of the stem but is followed by one of the pharyngealized consonants (e.g., *qiṛṭās, miṛṣād*); 4. if it is silent after an epenthetic /i/ or any /i/ which is not part of the stem (e.g., the /i/ of the imperative form, *iṛkabu*); 5. if a geminate /r/ is followed immediately by /a/ or /u/ (e.g., *šaṛṛun*).

Since pharyngealization in Qur'anic pronunciation works in a much more limited area, the effect is of a much quicker alternation between the pharyngeal and the nonpharyngeal sounds. Compare the Qur'anic pronunciation of the first line with the standard pronunciation of the second:

> *sayaṣlā nāṛạ(n) ḏāta lahabiw wa mṛạ' atuhu ḥammālat al-ḥaṭạbə*
> *sayạṣlạ nạṛạn ḏāta lahabin wa mṛạ' ạtuhu ḥammālat al-ḥạṭạb.*

Madd

Arabic prosody classifies the syllable into long and short durations, one long being approximately equivalent to two short. The durations of syllables in Qur'anic recitation range from one to six beats (*ḥarakāt*) or longer.[10] The rules governing duration are detailed and comprehensive and account for an overall rhythm unique to the recitation of the Qur'an.

The rules of *tajwīd* divide the syllables into two basic categories: the syllable with fixed duration and the syllable with variable duration. It is assumed, but not explicitly stated, that the minimum unit of duration is one beat, and this is applied to the short, open syllable (CV), (e.g., ***ki****tāb*, ***hi****jā****ra****tun*). Also assumed, but not dealt with in the manuals, is the short closed syllable (CVC), which is given two beats (e.g., *lam*, ***mur****salīn*).

Primary Duration. The rules of *tajwīd* define the syllable of fixed or primary duration (*madd aṣlī* or *ṭabīʿī*) as a long open syllable (CV̄) with a constant duration of two beats (e.g., ***qā****la*, *ya****kū****nu*, *alla****ḏī****na*). Because the obligatory six-beat syllable (CV̄ geminate C, *madd lāzim*) is defined by a syllable-final consonant (the first of a geminate consonant—***ḥāqq****ah*), it is usually categorized with those syllables of variable duration which are also defined by the syllable-final consonant (see below).

A. The syllable of variable or secondary duration (*madd farʿī*) takes two to six beats and contains either a glottal stop or a syllable-final consonant. The syllable characterized by the glottal stop may be long and closed with glottal stop (CV̄ʾ), long and open but followed by a syllable with initial glottal stop (CV̄ ʾV), or long and open with initial glottal stop (ʾV̄C). Three contexts, then, are delineated for these syllables: 1. conjunct (*munfaṣil*), that is, within a word (e.g., *sa****mā***, ***jā****ʾa*); 2. disjunct (*muttaṣil*), that is, between two words (e.g., ***yā*** *ʾayyuhā*, *lam yalba****ṯū*** *ʾillā*); 3. reverse position (*badal*), that is, the glottal stop precedes the long vowel (e.g., *ʾ****ā****manu*, *ʾ****ū****tu*).

B. The variable syllable defined by syllable-final is long and closed (CV̄C, C diphthong C, or CV̄ geminate C), and may be uninflected for reasons of pause (*li-ʿāriḍ al-sukūn*) (e.g., *al-ra****ḥīm***, *yaʿla****mūn***, ***bayt xawf***) or may be an essential feature of the word itself. Most of these essentially uninflected syllables (CV̄C) are names of the letters of the alphabet and introduce some of the *suwar* of the Qurʾanic text. Their extension (two to six beats) is called *madd ḥarfī muxaffaf* (e.g., *Yā Sīn*, *Ḥā Mīm*, *ʾAlif Lām Rā*). The single exception is the word *ʾālʾān* which occurs twice in *Ṣūrat Yūnis* (v. 51). This particular extension is called *madd kalimī muxaffaf*.

C. Another type of closed syllable is that characterized by long vowel and geminate consonant (formed by the following syllable) (e.g., ***ḥāqq****ah*, ***ḍāll****īn*). It is called *madd lāzim* and has a fixed duration of six beats. If it occurs within a word it is called *madd kalimī* *muṭaqqal.* If the geminate consonant is the result of the conjunction of the final consonant of the uninflected syllable with the initial consonant of the following word (due to assimilation or repetition of the consonant), this is also an obligatory six-beat extension called *madd ḥarfī muṭaqqal* (e.g., *Ṭā* ***Sīm*** ***M****im* [from *Ṭā Sīn Mīm*], *ʾAlif* ***Lām*** ***M****īm*).

Third-Person Singular Masculine Pronominal Suffix. The third-person singular masculine pronominal suffix (*hu, hi*) is the one short, open syllable (CV) that is variable in duration: when framed by two short open syllables the suffix acts like CV̄ in that it takes two beats (more if followed by a glottal stop), for example, *inna hū huwa,* versus *fī hi hudā.* The one exception is in *sūrat al-Furqān* (v. 69), *fī hī mihānan* (extended, although preceded by a long syllable).

An extension less generally used and characteristic of *qirāʾat Warš* is the transformation of the CVC of the second syllable of the second-person plural independent pronoun (*ʾan****tum***) and of the second- and third-person plural pronominal suffixes (*-kum* and *-hum*) into CVCV̄ (*ʾantu****mū****, kum → kumū* and *hum → humū*) when followed by an initial glottal stop (e.g., *yurīku****mū*** *ʾāyātih* and *fa lahu****mū*** *ʾajəruhum*). The syllable /*mū*/ may be from two to six beats' duration.

Actual Durations. The actual durations of these secondary extensions vary between two beats (called *qaṣr*), three to five beats (called *tawassuṭ*), and six beats (called *ṭūl*). To some extent, the options are regulated by the *qirāʾāt*: *badal* (ʾV̄) is two beats in all of the *qirāʾāt* except *Warš*, where it may be two, four, or six beats. The *qirāʾāt* of *Hamzah* and *Watš* tend to use the longer durations, in general. Otherwise, the reciter is free to choose his durations: it is required only that he be consistent within a single recitation; for example, if he begins his reciting with a pausal duration (the technical term is *madd li-ʿāriḍ al-sukūn*) of six beats, he may not shorten it during the rest of the recitation. In practice, although the underlying pulse is set by the shortest duration (CV), the 2:1 ratio of the long and short syllables is tempered by *gunnah* and stress (see note 8).

Conventions. Certain conventions do prevail as regards choice of durations in the melodic style, *mujawwad.* Rarely does a reciter use the shorter pausal duration, for example. In fact, a general tendency toward longer durations is a characteristic of this style: one can see that the longer the duration of the syllable, the greater the possibility of melodic play unrestricted by considerations of fitting the melody to a set rhythmic pattern. This is an example of music affecting *tajwīd*. I have noticed that the longer extensions tend to be multiples of the two-beat unit rather than of the single beat. Thus a *madd lāzim* is in fact twelve single beats, counted as six double beats.

Waqf and *Ibtidā'*

The reciting of the Qur'an is also characterized by the single-breath phrase. The rules of pause and beginning (*waqf* and *ibtidā'*) divide the Qur'anic text into four basic types of phrases which are characterized by their syntactic and semantic independence or dependence on what follows. The type of phrase determines where the reciter may begin his next phrase, that is, whether he may continue with what follows in the text, or whether he must begin the next phrase with a repeat of part of the last phrase.

This set of rules differs in nature from the other rules of *tajwīd*, because it acts to preserve the clarity of the meaning rather than the accuracy of the sound. And mastering the rules of *waqf* and *ibtidā'* requires an understanding of the subtleties of meaning in the text; the rules cannot be learned solely by imitation and rote memorization. The inclusion of these rules in the science of *tajwīd* demonstrates the comprehensiveness of the ideal of correct recitation: it is not enough to reproduce the sound—one must convey the meaning of the language. Thus it is required of the reciter that he understand what he is reciting in order to convey that message most clearly, and he uses knowledge of the pauses as a tool to achieve clarity. One authority states: "Whoever does not know the [proper] pause does not know the Qur'an" (Abū Ḥātim, as quoted in al-Ḥuṣarī 1967: 9). Al-Ḥuṣarī further quotes the Prophet himself: "The ideal recitation is the beautification of the phonemes and knowledge of the pauses" (al-Ḥuṣarī 1967: 9).

That pause can affect meaning is a reality marked in the written text. The sign ∴ indicates pause, and the word so marked may be taken to belong with equal validity either to what follows or to what precedes. This sign occurs twice in a given phrase, and the reciter chooses between the two places of pause, breaking the phrase according to the meaning he wishes to elicit. For example, the opening of *sūrat al-Baqarah* (v. 2) can be read: "This is the Book, without doubt. ∴ In it is guidance for those who fear God" (*Ḏālika l-kitābu la ṛaybə. ∴ Fīhi hudā li l-muttaqīn*) or: "This is the Book in which there is no doubt. ∴ [It is] a guide for those who fear God" (*Ḏālika l-kitābu la ṛayba fīh. ∴ Hudā li l-muttaqīn*).

Scholars recognize that the rules of pause and beginning were developed after the early period of Islam (*ṣadr al-Islām*) and are not based on any chains of transmission going back to the actual recitation of the Prophet, his companions, or followers: rather, the rules were formulated to guarantee clarity. There are ten, some say seventeen, pauses called *sunnah, jabrīl*, or *ibtāʿ* believed to have been observed by the Prophet Muhammad,[11] but even these are not authoritatively prescriptive. Differences of opinion are therefore inevitable and accepted, and scholars differ both in classification systems and in detail, just as the written texts may vary in the placing and nature of the written signs which guide the reader in his pause and beginning.[12]

It is impossible to give a consensus of the various rules for pause and beginning. Most scholars agree that there are four basic types of pause.

Waqf tāmm. *Waqf tāmm* or *lāzim* (complete or obligatory) is characterized by semantic and syntactic independence of what precedes or follows. Thus the phrase preceding the obligatory pause is self-contained and takes the form of an epigram or summation and most commonly signals the end of a subject matter.

> And they have been commanded
> No more than this: to worship God,
> Offering Him sincere devotion,
> Being true; to establish regular prayer;
> And to practice regular charity;
> And that is the religion, Right and Straight. [*Waqf tāmm*]
> Those who reject (truth) among the People of the Book . . .
> (Qur. 98/5–6)

> But God did punish him, and made an example of him,
> in the Hereafter as in this life.

Verily in this is an instructive warning
for whosoever feareth (God). [*Waqf tāmm*]
What! Are ye the most difficult to create
Or the heaven above?

(Qur. 79/25–27)

Although pause is preferred at the end of such a phrase (beginning the next phrase with what follows), it is obligatory (*lāzim*) if to continue would distort the meaning.

It is recommended that the reciter keep separate the various moods of the verses, for example, that he not mix a verse dealing with punishment with one dealing with mercy. If the reciter continues from the end of one *sūrah* into the beginning of the next without pause, he must not pause after the *basmalah*, for this is to be associated with the beginning of the *sūrah*, not the end.

Waqf, kāfin. *Waqf kāfin* is characterized by syntactic independence, but is linked to what follows semantically. This is the most common type of pause: "Oh ye who believe, put not yourselves forward before God and his apostle. [*Waqf kāfin*] But fear God" (Qur. 49/1). Like the *waqf tāmm*, pause and beginning in sequence is preferred, but it is permitted to continue, as in: "Say, 'My Lord knoweth best their number; it is but few that know their real case. [*Waqf kāfin*] therefore, enter not into controversies concerning them . . . (Qur. 18/22).

Waqf ḥasan. *Waqf ḥasan* is characterized by syntactic and semantic dependence on what follows, yet it may be a complete phrase, for example: "Praise belongs to God. [*Waqf ḥasan*] Lord of all the worlds" (Qur. 1/2). Pause and beginning in sequence is permitted here, but continuation is preferred, especially if the phrase is the first half of a conditional sentence, or similarly syntactically dependent on the following phrase.

Waqf qabīḥ. *Waqf qabīḥ* is characterized by total semantic and syntactic dependence on what follows to the extent that a pause would render the text unmeaningful, or actually mislead the listener as to the intended meaning, for example,

Grant us [*waqf qabīḥ*]
the path.

(Qur. 1/6)

> Verily God guideth not [*waqf qabīḥ*]
> people who do wrong.
>
> (Qur. 6/144)

Continuation is definitely preferred.

Since a reciter may, in fact, pause whenever he needs to draw breath, sneeze, or cough, or for other physiological reasons, he should be aware of the type of pause he has effected so as to know where to begin again. In the case of the *waqf qabīḥ*, for example, the reciter must repeat the end of the phrase just finished and carry it into the new phrase to realize the desired continuity. Such sectioning might read:

> Verily God guideth not [*waqf qabīḥ*] guideth not
> people who do wrong.
>
> (Qur. 6/144)

Application of the Rules of Pause and Beginning. Mastery of the rules of pause and beginning clearly involves more than the faculty of memory. These rules are introduced into the *tajwīd* curriculum in institutes administered by al-Azhar only in the second year, after the student has studied grammar and rhetoric. The reciter learns not only the obligatory places of pause and beginning, but the places enhanced and distorted by it. He learns how to use pause and beginning to the best advantage: a skilled reciter can illuminate the meaning of the text for the listener who has perhaps heard the same text hundreds of times before.

Šayx Ibrāhīm al-Šaʿšāʿī considers this knowledge essential to good reciting and attributes the excellent reputation of his father (Šayx ʿAbd al-Fattāḥ al-Šaʿšāʿī) to his command and manipulation of pause. As regards his own reciting, Šayx al-Šaʿšāʿī feels that his nine-year study of exegesis, grammar, and rhetoric at al-Azhar university is of great benefit, and gave the following report as an example:

> This morning I had a recording session at the television station at 11 for the series "The Illumination of the Qur'an" (I am doing four episodes for them). I recited from, "never should a believer kill a believer, except by error. (pause) And whoever kills a believer by error, then [incumbent upon him is] the free-

ing of a believing slave, and bloodwit delivered" (4/92), and I paused. It suddenly struck me that this wasn't as it should be [*miš huwwa*] . . . the better pause, since my breath wasn't enough to complete the verse, was, "the freeing of a believing slave and bloodwit." Then I began again, "bloodwit delivered to his family unless they remit it freely." . . . "Bloodwit" is the general, and the rest specifies it. The rest is connected as a unit, that is, which bloodwit? The one to be paid to his family unless they remit it freely.

(al-Šaᶜšāᶜī)

Šayx al-Šaᶜšāᶜī emphasized that he was the one who noticed the "fault" ("it wasn't wrong, but the other was better"), and that he asked the recording engineer to let him redo the passage. He also stressed that it is the responsibility of the reciter to know what he is reciting at every moment, that one's reciting should be dictated by understanding and not just by breath capacity.

In the above example it is the clarity of the meaning which is enhanced by the reciter's understanding. A skilled reciter may also use the rules of pause and beginning to emphasize a part of the text, to bring out multiple meaning, to heighten dramatic tension, and thus to enhance the emotional participation of his listeners. This is done essentially by means of repetition and isolation (framing a word or phrase with silence) of parts of the text. In this sense, *waqf* and *ibtidā᾽* can be seen as "the ornament of recitation and the embellishment of the reciter, as well as [the mark of] his competence" (al-Ḥuṣarī 1967: 10).[13]

The correct recitation of the Qur᾽an, as regulated by the rules of *tajwīd*, clearly involves the correct transmission of the semantic message. But the unmistakably unique sound of *tajwīd* also signals a text and an event set apart from all other texts and experiences. Moreover, *tajwīd* serves to separate this heightened experience from the aesthetic experience in general. Although the reciter's manipulations of the options within the rules of *tajwīd* do enhance the aesthetic effect of Qur᾽anic recitation, it is *tajwīd* itself which encodes and makes perceptible both the unique nature of the text and the unique significance of the sound.

3. The *Samāᶜ* Polemic

The impulse to render the Qur'anic text melodically has been irresistible from the beginning of its practice, although, apart from phonetics and rhythm, we do not know how Qur'anic recitation sounded before the advent of recording technology.[1] Evidence for the early alliance of Qur'anic text and vocal artistry can be found in the literature of *samāᶜ*, a debate carried on by Muslim legists, litterateurs, Sufi thinkers, and others concerning the permissibility of musical audition of any sort.

Samāᶜ is, more generally, "audition," or "listening," but it has come to refer to listening to music and musical recitation of the Qur'an. In some Sufi treatises dance is discussed in the same context, since music, as a means to spiritual union with the divine (and thus spiritual ecstasy), may lead the listener into a physical response: "Know that the listening comes first, and that it bears as fruit a state in the heart that is called ecstasy, and ecstasy bears as fruit a moving of the extremities of the body" (al-Ġazālī n.d.: 8/1121).

The effect of the *samāᶜ* issue on Qur'anic recitation has been, on the one hand, to keep alive the resistance to associating the Qur'an with the musical art in any way, and, on the other hand, to inspire discussion on the acceptable limits of the use of melody in recitation. The result has been an authoritative body of guidelines regulating the melodic recitation of the Qur'an.

At the heart of the *samāᶜ* polemic is an attempt to deal with a strong suspicion on the part of many Muslims that the recognized power of music is somehow antithetical to the ideals of Islam. However, the argument for or against the enjoyment of music in an Islamic context is not simplistic. It has been fueled by a number of different factors, such as the interrelationship of music and poetry and the contrasting status of each art in Islamic and pre-Islamic society, the popularity of music and recognition of its affecting power, a romantic nostalgia for the pre- and early conquest days of Islamic society, and the role of music in religious devotion as it has been championed by the majority of Sufi brotherhoods.

The *samāᶜ* polemic has run for centuries, and it is unlikely that it will ever be resolved. The ultimate authority of the Qurʾan and the *Ḥadīṯ* offers no clear resolution,[2] nor has the flourishing practice of music been able to dispel those attitudes which led Muslims to censure it.[3]

Even in today's Egypt, where a variety of musical traditions are supported, the controversy is still very much alive. In 1977 the newspaper *al-Ahrām* published an article on the state of Qurʾanic recitation in Cairo today in response to a controversy (in the form of letters to the editor of the religious page) created by a specific performance of recitation that seemed to many to be almost indistinguishable from singing (Diyāb 1977: 11). The magazine *al-Iḏāᶜah wa l-Tilifizyūn* in 1978 published a report of a Ph.D. thesis from Cairo University entitled: "Music: Lawful or Unlawful?"[4] And in the summer of 1982 the magazine *al-Kawākib*, a popular magazine which features the world of show business, published interviews with two respected religious scholars who discussed melodic recitation and the status of the arts, respectively, vis-à-vis Islam.[5] Most contemporary books on the history of Arabic music include such discussions as "The Position of Islam with Regard to Music,"[6] or "Music in Islam."[7] The authors of such works usually acknowledge the *samāᶜ* polemic in that they present evidence in support of *samāᶜ*. It is clear not only that the polemic is part of the history of Arabic music, but that even today nothing may be taken for granted regarding the status of music, for the case continually must be made anew.[8]

The key word in the polemic is authority, for the debate represents an attempt either to bring music under the mantle of Islam, or to justify its repudiation through its incompatibility with the ideals of the Islamic community. For this reason the *samāᶜ* literature draws on four kinds of sources, which, in descending order of authority, are: 1. Qurʾan, 2. *Ḥadīṯ*, 3. pronouncements and behavior (*sunnah*) of companions of the Prophet and their associates, founders and legists of the legal schools, and men of pious reputation in general, and 4. scholarly and scientific observations of the effect and influence of music on all living creatures.[9] The *samāʿ* literature itself is found in works on Sufism and on the Qurʾanic disciplines in general, and, in modern times, in music history books and in the media.[10]

The status of music and poetry and the ideals of Islam are the raw materials of the *samāʿ* polemic. To begin, the musical tradition at the center of the controversy is a very specific one, that of the professional musician. It is this tradition which was carried by patronage into the most elite circles of Islamic society since pre-Islamic times.[11] Its theoretical foundations were developed and articulated by Islamic philosophers/musicians such as al-Fārābī (d. ca. 950) and al-Kindī (d. ca. 874). It is this highly self-conscious "art music" which is referred to by the term *al-mūsīqā l-ʿarabiyyah*, Arabic music.

In pre- and early Islamic Arabia this tradition was carried by the *qaynah*, a slave or freedwoman trained in the art of singing. There were two contexts in which she performed: the taverns or pleasure-houses, where she served paying customers wine and entertained them, and the court or the home of the urban or tribal elite, where her duties were the same, but the audience more select.

During the reign of Caliph ʿUṯmān (644–56) a new kind of singer appeared and shared the role of professional singer with the *qaynah*. This was the *muxannaṯ*, the effeminate male singer, apparently a common phenomenon in Persia, Byzantium, and Syria (Farmer 1973: 44). Like the *qaynah*, the *muxannaṯ* found patronage among the elite and powerful: he had patrons and even composers among the caliphs themselves.

The subsequent flowering of musical life as it was opened to the Persian and Greek influences through the Islamic conquests is described in *Kitāb al-Aġānī* (The Book of Songs), written in the tenth century by Abū l-Faraj al-Isfahānī.[12] In this work we learn that music was no longer solely the arena of slaves, menials, and social deviants. The nobility joined the ranks not only as patrons and composers, but also as performers and theorists.[13] Further, singers acquired prestige and a higher status in society, sharing rank with the prestigious poets, literati, and savants (al-Isfahānī 1927–74: 5/286–87). Al-Isfahānī depicts a people infatuated with music.

But from the same source we learn that this florescence was tempered by an official disapproval of music.[14] Al-Isfahānī is not concerned with defending the art; thus the theme is woven through the fabric of his text with no special emphasis. In the following anecdotes from al-Isfahānī himself, however, the implications are clear. The first story concerns the *muxannaṯ* Ṭuways (632–711). It is related that the governor of Medina, Marwān ibn al-Ḥakam, offered a reward for every *muxannaṯ* put into his hands, and one was indeed put to death for making light of not reading the Qurʾan. Ṭuways had to seek refuge and lived out the rest of his life bitterly resenting the fact that his great musical reputation had not saved him from persecution (al-Isfahānī 1927–74: 3/29–30). The other story concerns Isḥāq Ibrāhīm al-Mawṣilī (767–850), chief musician of the court of Caliph al-Maʾmūn. He was famous for his wit and learning as well as for his music. The caliph is reported to have said concerning al-Mawṣilī's moral virtue, "Were he not so publicly known for his singing, I would make him a *qāḍī* [Islamic jurist]" (al-Isfahānī 1927–74: 5/272–73). The *qāḍī*, as dispenser of justice and upholder of the Islamic law, must be an example of righteousness, and it was felt that a righteous musician was a contradiction in terms.

The negative image of music can be better appreciated if we contrast the position of music with that of poetry, for although the two are intimately connected, poetry has escaped the opprobrium directed at music.

The interconnection of music and poetry cannot be overemphasized. Al-Isfahānī was not being whimsical or innovative when he chose to write equally about poets and singers. Although it is poetry which has been considered the great heritage of the Arabs since pre-Islamic times, and which has given vocal music more prestige and popularity than instrumental music, it is recognized that the effect of a poem is heightened by music:

> . . . and when a pleasant voice and measured tunes are added to it [poetry] then its effect increases. Then, if a drum and *šāhīn*

> and the movements of rhythm be added to it, the effect increases [still more].[15]
>
> (al-Ġazālī n.d. 8/1133)

A modern scholar says, "Probably much of pre-Islamic poetry was sung. . . . Only by this means could full justice be done to the poetic language."[16] Certainly countless references in Arabic writings support this and testify to the continuation of the practice after the advent of Islam: ". . . and most of the poetry of Ḥassān ibn Ṯābit is sung" (Ibn ʿAbd Rabbih 1968: 6/6),

> . . . and the Prophet had al-Šarīd mounted behind him, and asked him to recite some of the poetry of Ummayyah. So he recited a hundred rhymes and he [the Prophet] was saying, "well done," thinking them good. Then, when the satire in the poetry, and the talking about it, tired them, they said, "poetry is good, and we do not see that a beautiful melody detracts from it."
>
> (Ibn ʿAbd Rabbih 1968: 6/7)

We read a report that the famous pre-Islamic poet Imru l-Qays sang his poetry to his (female) cousin (al-Ixtiyār 1953: 13), and, in *Kitāb al-Aġānī*, that a poet would go into partnership with a singer, that he would hire a singer to sing his texts (al-Isfahānī 1927–74: 6/65). Most of the poetic texts cited by al-Isfahānī are identified not only by author, but by composer/performer. For example, al-Isfahānī reports that a poem by the pre-Islamic poetess al-Xansāʾ was set to music by Ibrāhīm al-Mawṣilī (al-Isfahānī 1927–74: 15/75).[17] Thus the distinction made between song and poem seems unclear, and the differentiation was probably made at the level of performance. It seems to have been the rendering of the poem by a professional musician (possibly with characteristic instrumental accompaniment) as much as the style of melodic rendering (i.e., more consciously ornamented) that transformed the poem into song.

Further evidence for the close association of poetry and music lies in the anecdotes and verses that, in testifying to the magical skill of the early singers, praise their language and poetic skills.[18] They evidenced a mastery of the Arabic language as well as superior knowledge of the poetic language, for the material of their songs was some of the greatest poetry of the time.[19]

In Egypt today good pronunciation and correct inflection (*iʿrāb*) are among the singer's criteria for excellence. Students at the Music Conservatory in Cairo study *tajwīd* with a religious scholar to improve their diction. One of the questions given to students taking their oral exams at the Music Institute of Cairo (June 1978) was "What distinguishes a singer who has studied *tajwīd* from one who has not?"—the correct answer is "Good pronunciation." One of the common complaints directed against singers of today is that, lacking traditional education (and therefore not drilled in correct pronunciation and inflection), they mouth their words unintelligibly. This is not merely a reflection of modern taste: Ibn Surayj (ca. 634–726) listed what was expected of a good singer, and among his points were good pronunciation and correct inflection (al-Isfahānī 1927–74: 1/315).

In spite of their close association, poetry and music retain separate images. Moreover, it seems that attitudes which award poetry a high status and music a low status are not dictated by Islamic authority, but only justified after the fact. For although the status of music is not authoritatively regulated in the Qur'an, we do find there explicit warning against listening to the poets:

> And the poets, the perverse follow them;
> hast thou not seen how they wander in every valley
> and how they say that which they do not?
>
> (Qur. 26/224–26)

However, these verses are generally interpreted to be not an injunction against poetry as such, but a recognition of its power, and a warning to those who would use it against Islam.[20]

Poetry was indeed a powerful art; the tribal poet and later the court poets of the caliphate used poetry as an offensive and defensive weapon in the service of tribe and patron. Through skilled use of insult or praise poetry could build and destroy reputation and honor. It gave courage to warriors as they charged into battle, and since it was inspired by the jinn, the spell of its magic might very well make truth seem false. That power harnessed in the service of Islam is certainly acceptable, as the many stories of the Prophet's fondness for poetry testify. Islam had its own poetic champion, Ḥassān ibn Ṭābit, to whom, it is reported, the Prophet once said,

> Pour out [an incitement to] the raid against the Banī ʿAbd Manāf, for by Allah your poetry is more potent than falling arrows in the darkness of dawn.
>
> (Ibn ʿAbd Rabbih 1968: 6/6)

The disparity in the status of poetry and music seems, then, to be a matter of role and context. Poetry in pre-Islamic Arabia was linked to the highest ideals of honor and manhood: "It is the register of the Arabs and declares precepts, and is the witness of their noble actions" (Ibn ʿAbd Rabbih 1968: 6/9–10). In pre-Islamic Arabia it was poetry that upheld the honor of the tribe, that gave meaning to its way of life. Thus, it was the heroic odes and not the love lyrics that defined poetry as an art par excellence, and the story that the emergence of a poet was celebrated with the same joy as was the birth of a son or a mare is a much-quoted testimony to the importance accorded the profession.

Singing, however, was a mere pastime: whereas the poet could heighten the events and thus the meaning of his or her listeners' lives, the *qaynah* could only heighten the effect of the particular text and help her listeners to while away the time. It is significant that it is the entertainment genre of the professional musician that is specifically singled out to bear the brunt of a general disapproval of music, and not the war songs, pilgrim chants, laments, and riding songs.

That disapproval was leveled most specifically at professional music might be due in part to its association with the cosmopolitan influences of postconquest times, for the simpler songs of a pre-Islamic, preconquest way of life were identified with an idealization of these Arabs as pure and uncorrupted by artifice or foreign influence.

Finally, with the coming of Islam we see that poets could exchange their old loyalties and high ideals for those of Islam: the context and function of pre–Islamic poetry were compatible with the new religion. But musicians found themselves and their art in an ambivalent position. Although the practice of music increased, it was felt by many Muslims that music was essentially a frivolous, if not abhorrent, vanity having little to do with the things that matter in this life or the next. The appearance of the *muxannaṯ* must have added to censure of this art, for taking up the profession of music was considered to lead to loss of *murūʾah* (manly, chivalric virtues):

> And as for al-Šāfiʿī his school does not pronounce singing unlawful as a fundamental principle.[21] Al-Šāfiʿī laid down a rule, and said of the man who takes up singing as a profession that his testimony is not allowable [in court]. And that is because it belongs to the dubious amusements and resembles what is vain, and he who takes it up as a profession is put in a relationship to folly, and the loss of *murūʾah*.
>
> (al-Ġazālī n.d.: 8/1147)[22]

In the Šāfiʿī law manual, *al-Tanbīh*, persons whose testimony must be rejected are listed as follows: "deranged persons, heedless persons or simpletons, those who have no *murūʾah*, such as scavengers, rag gatherers, sweepers, bathmen, those who play in the bath and singers, dancers, jugglers, those who eat in the streets and make water in public and play at chess on the highway."[23]

Ultimately one should be able to look to the authority of the Qurʾan to reconcile the un-Islamic image of music with its widespread practice. But as there is no explicit mention of music in the text, it cannot be employed in legislating the propriety of *samāʿ*. However, attitudes need no legislation and can rely on inference and interpretation to justify themselves. Thus the verses of the Qurʾan are interpreted according to the point of view presented. Those verses most commonly cited and interpreted by the opponents of *samāʿ* are:

> Prosperous are the believers
> who in their prayers are humble
> and from idle talk [*laġw*] turn away.
>
> (Qur. 23/1–3)

> . . . and those who bear not false witness
> and, when they pass by idle talk [*laġw*], pass by
> with dignity.
>
> (Qur. 25/72)

> When they hear idle talk [*laġw*], they turn away from it.
>
> (Qur. 31/5)

On the surface these verses do not appear to be directly concerned with music. However, Ibn Masʿūd (d. ca. 652–54) and al-Ḥasan al-Baṣrī (d. 728) are cited for the interpretation that "idle talk" refers to music (al-Ġazālī n.d.: 8/1148). Likewise, opponents of *samā*ʿ, starting from the point of view that music is futile folly, have no trouble accepting the interpretation that "idle talk" applies to music.[24]

These interpretations do not go unchallenged. Referring to Qurʾan 31/5, Ibn ʿAbd Rabbih says:

> . . . and they err in their interpretation. This verse was revealed only about people who were purchasing story books of biographies and tales of the ancients, and compared these with the Qurʾan and said that they are better than it. But he who listens to singing does not take the verses of Allah for mockery.
>
> (Ibn ʿAbd Rabbih 1968: 6/9)

Al-Ġazālī counters the above interpretations by challenging their implication with the report that Ibn Jurayj (d. 767):

> was wont to allow listening to music and singing, and that it was said to him, "Will this be brought on the day of resurrection among thy good deeds or thy evil deeds?" He said, "Neither in the good deeds nor the evil deeds, for it is like idle talk [*laġw*], and God Most High has said, 'Allah will not call you to account for thoughtlessness [*laġw*] in your oaths'" [Qur. 2/225, ʿAlī 1946].
>
> (al-Ġazālī n.d.: 8/1124)

Al-Ġazālī goes on to point out that if idle talk is not censured with regard to something important like oaths, then how can it be censured in less important contexts? In other words, even if music were to be labeled as folly and vanity, that is no reason for censure, for "it is said that music and singing are amusement and play, and so they are, but the whole of this world is amusement and play."[25]

Another verse cited in support of the censure of music as vanity is:

> And will ye laugh and not weep, wasting your time in vanities [*sāmidūn*]?
>
> (Qur. 53/60–61, ʿAlī 1946)

Opponents of *samāʿ* interpret *sāmidūn* to mean singing.[26]

The following verse seems to be the least subject to variant interpretation with regard to the polemic, and it is unchallenged in the *samāʿ* literature:

> [Allah speaking to Satan] Lead to destruction those whom thou canst among them with thy voice [*ṣawt*].
>
> (Qur. 17/64, ʿAlī 1946)[27]

Those in support of *samāʿ* justify their view with their interpretations of the following verses:

> He adds to Creation as He pleases.
>
> (Qur. 35/1, ʿAlī 1946)

It is generally accepted in the *samāʿ* literature that the reference here is to the beautiful voice (*al-ṣawt al-ḥasan*),[28] and, as al-Ġazālī elaborates, "The permissibility of hearing a beautiful voice is shown by the fact that Allah has granted such to His creatures" (al-Ġazālī n.d.: 8/1125).

> The most hideous of voices is the ass's.
>
> (Qur. 31/19)

The argument here (and none of the sources is more specific) is that this is implicit praise of the beautiful voice.[29]

> Then those who have believed and worked righteous deeds, shall be made happy [*yuḥbarūn*] in a Mead of Delight.
>
> (Qur. 30/14, ʿAlī 1946)

The term *yuḥbarūn* is generally interpreted by proponents of *samāʿ* to mean "singing," or, more specifically (according to Mujāhid as quoted in al-Qušayrī 1959: 169), "listening to the voices of the houris."[30]

The evidence of the other authoritative sources such as the *Ḥadīṯ* is clear yet contradictory. For example, concerning the *mizmār* (a reed or pipe or flute),[31] the following is attributed to the Prophet (on the authority of Abū Umāmah [d. 700]):

> Allāh's apostle said, Allāh sent me as a blessing and guidance to all creatures. He sent me to annihilate the stringed instru-

> ments and the *mazāmīr* [plural of *mizmār*] and to destroy the *Jāhiliyyah* and the idols.
>
> (al-Dunyā/Robson 1938: 52)

It is also reported that Muhammad said, "There are two cursed sounds, the sound of wailing at a disaster, and the sound of a *mizmār* in a melody."[32] A much debated *ḥadīṯ* is the following on the authority of Nāfiʿ:

> I was with Ibn ʿUmar on the road, and I heard the *zammārah* [playing of the *mizmār*] of a shepherd, and he put his fingers in his ears, then turned from the road, and did not cease saying, "Nāfiʿ, do you hear it?" until I said, "No." Then he took his fingers out and said, "Thus I saw the Apostle of God do."
>
> (al-Dunyā/Robson 1938: 52; al-Ġazālī n.d.: 8/1151)

The implications of this as discussed in the *samā*ʿ literature are as follows:

> But as for the mizmār, it is forbidden to listen to it on account of what has come down in the tradition that he [Muhammad] heard the sound of the mizmār and stopped his ears.
>
> (al-Dunyā/Robson 1938: 52)

And on the other hand:

> Again, in the stories of particular cases, the possible views are many. For example, opposed to his putting his fingers in his ears is the fact that he did not command Nāfiʿ to do the like and did not disapprove of his listening. He only did it himself because he considered that he should guard his ear in its then condition, and his heart from a sound which would usually provoke amusement [*lahw*], and so might hinder him from a thought he was engaged in or a recollection that was more important.
>
> (al-Ġazālī n.d.: 8/1151)

Many sources cite the tradition that Muhammad, on hearing Abū Mūsā l-Ašʿarī reciting the Qurʾan, said to him, "Verily thou hast been gifted with a *mizmār* like the *mazāmīr* of David" (who, of course, was known for his beautiful voice).[33]

Similar contradiction is found regarding the allowability of listening to the *qaynah*. There are a number of *ḥadīṯ* which show the Prophet listening to their singing. In one of the more commonly cited of these, Abū Bakr comes in and, finding two girls singing, rebukes them. But Muhammad says, "Leave them alone for these are feast days."[34] Contrary to this evidence is the *ḥadīṯ* given on the authority of Abū Umāmah, who said, "Allāh has forbidden the singing-girl and selling her and her price and teaching her and listening to her" (al-Dunyā/Robson 1938: 46). Abū l-Ṭayyib al-Ṭabarī quotes al-Šāfiʿī: "If the owner of a female slave gather men together to listen to her, he is of light understanding and you shall repudiate his testimony" (al-Ġazālī n.d.: 8/1121).

These latter *ḥadīṯ* are subjected to interpretation by the proponents of *samā*ʿ. Al-Ġazālī says that the *ḥadīṯ* by Abū Umāmah only applies to "the female slave who sings to men in a place where there is drinking, for we have mentioned that the singing of a strange woman to the dissolute and to those for whom temptation is something to be feared is forbidden" (al-Ġazālī n.d.: 8/1148). Majd al-Dīn bases his argument for *samā*ʿ on the existence of those well-documented stories of the Prophet and his companions and saintly men listening to music and accuses those who would censure music of finding fault with the Prophet, undermining the authority of the sources, and rejecting the guidance of established authority (Majd al-Dīn/Robson 1938: 126–56)!

As to the type of evidence drawn from general human observation by scholars and scientists, there are reports that singing "decreases shame, increases desire, and destroys murūʾah, and indeed, takes the place of wine and what drunkenness does" (al-Dunyā/Robson 1938: 49), that singing "is the amulet of fornication" (al-Dunyā/Robson 1938: 49), that it "makes hypocrisy to spring up in the heart."[35] But we also read that "the beautiful melody is a spirit from God which revives burning hearts" (al-Sarrāj al-Ṭūsī 1960: 339), and that one may apprehend

> the blessings of this world and the next by means of beautiful melodies. And proof of that is that they induce generosities of character in performing kindnesses and observing family ties, and defending one's honor and overlooking faults. And sometimes man will weep over his sins by means of melodies, and

> the heart will be softened from hardness and man will remember the joy of heaven and picture it in his mind.
>
> (Ibn ʿAbd Rabbih 1968: 6/5)

Al-Ġazālī states:

> The consequence of hearing music and singing is that he who was weak in counsel is set to work, and he who was distant from meditation is driven forward, and he who was wearied on account of worries and plans is sharpened.
>
> (al-Ġazālī n.d. 8/1132)

Music quiets and calms the child,[36] and refreshes the camel on the long journey.[37] In conjunction with references to the responsiveness of the camel to singing, al-Qušayrī quotes the Qur'anic verse "Have you not considered how the camel was created?" (Qur. 88/17) to indicate not only God's approbation, but His will for this responsiveness (al-Qušayrī 1959: 167). Finally, in a medical-ethical treatise on maintaining the health of the body and the soul, we find a chapter devoted to *samā*ʿ, which, "since it is equally useful for the soul and the body," has been put at the end (Biesterfeldt 1976: 31–32).

Closer examination of the attitudes that shape all this material makes it clear that they are not starkly opposed.[38] Although the attitude of opposition to *samā*ʿ is uncompromising, the majority of those writers who support *samā*ʿ do so with various reservations and qualifications.

The first of these attitudes, the one which unequivocally repudiates music, is characterized by a puritanical suspicion of everything pleasurable. These are the people, explains Ibn ʿAbd Rabbih, who object to pleasures, refusing such foods as white flour, in a general abstinence from this world (Ibn ʿAbd Rabbih 1968: 6/10). It is the view of those who regard all which does not contribute directly to salvation as frivolous. We have seen evidence of this in the defining of music as amusement, idle talk, and nonsense. Ibn Abī al-Dunyā, whose treatise *Ḏamm al-Malāhī* (1938) reflects this view consistently, quotes a characteristic report:

> A man asked al-Qāsim ibn Muḥammad about singing and he said, "I forbid you it and make it abhorrent to you." He said, "Is it unlawful?" He said, "Look, O son of my brother, when

> Allāh distinguishes the truth from what is vain, in which of them will he put singing?"[39]
>
> (al-Dunyā/Robson 1938: 47)

The second attitude is held by those who accept the pleasure of listening to music:

> Anyone who says that he finds no pleasure in sounds and melodies and music is either a liar and a hypocrite or he is not in his right senses, and is outside of the category of men and beasts.
>
> (al-Ḥujwīrī/Nicholson 1976: 401)

But even this acceptance of music is qualified. Music must be handled carefully and sparingly, not because it is pleasurable ("for there is no one who regards the voice of the nightingale or those of the other birds as forbidden," al-Ġazālī n.d.: 8/1126), but because it is possible to respond to it in ways unacceptable to Islam; "its lawfulness depends on circumstances and cannot be asserted absolutely: if audition produces a lawful effect on the mind, then it is lawful; it is unlawful, if the effect is unlawful" (al-Ḥujwīrī/Nicholson 1976: 401–2).

According to this attitude, music is itself a neutral, if potent, power; it is the spiritual state of the listener that transforms its influence into a tool for good or evil. Most of those holding this view are Sufis, who, since (with the exception of the Naqšabandī order) they use music "as a vehicle for the ascent of the spirit to the transcendent world,"[40] address themselves particularly to the regulation of *samāᶜ*, setting out the contexts, circumstances, and states of mind in which *samāᶜ* is to be considered welcome, permitted, or forbidden.[41]

Even with regulation, music can be too much of a good thing according to al-Ġazālī. He likens it to a mole on the cheek, which is considered a mark of beauty, whereas a face covered with moles is repulsive (al-Ġazālī n.d.: 8/1146).

A dissident voice in the issue of regulating *samāᶜ* is that of Majd al-Dīn, brother of al-Ġazālī. His acceptance of music is not so wary:

> Then if he who disapproves says, the audition of the *fuqarā'* [spiritually motivated] is allowable according to the conditions

> you have mentioned, but the audition of the common people is unlawful we say, no one has a right to declare anything lawful or unlawful in the Law as long as the lawgiver has laid down no statute about it according to what has come down in the tradition . . . further, regarding the audition and dancing of the common people, their recreations in gardens compare with the audition and dancing of the Abyssinians in the presence of Allāh's apostle and there is no dispute about the permissibility of that.[42]
>
> (Majd al-Dīn/Robson 1938: 150–1)

Despite a more liberal view, the polemicists who hold that it is context which determines the lawfulness of *samāᶜ* cannot deny the salacious associations of music, and proponents and opponents of *samāᶜ* meet on the liability of the early context of music. Most of the polemicists agree that stringed instruments, the *kūbah* drum,[43] and the *mizmār* are forbidden. Al-Ġazālī elaborates characteristically, arguing that the proscription has nothing to do with their being pleasurable, but is because they are a prelude to drinking wine, and so forth, "and a little wine is forbidden, even though it does not intoxicate, because it invites to intoxication" (al-Ġazālī n.d.: 8/1127). Moreover, since "he who becomes like to a people becomes one of them" (al-Ġazālī n.d.: 8/1127), the *kūbah* drum is prohibited because it was used by the *muxannaṯ*.

A second but related kind of discrimination on the part of *samāᶜ* writers leads to such statements as "We grant the permissibility of playing the tambourine which has no metal plates for the tambourine of the Arabs was like that, but we do not admit the permissibility of playing the tambourine with metal plates" (Majd al-Dīn/Robson 1938: 154) and "The only song to which one may listen is that of the camel drivers. All other unaccompanied singing is disapproved."[44] This may be attributed to a chauvinism which championed the simple desert life of the tribes in the face of a flood of foreign importations dictating speech, etiquette, dress, and so forth, and reflects a romanticization of the language and way of life of those Arabs uncontaminated by the cosmopolitan and urban decadence of postconquest Islamic society.[45]

A third theme or issue shaping the polemic exploits the link between music and poetry. The more liberal of the polemicists consider the widespread support of poetry as a very persuasive factor in the support of music. We are told that the Prophet not only enjoyed poetry but was close to being a poet himself: "It has happened that the expression of the Prophet . . . was close to poetry, even though he did not intend it to be poetry" (al-Qušayrī 1959: 166). Ibn ᶜAbd Rabbih is more explicit: ". . . and one argument of those who permit it [*samāᶜ*] is that it has its origin in poetry, which the Prophet commended: he incited to it and urged his companions to it, and found help in it against the unbelievers" (Ibn ᶜAbd Rabbih 1968: 6/6).[46]

An argument of those defending the neutral power of music, and exploiting the close identification of music with poetry, is that a song is judged lawful or not on the basis of the lawfulness of the meaning of its text.[47] The burden of disapprobation is carried in this case by the poetry.

These attitudes show an aspect characteristic of the body of medieval *samāᶜ* literature which is available to the scholar. We see that, with the exception of Ibn Abī l-Dunyā's treatise *Ḏamm al-Malāhī* (1938), all the evidence used by the opponents of *samāᶜ* is to be found in the more equivocally pro-*samāᶜ* works. Those who advocate *samāᶜ* in the literature tend to use the evidence of the sources as the basis of logical persuasion, and one of the tactics of this persuasion is to disqualify or disarm the opposing evidence. When contrasted with the single-minded work of Ibn Abī l-Dunyā (who is content to let the evidence speak for itself with little or no analysis of his own, and certainly no reference to any divergent opinions), the effect is that *samāᶜ* supporters seem to be working from a less secure position which requires of them a more defensive posture.

In current Egyptian treatment of and references to the question of *samāᶜ*, this defensive tone has significantly weakened. In fact, although the question of the propriety of music in an Islamic context is still being asked in the media and in scholarly discussions, the only voices responding belong to those who accept its legitimacy, and the status quo of a society in which music is vigorous and pervasive goes unchallenged. For now it is the proponents of *samāᶜ* who are secure enough in assuming the basic acceptability of *samāᶜ* to let their case rest on the authority of their sources.

Given that listening to melodies is acceptable and even regarded as having a positive virtue in the right circumstances, and that the lawfulness of song depends on the text used, what kind of text can best effect this virtue? This issue in the polemic brings us back to Qurʾanic recitation, since the texts in question are the Qurʾan and poetry. There is some difference of opinion, and the arguments vary in their complexity. Al-Ḥurwīrī and al-Makkī both assert the supremacy of the Qurʾan in everything, holding that:

> The most beneficial audition to the mind, and the most delightful to the ear is that of the Word of God. . . . It is a miraculous quality of the Qurʾan that one never grows weary of reading and hearing it.
>
> (al-Ḥujwīrī/Nicholson 1976: 394)

and:

> Listening to the Qurʾan is lawful, listening to singing unlawful, listening to odes of a religious nature doubtful.[48]

A number of stories in the literature testify to the power of the recited Qurʾan: swooning or even dying are among its most extreme effects.[49]

Others find poetry more effective. Al-Sarrāj al-Ṭūsī argues that the preference for poetry set to music shows respect for the Qurʾan, as it is of divine origin and can therefore not be adorned by music, which is of human origin, "rather, it is by means of it that things are adorned" (al-Sarrāj al-Ṭūsī 1960: 356).

This is also the basis of al-Ġazālī's argument for the effectiveness of poetry over the Qurʾan. He argues further that the immutability of the Qurʾan makes it an inappropriate medium for *samāʿ* for the following reasons. First, because poetry is subject to interpretation by the individual, but "It is not allowable to apply the word of God Most High except to what He intended" (al-Ġazālī n.d.: 8/1175). Second, what is recited from the Qurʾan may not suit the state of the listener, and he may not (as with poetry) reject it or pervert it in any way (al-Ġazālī n.d.: 8/1175). Third, it is not permitted to play around with the given durations of the syllables of the Qurʾanic text, and it is precisely this play in poetry that has such an effect on the soul (al-Ġazālī n.d.: 8/1174).

But the essence of al-Ġazālī's argument is his insistence on the separation of the Qurʾan from the human sphere. He feels the Qurʾan should be kept at a distance from music and its soiled associations (al-Ġazālī n.d.: 8/1174). He quotes al-Sarrāj: "The Qur'an is the word of God and one of His qualities; and it is a truth which humanity cannot comprehend" (al-Ġazālī n.d.: 8/1175, original in al-Sarrāj al-Ṭūsī 1960: 356). He elaborates this point, carrying it further:

> A new verse will rouse from them what the recital of the Qur'an does not rouse. It is because of the measure of the poetry and its being in accord with natural qualities that human beings have the power of composing poetry. But the composing of the Qur'an lies outside of the paths and tracks of speech, and on account of that it is a miracle which does not enter into the power of human beings because of its not being in accord with their nature.
>
> (al-Ġazālī n.d.: 8/1176)

The mutual exclusivity of the divine and human spheres (in this case, the Qur'an and poetry) explains what would otherwise be a definite inconsistency in the argument. Thus, some points of al-Ġazālī's argument come close to undermining the overall superiority of the Qur'an which he is trying to maintain. For example, he says that the first hearing of a text has the most profound effect, and since most believers have memorized the Qur'an, they are indifferent to its power (al-Ġazālī n.d.: 8/1173). Likewise, several scholars cite and defend, without a hint of blasphemy, the story of Yūsuf ibn al-Ḥusayn al-Rāzī, who was deeply moved on hearing a verse of poetry and upset to realize that he had been reading the Qur'an for hours with no such response.[50]

This issue in the polemic is, of course, testimony for the widespread practice of melodic recitation of the Qur'an. This is not surprising, given the link of poetry with music and the inherent musicality of the text itself in terms of rhyme, rhythm, and assonance. The many studies of, and allusions to, Qur'anic style, as well as the *iʿjāz* works, make use of poetic terminology in describing the style of the Qur'an, employing poetic style as a reference point in general.[51]

To summarize, then, the *samāʿ* polemic is an attempt to define the position of music with respect to the values of the Islamic community. That there is a need to do so can be attributed to several factors: 1. the popularity of music was such that it was felt to be important to explain its attraction rather than ignore it; 2. music and musicians had associations with contexts and lifestyles unacceptable to Islam; 3. to a lesser degree the polemic was also one of the forums in which the traditional values of an ideal age were upheld against the corruptions of foreign innovation.

There are basically two positions in the polemic: those who reject *samāʿ* unconditionally and those who accept it conditionally. However sharp their apparent divergences in the debate, these two positions share the basic premise that music is a powerful and affecting force. For the opponents of *samāʿ*, it is a force which distracts from—if not actually interferes in—the struggle to achieve God's will. For *samāʿ*'s proponents, most notably the Sufis, music is a neutral force which, channeled and regulated, can just as well lead to God as away from Him. It is human response and poetic text which are variously held responsible for the un-Islamic influence of music.

The arguments of those who reject *samāʿ* are characterized by a simple enumeration of statements supporting their position. Those who accept *samāʿ*, however conditionally, not only present their own evidence but respond to the statements of their opponents in the polemic with careful and logical argument for their position. Their arguments can be classified by issue, whereas it is attitude that is most prominent in the presentations of the first group.

The two main bases of support with which polemicists justify *samāʿ* are the acceptance of the beautiful voice (*al-ṣawt al-ḥasan*) in Islamic contexts, and the close identity of music with poetry. The first rests on numerous religious authoritative references in praise of the beautiful voice. The second exploits the more positive image of poetry and its close ties to music, drawing on the prestige of poetry to make the case for music. The widespread practice of melodic recitation is used as justification in the same way.

Finally, the polemic cannot be definitively resolved, as the ultimate authority, the Qurʾan, is not specific on the subject of music, and its verses have been variously interpreted by the polemicists. The *Ḥadīṯ* contain material supporting both points of view, and the pronouncements of leading figures differ.

Perhaps because of the lack of any authoritative resolution of the *samāʿ* debate, both the popularity of music and the perception of it as un-Islamic have persisted side by side through the centuries. In current Egyptian practice, the polemic seems to have been resolved in favor of the view of music as essentially morally neutral. But the ambivalence persists: the legacy of *samāʿ* is such that although most Egyptian Muslims never question the compatibility of music with Islamic principles, they do instinctively resist its association with the Qurʾan. And just as music flourished in the face of official disapproval, so has the melodic recitation of the Qurʾan continued as a widespread practice and even, in Egypt, a source of pride. This state of affairs has no doubt played a role in shaping the perception of melodic recitation as a unique art, separate from music.[52] In looking at the principles by which scholars have accepted and regulated melody in the ideal Qurʾanic recitation we confront both an awareness of the power of music and its controversial status vis-à-vis Islamic ideals.

4. The Ideal Recitation of the Qur'an

Because of the *samā'* polemic, Western scholars of Islam, as well as most Muslims, have assumed that acceptance of melodic recitation of the Qur'an, however widespread, is basically a compromise of Islamic principles and a submission to the pressure of its popularity. Many non-Egyptian Muslims, especially, suspect the acceptability of the Egyptian tradition of recitation in view of its great appeal, and some have even declared to me that Egyptians are not really Muslims if they condone it.

However, an examination of the ideal Qur'anic recitation, as it is treated in the long tradition of authoritative religious scholarship, proves that this prejudice cannot be justified. We find that the ideal recitation is defined according to an intent which not only accepts, but depends on the melodic element for its fulfillment. The melody draws the listener more deeply into the experience, and there is no sense of a separation between the aesthetic and the religious involvement.

The ideal recitation is a paradox. Participants in the tradition are not lined up on opposite sides of a line separating music from recitation. They all agree first, that the Qur'an is paramount in its divine uniqueness and perfection, and second, that melody is essential to the most effective Qur'anic recitation. The inherent contradiction between these two premises is accepted, even unquestioned, as long as the right balance of elements is maintained.

The issues and terminology which form the basis of the following discussion on the ideal recitation of the Qur'an are taken from fieldwork in Egypt and from a pertinent selection of the texts used in Egyptian institutions of Qur'anic learning, and/or those texts recommended to me by Egyptian Qur'anic scholars. The relationship of these sources to each other is the following: after a year of fieldwork, a year of listening to Egyptians talk about Qur'anic recitation, I was able to summarize what seemed to me to be the clear consensus of the Egyptian resolution of the issues involved in the acceptability of a melodic recitation. A subsequent study of the scholarly literature revealed that the Egyptian perception of melodic Qur'anic recitation is firmly grounded, in detail as well as in general principle, in the writings of generations of Islamic religious scholars, and that it is not solely an Egyptian or an Islamic sectarian accommodation of theory to practice.

Issues

The concerns and attitudes that shape Egyptian perception of Qur'anic recitation can be traced in the sources to two main areas of Qur'anic scholarship. These are the enumeration of the virtues of the Qur'an (*faḍā'il al-qur'ān*) and of the code of behavior regulating recitation (*ādāb tilāwat al-qur'ān*). The first establishes the importance of reciting the Qur'an, and the second describes how it should be done. From both we deduce the role which has been defined for recitation, and the intended aim of that role or, in other words, the expectations which shape its regulation.

Faḍā'il al-Qur'ān not only embraces the intrinsic virtues of the revelation itself, but fixes the importance of the believer's obligation vis-à-vis the learning, teaching, listening, and reciting of the Qur'an. The fulfillment of this obligation gains spiritual merit for the believer and assures the continued and correct transmission of the revelation (al-Zarkašī 1957: 456).

In the context of the *faḍā'il* we read such *ḥadīṯ as:*

> Verily he who has nothing to do with the Qur'an is like the deserted house.
>
> ('Uṯmān 1969: 15)

> The best of you is he who learns and teaches the Qur'ān.
>
> (al-Zarkašī 1957: 455)[1]

> To him who listens to a verse from the Book of God Most High are ten blessings.
>
> (al-Makkī 1961: 125)

> The superior worship of my community [*ummah*] is the *tilāwah* of the Qur'an.
>
> (Naṣr 1930: 246)[2]

Al-Zarkašī cites one of the companions of the Prophet: "Teaching the Qur'an is a collective duty, and therefore its memorization is incumbent upon the community."[3]

The central importance of recitation in all of this is clear: teaching and learning are oral, that is, the teacher recites, the student listens, memorizes, and recites back what he or she has heard. My teacher, Šayx ʿAbd al-Mutaʿāl, pointed out to me that there is divine recommendation of this mode of learning, not only in the fact that this is how Muhammad learned the revelation, but in the verse:

> Move not thy tongue with it to hasten it;
> Ours is to gather it, and to recite it.
> So when We recite it, follow thou its recitation.
> Then Ours is to explain it.
>
> (Qur. 75/16–19)

According to Šayx ʿAbd al-Mutaʿāl, this is essentially a command to listen as the best way to learn. And what is listened to is recitation. Šayx Aḥmad al-Ruzayqī, explaining the style of reciting called *murattal*, said that it is for worship and for learning, and that it is not possible to learn to recite the Qur'an, or to memorize it, on your own. Indeed, the unprecedented recording and subsequent broadcasting of the *murattal* style (1960, see chapter 5) was done with the aim of providing an oral model for learning and memorizing the Qur'an. And a primary justification given for this official project was that the loss of the art of recitation was feared, since it is not possible to learn and memorize the text from the more widely broadcast melodic style.

Listening is followed by active learning: *ḥifḍ*, "memorization." Memorization is still the starting point for Qur'anic studies in the Muslim world. Indeed, some of the more advanced texts, such as those on the *qirā'āt*, presuppose a memorization of the Qur'an in the way their material is organized. Although it is no longer a requirement for admission to al-Azhar university, memorization of the Qur'an is still a basic requirement for admission to the Institute of Qirā'āt, an affiliate of al-Azhar.[4]

The role of *ḥifḍ* in Islamic learning presupposes a concept of knowledge as "fixed, memorizable truths" (Eickelman 1978: 491). I had personal experience with this concept in the course of my own studies in Egypt. My lessons in *tajwīd* were conducted without the aid of any text other than the Qur'an. When I was called upon to state a rule, it was not enough to give the basic principle; I was expected to quote it verbatim, as I had received it from my teacher. Toward the end of my studies I asked my teacher to help me acquire the basics of the *qirā'āt*, and he very capably summarized a great deal of the material for me. But when I told a reciter that I had begun a study of the *qirā'āt* and mentioned the title of the text I was using as reference, he asked me, "To which line have you memorized?"

Ḥifḍ means "to preserve," both literally and figuratively (as in the expression *ḥifḍ ʿala ḍahr al-qalb*, "learning by heart," that is, "preserving on the back of the heart"). In much of the Islamic world, the Qur'an reciter is called *ḥāfiḍ* or *ḥāfiḍah*, "preserver," "memorizer," for he or she is an important link in the transmission—and thus the preservation—of the Qur'an; the first requirement for the professional reciter is to have the complete text in his memory. The author of a text on the *qirā'āt* writes that *ḥifḍ* is necessary to anyone wanting to recite (*qara'a*) a book, not only to be able to distinguish personal differences in reciting, but so as not to deviate too much from the text (al-Safāqisī 1934: 13). And in a section entitled "Concerning Continuing to Recite the Qur'an after Learning It" al-Zarkašī cites two *ḥadīṯ* which exhort the believer to keep a firm grip on the Qur'an, for it is more likely to bolt (from the mind) than a camel from its halter (al-Zarkašī 1957: 458; see Naṣr 1930: 242 for a variant). Naṣr cites the *ḥadīṯ* "He who recites the Qur'an and then forgets it will meet God on the Day of Resurrection in a mutilated state" (Naṣr 1930: 242).

That memorizing involves reciting is to be expected in this context and is well documented in the sources. For example, the following passage describes the memorizing process:

> Recite a single verse or a few verses to someone who knows the Qur'an. Then transcribe it on paper or a slate. Then repeat

> it to yourself or recite it on your own until you feel it is fixed in your mind. Then ask your teacher or a colleague of yours to listen to you, for it may be that you have made a mistake in it. Then after that, make it a part of your recitation in prayer until you feel it is firmly with you. Then take another part, add it to the first, and so on.
>
> (Ṣaqr 1976: 49)

The virtues of reciting the Qur'an are the subject of many *ḥadīṯ*:

> You must recite the Qur'an for verily it is a light for you on earth and a treasure for you in heaven.
>
> (al-Ḥuṣarī 1966: 24)
>
> Whoever recites a single letter from the Book of God has benefit.[5]
>
> The superior worship of my community is the reciting of the Qur'an.[6]
>
> Illuminate your homes with prayer and Qur'anic recitation.[7]

A common theme in discussions of the virtues of Qur'anic recitation is that of recitation as intercessor on the Day of Judgment.[8] And in the Qur'an itself we read:

> Surely those who recite the Book of God and perform the prayer, and spend out of that which we have provided them, secretly and in public, look for a commerce that comes not to naught, that He may pay them in full their wages and enrich them of His bounty; surely He is all-forgiving, all thankful.
>
> (Qur. 35/29)

Given that the Qur'an is to be recited, how shall it be done? This leads to a number of issues in the discussion of recitation itself, such as how long one should take to complete the reciting of the entire text, and how often it should be done, whether it is preferable to recite from memory or by looking at the text, whether it is better to read aloud or in a low voice, how one should dress, where one should sit, and so forth. We also find in this context discussion of what musical elements are appropriate to recitation, and the recommendation of *ḥuzn* (see below) as the proper state for listening and reciting. These issues form part of an elaborate code which regulates not only the listener's attitude and response (as is done in some Sufi orders with regard to *samāʿ*), but the intent of the reciter and listener. This code is known as *ādāb al-tilāwah*, or, more specifically, *ādāb al-qāri'* (code of behavior for the reciter) and *ādāb al-mustamiʿ* (code of behavior for the listener).

The foundation of this code, and what links all of these issues, is, again, a concern for the accurate preservation and transmission of the Qur'an and, equally, for its meaningful and effective recitation.

Over and over again it is stressed that going through the motions of fulfilling one's religious duties is not enough, that the true act of worship involves the believer body and soul.

> Verily God does not accept an act of anyone until his heart bears witness to what his body bears witness to.
>
> (Naṣr 1930: 236)

> The intent with regard to listening to the Qur'an is attendance of the heart, and contemplation and thought.
>
> (al-Sarrāj al-Ṭūsī 1960: 355)

> The necessary, obligatory recitation is the thoughtful one which engrosses the whole self.
>
> (al-Saʿīd 1967: 310)

Al-Sarrāj al-Ṭūsī cites commentary on several verses from the Qur'an (5/83, 8/21, 47/16):

> Those who would listen to the Qur'an with their ears, not attending with their hearts, God faulted them for that.
>
> (al-Sarrāj al-Ṭūsī 1960: 353)

The value of the gesture is in the attitude and intent of its executor, and these are explicitly defined:

> It is incumbent upon the reciter that he be pure and sincere and without hypocrisy in his reciting and that he have in mind the purpose of God Most High, and that he not intend by it to reach anything but that.
>
> (Naṣr 1930: 236, quoting from al-Durr al-ʿAḍīm)

I was told that the basis of Šayx Muḥammad Rifʿat's successful effect in reciting was his "perfect faith" (*īmān kāmil*). Several reciters stressed to me the importance of sincerity and piety on the part of reciters, especially if they are to reach their listeners:

> The Qur'an, when recited from the heart, reaches the heart.
> (Šayx ʿAbd al-Bāsiṭ ʿAbd al-Ṣamad)

> What comes from the heart penetrates the heart.
> (Šayx Muḥammad al-Ṭablāwī)

In a letter to the editor of *al-Ahrām* a writer characterizes a particular reciter as leading a pious and ascetic life: when he recites "you feel that this recitation has its source in the heart so that hearts seize it before ears . . ." (Ismāʿīl 1978: 9).

Yet another scholar defines the effective recitation as follows:

> The affecting recitation is that which the reciter recites with heartfelt and present enthusiasm, true concentration of the mental faculties, and readiness of the soul, not languidly or listlessly. Perhaps the *ḥadīṯ* "Recite the Qur'an as long as your hearts are united with it, and when you differ then arise from it" is a command to this reciting, for it calls for reciting as long as the heart is accepting and the mind alert, and the soul responsive, and if not, postponement is best.
> (al-Saʿīd 1970: 88)

This recommendation to heedful listening has a divine source: "And when the Qur'an is recited, listen and be silent that you may receive His mercy" (Qur. 7/204). Al-Ḥuṣarī explains that "being silent" leads to influencing the heart, bringing it to obedience and reverence, and gaining His content and mercy (al-Ḥuṣarī 1966: 45).

Concern with the proper spirit and intent (*niyyah*—see note 24) is applied to all acts of worship and religious duties, but the significance of the Qur'an in Islamic society makes proper recitation of it particularly crucial. A Western scholar has clarified why this is so:

> It [the Qur'an] was never designed to be read for information or even for inspiration, but to be recited as an act of commitment

> in worship; nor did it become a mere sacred source of authority. . . . it continued its active role among all who accepted Islam and took it seriously. What one did with the Qur'an was not to peruse it, but to worship by means of it; not to passively receive it, but in reciting to reaffirm it for oneself; the event of revelation was renewed every time one of the faithful, in the act of worship, relived [that is, respoke] the Qur'anic affirmations. . . . it continued to be an event, an act rather than merely a statement of facts or norms.
>
> (Hodgson 1974: 1/367)

Muslim scholars would agree that recitation is more than information conveyed, that it is something to be experienced and felt (al-Zarkašī 1957: 454), but would add that recitation should communicate specific meaning as well as general significance; this is central to their conception of the ideal recitation.

> Know that the memorization of the Noble Qur'an is required . . . the desire to beautify the voice by means of it . . . but above all, what is most important . . . is the understanding of its meanings, its contemplation, acting according to it, stopping at its limits, and following its moral example.
>
> (Naṣr 1930: 235)

> There is no blessing in a recitation in which there is no contemplation [of its meanings].[9]

We read that it is better to read a few short chapters of the Qur'an with contemplation (*tadabbur*) than to read several long chapters, or even the whole text, without it.[10] So that my own recitation would not be unthinking, my teacher insisted that, in addition to memorizing the text and learning the rules of *tajwīd*, I devote study to the meaning. Indeed, more than half of each lesson was taken up with discussion of the meaning of the verses I had learned.

Of course, these attitudes bear on the issues in the *ādāb* of recitation. For example, as regards the recitation of the complete text (*xatm*),[11] sources vary as to how often it should be done, and how long it should take. It was the practice of ʿUṯmān to do the *xatm* in a single night (al-Zarkašī 1957: 471), and, according to al-Suyūṭī, the record is eight times in twenty-four hours (1910: 1/106), but there are a number of *ḥadīṯ* which testify to the Prophet's disapproval of the *xatm* being completed in less than three days.[12] One of these *ḥadīṯ* specifies the reason: "Whoever recites the Qur'an in less than three days does not understand it" (al-Qārī' 1948: 23). Al-Nawawī (cited in al-Suyūṭī 1910: 1/100) states the regulating principle: as long as the reciter is attentive to the fine points of meaning, the speed of his reciting may vary. According to al-Zarkašī (1957: 471), this variance accommodates the enthusiasm, frailty, concentration, and indifference of the individual reciter, all of which must be taken into consideration if the recitation is to be meaningful and not, in the words of al-Ḥuṣarī, "merely the passage of words by means of [the act of] reciting" (al-Ḥuṣarī 1966: 21).

Regarding reciting from memory or from the text, scholarly consensus seems to be in favor of the text.[13] This is a guard against change which imperfect memory may cause. However, it is not the general practice of professional reciters in Egypt today to recite from the text. They pride themselves on their mastery of the text and on their ability to comply with any on-the-spot request for recitation. There are examples, admittedly rare, of faulty memory in performance. A reciter whose taped performance was being reviewed by the Reciters' Committee (Lajnat al-Qurrā') made such a slip (*wa ḏkurū* for *wa škurū*), and several of the members of the review board exclaimed that they wished he had had the text in front of him so he could have corrected himself. As it was, the recitation, which was otherwise excellent, had to be rejected for broadcast.[14]

Another reason for preferring the text concerns total involvement in the recitation. A number of scholars have said that reciting from the text is preferable because the eye on the text is itself an act of worship, and thus the oral (reciting) and the visual (looking at the text) are brought together.[15] Makkī Naṣr adds that this increases humility (*xušū'*) and the attending of the heart to the reciting (Naṣr 1930: 244).

Finally, there is the question of whether it is better to read the Qur'an aloud (*bi l-jahr*) or in a low and inaudible voice (*bi l-isrār* or *bi l-ixfāt*). The evidence of the *ḥadīṯ* is varied: some are against *jahr*,[16] some support it.[17]

The objection to *jahr* seems to be that it is a tool used to draw attention to oneself, to proclaim one's piety. Al-Makkī cites the story of a man who, when he had finished his reciting, was visited by a heavenly being who showed him the text of what he had recited. When he asked why a part of it was blank, the angel answered that at that point the reciter had raised his voice because a man was passing by (al-Makkī 1961: 127). The following statement of the Prophet is often quoted in the discussion of *jahr*: "The virtue of a secret recitation over a publicly proclaimed one is like the virtue of secret over publicly proclaimed charity."[18] Al-Zarkašī mentions that some people like to vary the two, "because *isrār* may be tedious, so *jahr* will delight, and *jahr* may fatigue, so *isrār* refreshes."[19] Al-Makkī makes the link between *faḍa'il istimaʿ al-qur'ān* (the virtues of listening to the Qur'an), stories of the Prophet and his companions listening to each other's reciting,[20] and *jahr*, by saying that reciting in a low voice only benefits oneself, whereas reciting aloud benefits others.[21]

In fact, the whole issue revolves around attitude and intent, and, to a lesser degree, circumstance. Thus, in the following account, both reciters are judged correct: Abū Bakr was reciting in a low voice, and the Prophet asked him about it, and he replied, "verily He in whom I confide hears me." And ʿUmar, who was reciting in a raised voice, when asked, replied, "I awaken the sleepy and drive away Satan."[22] Al-Nawawī (1971: 46) prefers *jahr* as long as it does not disturb the sick, the praying, or the sleeping. Al-Suyūṭī, quoting al-Nawawī, gives the same conditions, adding that as long as no hypocritical intent is present, *jahr* is preferred because more is involved (*al-ʿamalu fīhi akṯar*), and the benefit extends to the listeners. Moreover, it "rouses the reciter's heart and collects his cares for thought, and directs his ear to it, drives away sleep and increases enthusiasm" (al-Suyūṭī 1910: 1/109). Naṣr concurs that *jahr* is best except "where there is risk of hypocrisy or annoyance" (Naṣr 1930: 238). This explains the preference for *isrār* by day (when the reciter may be tempted to show off to others) and in the prayer ritual.[23]

Al-Makkī gives a list of seven "intents,"[24] which, if performed with sincere desire to draw near to God, make *jahr* the preferred mode of recitation, and which, if not present, make the reciter prey to the hypocrisy of the empty, vain gesture. These are: 1. correct and contemplative reciting (*tartīl*), 2. beautification of the voice (*taḥsīn al-ṣawt*), 3. full attention of ears, heart, and mind, 4. driving away of Satan and sleep, 5. rousing the sleeper to consciousness and awareness of the creator, 6. spurring the indifferent and idle to service and piety, and 7. increasing the recitation, and continuing the habit of it (al-Makkī 1961: 125–7). The implication is clear that the most meaningful recitation, the one which "captures the attention of the ears, and rouses the heart that the words may be contemplated and the meanings understood . . . all of that cannot be except by means of *jahr*" (al-Makkī 1961: 125).

There is also the implication (and we find it elsewhere) that *jahr* is more than a louder-voiced version of *isrār*. Once the voice is raised, it seems some sort of heightened speech must follow, and *jahr* is often associated with vocal artistry and the beautiful voice:

> God does not listen to anything as He listens to the Prophet beautiful of voice, singing and raising his voice [*yataġannā wa yajharu*] with the Qur'an.[25]
>
> He heard ʿUmar ibn ʿAbd al-ʿAzīz reciting aloud [*yajharu*] in his prayers and his voice was beautiful.
>
> (al-Makkī 1961: 124)

A synonym for *jahr*, *rafʿ al-ṣawt* (raising the voice) seems to be particularly associated with music. Al-Qurṭubī lists those who disapproved of any sort of music in Qur'anic recitation, saying, "They all disapproved of raising the voice and making music in reciting the Qur'an [*rafʿ al-ṣawt bi l-qur'ān wa l-taṭrīb fīhi*]" (al-Qurṭubī 1968: 10). Al-Qurṭubī, in fact, disassociates *jahr* from the enchantment of music (*ṭarab*) but not from singing (*taġannī*) or vocal artistry in general (*taḥsīn al-ṣawt*).[26]

The concept of the ideal Qur'anic recitation as an act or an experience of total involvement and awareness on the part of both listener and reciter is the basis on which the acceptance of melody and vocal technique into recitation rests. It is the responsibility of the professional melodic reciter to make his skill the instrument of his understanding in order to bring out the meanings of the text and to evoke a more total response in his listeners.[27]

Correlating melodic mode (*maqām*) and vocal technique to meaning is termed *taṣwīr al-maʿnā* (picturing the meaning), and is considered an essential element of the ideal recitation. A writer responding officially to public criticism of some recitation as being too much like singing quotes from a *ḥadīṯ* that when the Prophet recited a passage of praise he would praise, and if it was a verse in which there was a question, he would question, and so forth, concluding that this "can only mean that the Prophet praised, asked, and took refuge, and so forth, with a voice suited to praising, asking, and taking refuge, and that this is the recitation which makes clear the meanings" (ʿAbd al-Wāriṯ ʿAṣr quoted in Diyāb 1977: 11). Elsewhere we read that the recitation must be suited to the meaning (al-Makkī 1961: 99), that melodic recitation began as a response to the recognition that there must be variety in voice and melody to reflect the text (Anonymous 1974: 29), and that "it would not be natural to express all the subjects of the Qur'an in the same way. . . . what is acceptable is the 'intoning' [*tarannum*] which suits the meaning and demonstrates it" (al-Saʿīd 1967: 319). Labīb al-Saʿīd refers to this recitation of the Qur'an with melody (*talḥīn al-qur'ān*) as "expressive recitation" (*qirā'ah muʿabbirah*) (1967: 319). In another work he refers to the "descriptive music" of the Qur'an,[28] "and it is that which pictures the meaning and indicates the idea by means of the inspiration of the melody and matching of the voice to that harmony which is between music and the meaning which inspires it" (al-Saʿīd 1970: 69). The point of all this is to better affect the listener:

> And it is necessary that affecting the worshiper with recitation reach the point described by the Imām al-Ġazālī: "that he should become one with the character of the recited verse. Thus when he hears about threats and the conditional withholding of forgiveness he shrinks with fear as if he were dying, and when he hears about magnanimity and the promise of forgiveness he rejoices as if he were flying with joy . . ."
>
> (Anonymous 1974: 28)

Reciters themselves are explicit on the necessity of using melody in this regard:

> Reciting with melody [*naġama*] is like giving commentary: he who recites with correct melody and has a basic idea of the art . . . brings the listener closer to the Qur'an.
>
> (Šayx ʿAlī Ḥajjāj al-Suwaysī)

> The basis of the reciter's use of melody is meaning, and not custom or taste. He extracts the meaning for the people according to his understanding.
>
> (Šayx Muḥammad al-Ṭablāwī)

> The reciter needs talent and vocal technique [*ṣōt*] to bring different colors to different meanings. Not everyone can do this.
>
> (Šayx al-Ḥuṣarī)

Šayx Ibrāhīm al-Šaʿšāʿī described his father's reciting: "a verse with one meaning got a particular melody, and one with glad tidings got another." Šayx Rašād described how a reference to hell takes a full and heavy voice, while in a reference to heaven, the voice is bright, sharper, and lighter.

In this context the term *maʿnā* seems to refer more to mood or emotion than to meaning. Joy and sorrow, as evoked by the mention of heaven and hell, are the basic moods that feature in any mention of *taṣwīr al-maʿnā*. Still, the more subtle shades of these emotions are communicated as well. Basic to the concept of *taṣwīr al-maʿnā* is the association of the *maqāmāt* with a mood or emotion, and reciters are generally agreed in assigning a mood to a *maqām*. Thus, (*maqām*) *sīka* evokes joy, *girka*, awe, *ṣabā l-yatīm*, sublimity, and *ṣabā*, the sorrow of soulful yearning (Šayx Muḥammad Salāmah included joy in the emotions evoked by *ṣabā*). Šayx Aḥmad al-Ruzayqī demonstrated the role of the reciter in bringing out the mood of a verse when he recited the same verse in two different *maqāmāt*. The verse was "And Hell, that Day is brought (face to face). On that Day will man remember, but how will that remembrance profit him? He will say: 'Ah! would that I had sent forth (good deeds) for (this) my (future) life.'" (Qur. 8/23–24, ʿAlī 1946). Šayx Aḥmad first recited this text in *maqām nahawand*, "which brings out the pain and grief," and then he recited it in *ṣabā*, "which reflects the self-reproach and repentance." Other examples of the application of vocal technique to meaning were pointed out to me by listeners, such as the recitation which changed from low register and quiet delivery to higher-pitched and increased volume when the infant Jesus stands up to speak (in *sūrat Maryam*), or a reciter's manipulation of the register to set off the two voices of a dialogue.

Techniques for correlating melody with meaning are limited only by the imagination of the reciter, and evaluations of reciters and recitations reflect an appreciation of this skill. One reciter was praised because "he has a sensitivity for expressing the meaning," "he demonstrates the distance [referred to in a verse] with his voice." Likewise, another was criticized for lack of sensitivity to meaning: "He rests his voice with *ṣabā* without regard to meaning."

Labīb al-Saʿīd reports that the musician Zakariyyā Aḥmad mentioned to him that he once heard a reciter recite with so little understanding of what he was saying that he evoked such a temptingly beautiful image of hell-fire (Qur. 74/28–32) that Zakariyyā Aḥmad said, "If hell is so lovely and pleasant, take me to it."[29] Another writer describes the recitation of Šayx Rifʿat:

> I heard him once evoking *ḥuzn* [sorrow and awe, see below] in his reciting, and I heard the *naġamat ṣabā* [which is famous among the Arabic modes for *ḥuzn*] coming out of his throat as if it were drowned in tears. Then he came to verses which required zeal and enthusiasm in their execution, and suddenly *naġamat rast* burst out like the beating of drums, and the capable Šayx, the great artist, moved from *ḥuzn* and meekness to power and ardor in the twinkling of an eye.
>
> (al-Najmī 1968: 175)

There is no doubt that the reciter who has mastered the subtleties of melodic and vocal technique is more effective in conveying the meaning. One reciter claims that the reciter skilled in correlating his technique to his understanding can convey the meaning of the text to someone who does not understand Arabic (Šayx Aḥmad al-Ruzayqī).

The clarification and enhancement of intellectual meaning is only one of two primary reasons for accepting the use of melodic and vocal artistry in Qur'anic recitation. The second reason acknowledges the affective power of music to touch the listeners' hearts and engage them more fully in the significance of the revelation. Qureshi puts her finger on this important aspect of recitation when she says that the idea of rousing people's hearts,

> in fact coincides with one primary definition of the function of music, that of "stimulating and expressing emotion in the performers and imparting it to the listeners" (Burrows, 1933, p. 54 as quoted in Merriam 1964, p. 219). Tarannum shares this musical function with religious chanting.
>
> (Qureshi 1969: 448)

There are numerous testimonies to this function or power of music. In al-Qurṭubī we read that making music in recitation is permitted by some and that this is because "when the voice is beautified thus it has greater effect on the soul, and it is more agreeable or welcome to hearts" (1968: 1/11). Al-Jawziyyah elaborates with the statement that embellishing (*tazyīn*), beautifying of the voice (*taḥsīn al-ṣawt*), and musical enchantment (*taṭrīb*) in recitation are more affecting and more stimulating to audition and attentiveness, for by means of these the praise is carried to the ear, and its meaning to the heart (1970: 1/167). He adds another nuance when he compares it to "sweetness which is put in medicine. . . . spices put in food, that the natural be more stimulating and acceptable. . . . and the perfume and adornments of the wife who beautifies herself for her husband" (1970: 1/167).

Labīb al-Saʿīd writes that there is a distinction between the singing (*ġināʾ*) in recitation "that takes the recitation from what should be [i.e., that state in which fear of God and dignity are present] and the beauty of the voice in the ideal recitation. This beauty is fixed overwhelmingly on the goal which is the stimulation of audition" (1967: 310).

Šayx Muḥammad Salāmah expressed this goal in another way when he told me that he learned music "for the sake of the Qur'an, in order to take possession of the hearts [of his listeners]." Šayx Ramaḍān, discussing the importance of evoking the mood and meaning of the text, said that "the reciter must insert it into the ear of the crowds." The effectiveness of the reciter Šayx Muḥammad Rifʿat has been attributed to the fact that "his voice overwhelms you, takes you over" (Saʿid al-Maṣrī, personal communication). And Mr. Ḥusayn Rifʿat, describing his father's recitation style, told me that Šayx Rifʿat felt that everyone has a *maqām* to which he or she is particularly responsive, so he tried to vary the *maqāmāt* in his recitation in order to touch a wider group.[30] Šayx Rifʿat indeed seems to have been especially effective in touching people's emotions with his reciting. A modern writer describes this effect:

> Šayx Rifʿat's voice was full of humility, tears, and sorrow, and it caused the listeners' tears to flow and evoked their humility, and he continued to make them weep and to soften their hearts with verses of divine reward and punishment for a long time, until he made them weep at the end of his life for himself, and their tears to flow for his voice.
>
> (al-Najmī 1968: 168)

In a letter to the editor of the newspaper *al-Ahrām*, the following tribute to Šayx Rifʿat appeared: "[He] touches the lips of the heart and fills our souls with awe and faith, and makes us feel the greatness of the words of God" (*al-Ahrām*, July 13, 1978: 11).

Some comments indicate that reciters have a responsibility to maximize their skill and talent in this aspect of recitation, for lack of fluency with the *maqāmāt* can jar the listener and obstruct an otherwise moving experience. Thus, Šayx al-Ḥuṣarī, who stands out among Egyptian reciters not only for his scholarship but for a style of recitation relatively free of musical artifice and artistry, told me that the reciter does not need to know *mūsīqā* and *ġināʾ*. He should, nevertheless, be aware of the *maqāmāt*, so that there is no discord (*našāz*) in his reciting. Two other reciters said that the skilled reciter changes his melodic patterns so as not to bore or annoy his listeners (Šayx al-Ṭablāwī, Šayx al-Suwaysī). Šayx ʿAlī Ḥajjāj al-Suwaysī added that a good voice (*ṣōt ḥasan*) is necessary to a reciter "so that people don't laugh." And Šayx Fatḥī Qandīl stated unequivocally that of those who study the Qur'an, only those with *ṣōt* (vocal talent) will become reciters—the others will end up as teachers. Šayx Muṣṭafā Ismāʿīl asserted not only that "the better one can use the *maqāmāt*, the more effective one's recitation," but that "recitation without melody is of no benefit."

The implication that the Qurʾanic text, on its own, is boring, that it needs melody to be effective, contradicts the idea of the supremacy and perfection of the text. Such contradictions do not undermine the tradition, but, rather, illustrate its paradoxical nature. Nor are reciters who express such sentiments censured.

Finally, official recognition of the value given to an affecting and meaningful recitation and the role of melody and vocal artistry in this is also exemplified by the presence of two musicians on the committee which auditions new reciters for radio employment and evaluates all recording of recitation submitted for broadcast (see chapter 5).

Terminology

The issues which shape the ideal recitation of the Qur'an can be further clarified by a discussion of the specific terms applied to it. Many of these carry with them a long history of varied usage, so that the same term appears in a confusing number of different contexts. Others have been the subject of much philological discussion in an attempt to reconcile their general usage with established ideals of Islamic practice. But ultimately, the value of looking at this terminology is not in determining the meaning of a word, but rather in elucidating what the particular usage reveals of the various perceptions, biases, and ideals of those who describe, define, or simply refer to the ideal recitation of the Qur'an.

I have selected the most frequent terms and those more specific to the topic of Qur'anic recitation as being most pertinent to the discussion. The following occur in both scholarly and modern Egyptian usage:

Al-Ṣawt Al-Ḥasan

In the context of the *samāʿ* polemic we encountered the term *al-ṣawt al-ḥasan*, "the beautiful voice." Evidence pointing to an Islamic acceptance, and even praise, of the beautiful voice is employed in support of both *samāʿ* and melodic recitation.

For example, in works on Qur'anic recitation we find many of the citations already encountered in the context of the *samāʿ* polemic:

> He adds to creation as He pleases [i.e., the beautiful voice; see chapter 3].
>
> (Qur. 35/1 [ʿAlī 1946], quoted in al-Saʿīd 1970: 10)

> Then those who have believed and worked righteous deeds, shall be made happy in a Mead of Delight [*yuḥbarūn*, "shall sing"; see chapter 3].
>
> (Qur. 30/14, [ʿAlī 1946], quoted in al-Saʿīd 1970: 10)

In his book on melodic recitation, *Al-Taġannī bi l-Qur*'ān, Labīb al-Saʿīd cites the report that Muhammad chided Abū Bakr for rebuking the slave women for their singing (see chapter 3). Works on recitation also note that the Prophet praised the voice of Abū Mūsā l-Ašʿarī, comparing it to the *mazāmīr* of David (see chapter 3).[31]

In turn, we find in the context of the *samāʿ* polemic many *ḥadīṯ* praising the beautiful voice reciting the Qur'an.

> Beautify [*ḥassinū*] the Qur'an with your voices. Verily the beautiful voice increases the beauty of the Qur'an.
>
> (e.g., in al-Sarrāj al-Tūsī 1960: 339)

> Embellish [*zayyinū*] the Qur'an with your voices.[32]
>
> (e.g., in al-Ġazālī n.d.: 8/1125)

> Everything has an ornament, and that of the Qur'an is the beautiful voice.
>
> (e.g., in al-Qušayrī 1959: 167)

> God does not listen [*aḏina*] to anything as He listens to a Prophet of beautiful voice.[33]
>
> (e.g., in al-Qušayrī 1959: 167)

> God listens [*aḏina*] more attentively to the man who beautifies his voice with the Qur'an than does the owner of the *qaynah* to his *qaynah*.
>
> (e.g., in al-Sarrāj al-Ṭūsī 1960: 338)

And a scholar writing in an Egyptian music journal states as a matter of fact that singers and reciters share two important aspects of music making, namely, creating and performing, and that, in both aspects, the beautiful voice figures prominently (Xašabah 1975: 11–12).

In works on recitation it is clear that the beautiful voice is desirable in reciting the Qur'an. The *ḥadīṯ* quoted above are invariably cited in this context. There are also references to the beautiful voice of the Prophet (Ibn Saʿd 1960: 1/375–76), and stories of the Prophet and his companions listening with pleasure and approval to recitations with beautiful voice.[34] On the authority of Abū Dāwūd, we are told that, in connection with the Prophet's statement that "there is none among us who does not sing [*yataġannā bi*] the Qurʾan" the question was asked, "What if one hasn't a beautiful voice?" and answered, "He must beautify as best he can."[35] Al-Suyūṭī says there are many *ḥadīṯ* in favor of the beautiful voice in recitation and, without quoting the whole story, makes the point that one must do the best one can (al-Suyūṭī 1910: 1/109). A modern scholar summarizes: "And the verifiable authoritative practice [*sunnah saḥīḥah*] has confirmed the desirability of beautifying the voice [*taḥsīn al-ṣawt*] with the Qurʾan" (al-Saʿīd 1967: 311).

The "beautiful voice" and "beautifying the voice" seem to express the same concept. From the contexts in which *ṣawt ḥasan* occurs, and from the associations its use evokes, it is clear that the term in Arabic also refers to more than a pleasant speaking voice. At the very least, some sort of heightened speech, if not actual vocal artistry, is involved. In *samāʿ* works, for example, the beautiful voice is almost synonymous with the pleasant melody (*laḥn ṭayyib, naġamah ṭayyibah*).[36] In *Al-ʿIqd al-Farīd* we read:

> And physicians assert that the beautiful voice moves in the body and flows in the veins. In consequence the blood becomes pure through it, and the heart is at rest. . . . and for that reason they dislike that the child should be put to sleep after crying unless it be danced and sung to.
>
> (Ibn ʿAbd Rabbih 1968: 6/4)

Frequent reference is made to the beautiful voice of David, the psalm singer and, in Islamic tradition, prophet. Farmer cites the story that Satan invented musical instruments because he was jealous of David's voice (1973: 78). The most widely told story is that when David would recite (*qaraʾa*) the psalms in their seventy tunes (*luḥūn*) the wild beasts and the birds would gather to listen and would be moved (*ṭaraba*) by his recitation.[37]

In a discussion of melodic recitation (al-Jawziyyah 1970: 1/166) we read that such and such a person "has the most beautiful voice in reciting the Qurʾan [*aḥsan al-nās ṣawtan bi l-qurʾān*]," and later in the same passage (al-Jawziyyah 1970: 167) that beautifying and embellishing the voice [*taḥsīn* and *tazyīn al-ṣawt*] lead to the emotional response effected by music (*ṭarab*, see below). Al-Qāri' (1948: 23) refers to stories of Christians and Jews converting to Islam as a result of listening to a certain reciter's recitation "and the beauty of his voice."

The term *ṣawt* (plural *aṣwāt*) itself not only denotes "voice" and "sound," but is a synonym in the literature for "melody," "song," "verses set to music":[38] for example, "Among the innovations people introduced into Qur'anic recitation are the tunes of music [*aṣwāt al-ġina'*],"[39] and "a man sang . . . a song [*ġannā . . . ṣawtan*]" (Ibn ʿAbd Rabbih 1968: 6/14). Ibn Qayyim al-Jawziyyah (1970: 1/168) refers to reciters who recite in the melodic style as *qurrā' al-aṣwāt* (i.e., melodic reciters.)[40] A similar term, *qurrā' fī l-aṣwāt*, was used by one of my informants to denote the same thing (Šayx ʿAlī Ḥajjāj al-Suwaysī).

In the context of modern Egyptian Qur'anic recitation it is clear that *ṣōt ḥilw*, *ṣōt gamīl*, or *ṣōt ḥasan* is the equivalent of *ṣawt ḥasan* in the literature. The root Ḥ S N is collocated with *ṣōt* in the verbal expression *istaḥsān iṣ-ṣōt*, "to consider the voice beautiful": a reciter related to me that he was singled out early in his studies by his teacher for melodic recitation "because he considered my voice beautiful" (Šayx Aḥmad al-Ruzsayqī). The same root also occurs in the phrase *ḥusn iṣ-ṣōt*, "beauty of voice." A synonym for this expression is *ḥalāwit iṣ-ṣōt* (cf. *ṣōt ḥilw*, above).

But most commonly the term *ṣōt*, alone, implies not only voice quality but some sort of vocal skill. One of the most common expressions denoting melodic recitation in use in Egypt today is *al-qirā'a bi s-ṣōt* (recitation with voice). For example, the reciter Šayx Maḥmūd Xalīl al-Ḥusarī used the term in this sense when he described his early training: "each student was asked to recite something from the Qur'an *bi-ṣōtu* [i.e., in the melodic style], and the acceptable student was given experience reciting in public." Other examples which demonstrate this sense are: "Those who want to hear *ṣōt* and melody won't listen to *murattal* [the speech-bound style of recitation] ever" (Šayx Muḥammad al-Ṭablāwī), and, "so-and-so has no *ṣōt*, no artistry" (Šayx Muṣṭafā Ismāʿīl).

The criteria by which candidates are judged in recitation at the

Cairo Radio are three: *hifḍ* (memorization), *adāʾ* (execution of the rules of *tajwīd*), and *ṣawt* (voice quality, general musicality, and melodic technique). Finally, this sense of *ṣōt* is used in the form *ṣōtī*, "pertaining to *ṣōt*," as in *qafalāt ṣotiyya*, "melodic or musical cadences."

Tilāwah (Plural *Tilāwāt*)

This is a generic term denoting Qur'anic recitation. It is used in the Qur'an in several senses: "to recite," "to relate" and "to follow":

> A messenger from God reciting pages purified . . .
>
> (Qur. 98/2)

> Will you bid others to piety, and forget yourselves while you recite the Book?
>
> (Qur. 2/44)

> . . . and when it is recited to them, they say, We believe in it; surely it is the truth from our Lord.
>
> (Qur. 28/53)

> And recite [relate] thou to them the story of the two sons of Adam truthfully . . .
>
> (Qur. 5/30)

> Say: Come, I will recite/relate what your Lord has forbidden you . . .
>
> (Qur. 6/151)

> By the sun and his morning brightness and by the moon when she follows him . . .
>
> (Qur. 91/1)

Some scholars would incorporate a second sense of the verb, that of "following," to imply that one not only recites the Qur'an but adheres to its precepts:

> The infinitive noun (*tilāwah*) especially signifies the following of God's revealed Scriptures, sometimes by reading or perusing, or by reciting, and sometimes by conforming therewith, for

every *tilāwah* is reciting (*qirā'ah*), but the reverse is not the case.

(Lane 1863: 1/313, citing al-Rāġib, *Tāj al-ʿArūs*)

Ibn ʿAbbās and Mujāhid (as cited in Naṣr 1930: 235) would interpret the verse "Those to whom we have given the Book and who recite it with true recitation [*tilāwah*] . . ." (Qur. 2/15) to mean "Those to whom We have given the Book follow it truly." Another translation reads "Those to whom We have sent the Book study it as it should be studied" (Qur. 2/21/, ʿAlī 1946).

Makkī Naṣr elaborates with a statement of al-Ġazālī to the effect that the true *tilāwah* "is that in which the tongue, the mind, and the heart share."[41] The tongue, mind, and heart deal with the sound, the meaning, and the emotional response to the human condition, respectively. This concept of a totally involving recitation is, of course, central to the definitions of the ideal Qur'anic recitation.

Perhaps because *tilāwah* is the only term applied to Qur'anic recitation which carries this ideal in its basic meaning (i.e., to follow), its usage is most often generic. The term carries no connotations of style, nor is it used in compounds specifying a certain style (as is *qirā'ah*—see below). In general the distinction in usage between *tilāwah* and *qirā'ah* is clear: they are both generic terms, but whereas *qirā'ah* may be specified, *tilāwah* is always general. *Tilāwah* is most commonly used in subject headings and titles:

The Virtue of *tilāwah* of the Blessed Qur'an

(Ismāʿīl 1978: 18; al-Ḥuṣarī 1966: 21)

On the *ādāb* [procedure] of Its [the Qur'an's] *tilāwah*

(al-Zarkašī 1957: 1/449)

On Continuing *tilāwah* of the Qur'an after Learning It

(al-Zarkašī 1957: 1/458)

On the Mention of the Conduct of the Worshiper with Regard to *tilāwah*

(al-Makkī 1961: 95)

How the Qur'an Is Recited [*yutlā*]

(ʿUṯmān 1969: title page)

> Chapter on the Manner of *tilāwah* of the Book of God Most High
>
> (al-Qurṭubī 1968: 1/4)

Compare the generic usage of the above with the following:

> Regarding the Disapproval of Reciting [*qirāʾah*] the Qurʾan without Contemplation
>
> (al-Zarkašī 1957: 1/455)

and the contrast of specific and generic within the same sentence:

> On the *istiʿāḏah* and the *qirāʾah* of the *basmalah* in *tilāwah*[42]
>
> (al-Zarkašī 1957: 1/460)

I have not seen the above distinction specified, but it seems to carry over into modern Egyptian usage in that *tilāwah* is the official and formal term for all Qurʾanic recitation. One might posit that this is because it is a neutral term and, unlike *qirāʾah*, carries no controversy. For example, although there is no lack of expressions denoting melodic recitation of the Qurʾan, the Egyptian media, in their announcements of such recitation, use the term *tilāwah*:

> Live broadcast, 8:30 P.M. . . . will include *tilāwah* of the Holy Qurʾan by famous reciters.
>
> (*al-Ahrām*, April 1, 1979: 2)

> The ritual of the Monday dawn prayer is broadcast from the mosque of the Imām al-Ḥusayn. Šayx Muḥammad ʿAbd al-Ḥakam will recite [*yatlū*] from the Blessed Qurʾan.
>
> (*al-Ahrām*, April 1, 1979: 2)

I can find no substantiation of Boubakeur's (1968: 388) definition of *tilāwah* as "recitation without the help of the text, with melody." It is true that *qirāʾah*, and not *tilāwah*, is the term used in the discussions of whether it is preferable to recite from the text or by memory, but nothing in the sources or in my fieldwork experience would seem to indicate that *tilāwah* specifically denotes a melodic recitation. The example of Šayx al-Ḥuṣarī's usage is typical: although he uses *tilāwah* freely throughout the rest of his book *Maʿa l-Qurʾān al-Karīm* (1966), in the chapter on melodic recitation only the term *qiraʾah* is employed (al-Ḥuṣarī 1966: 97–125).

Al-Faruqi, in her definition of *tilāwah*, equates it with *tarannum* (see below): "This word [*tilāwah*] was used in pre-Islamic Arabia to designate recitation of poetry. Such recitations involved a manner of simple humming or singing called tarannum" (al-Faruqi 1979: 107). The deduction is logical, but there is no evidence to substantiate the equation. On the contrary, we read that "the Arabs delighted in the *tilāwah* of poetry without *tarnīm* [synonym of *tarannum*] or *ġinā'*" (Kāmil 1973: 10).

Qirā'ah

This is yet another term denoting recitation.[43] Naṣr (1930) uses this term almost exclusively to denote recitation in both specific and general contexts. However, as we have seen in the story of David's reciting the psalms (see above), *qirā'ah* may take on musical connotations.[44]

Most commonly, the melodic sense of *qirā'ah* is specified with a second term, giving a compound such as *al-qirā'ah bi l-alḥān* (*laḥn*, plural *alḥān* or *luḥūn*, denotes, in this context, "melody," "air," "music"). The degree of association of *laḥn* with the elaborately formulated art music is what determines its unacceptability—from the scholarly point of view—in recitation, for there is a definite sense that *laḥn* is a composed rather than spontaneously improvised sound (al-Fīrūzabādī 1913: 4/266: *luḥūn* "are among the crafted and composed songs [*min al-aṣwat al-maṣūġah wa-l-mawḍū'ah*]").[45]

Thus, al-Safi'i's judgment was that *al-qirā'ah bi l-alḥān* was not objectionable, but commentators take care to point out that what he must have meant was that it is not objectionable as long as there is no distortion of the rules of *tajwīd*,[46] a definite risk when dealing with composed melodics (see chapter 6). Talbi (1958: 189) writes that the term *qirā'ah bi l-alḥān* has changed in connotation over the centuries, becoming more and more identified with the art music, to the point where the Qur'an was treated as any profane text, with the same intent to entertain. However, I did not find that the term carries particularly negative connotations in modern Egyptian usage; it seems to be used simply to distinguish the Egyptian style of melodic recitation from a more speech-bound style.

A related term, *al-qirā'ah bi l-talḥīn*, or *talḥīn al-qur'ān* (*talḥīn*, verbal noun of *laḥḥana*, "to sing, make music, set to music") is employed interchangeably (by scholars and informants) with the above terms to denote a musical inflection of the Qur'an.

The more common modern Egyptian equivalent to these expressions is *al-qirā'a bi n-naġama* or *bi t-tanġīm*, *Naġama* and *tanġīm* being synonymous with *laḥn* and *talḥīn*. *Naġama* also denotes "pitch" or "musical note" and, in colloquial usage, the *maqām*.

Another compound is *al-qirā'a bi l-taṭrīb*. *Taṭrīb* is the verbal noun of *ṭarraba*, "to make music, sing, delight." The musical connotations of the root Ṭ R B are well established: *muṭrib* is a common synonym for *muġanni* (singer). And *ṭarab* is both a synonym for music (as in *Al-Ṭarab ʿInd al-ʿArab*, "Music among the Arabs," the title of a book [al-ʿAllāf 1963] and *ālāt al-ṭarab*, "musical instruments"), and connotes the delightful effect of music, the stirring of the senses and emotions by means of music. H. H. Touma summarizes this meaning of *ṭarab*: "if the musician succeeds in inspiring his audience with enthusiasm, one speaks of what is called *ṭarab*, a term signifying the standard for assessing the creation of an emotional climate in music. When listening to Arabian music, *ṭarab* is the great musical experience par excellence" (Touma 1976: 35).

The association of *ṭarab* (and related terms) with Qur'anic recitation may be censured or not, depending upon the particular writer's interpretation of the term. The sense of "music" is unacceptable. In a contemporary Egyptian article we read that one of the effects of the Islamic conquests against which the Prophet warned was the development and flourishing of music to the point that "recitation became *taṭrīb*" (Anonymous 1974: 29). Here, *taṭrīb* is identified with the system and craft of the art music which developed under the influence of Persian music and flourished in a rather un-Islamic context of lavish indulgence.[47] Ibn Qayyim al-Jawziyyah indicates the acceptability of *ṭarab* in his argument for melodic recitation: "There is no escaping the soul's need for *ṭarab*, and its yearning for *ġinā'*, so it [Islam] has substituted for the *ṭarab* [i.e., the emotional delight] of *ġinā'* the *ṭarab* of the Qur'an, just as it has replaced all of what is forbidden and disapproved of with what is good" (al-Jawziyyah 1970: 1/167). He continues with examples of this kind of substitution (e.g., marriage for fornication) to show that our needs may be lawfully fulfilled.[48]

What is acceptable in the concept of *ṭarab*, with regard to Qur-'anic recitation, is the sense of stirring, affecting, and delighting the emotions, of provoking a response, for the ideal recitation is one which stirs and affects the listeners, involving them more totally in the experience. I rarely heard the term *al-qirā'a bi l-taṭrīb*, but I was told a number of times that *ṭarab* is a desirable quality in recitation. One reciter was praised because "there is *ṭarab* in his voice [*fi sōtu fī ṭarab*]," and a religious scholar, distinguishing between two reciters, expressed his preference for the first "because this one has *ṭarab*; the other is ordinary."

Al-Taġannī Bi L-Qur'ān

This is one of the most widely used terms in the literature denoting the melodic style of recitation. It is not current in modern Egyptian speech, but would be immediately understood. There is little ambiguity in the term: *taġannī* is the verbal noun of *taġannā*, "to sing, to chant,"[49] and is related, of course, to the term *ġinā'*, "music, singing." However, its positive association with Qur'anic recitation in several widely quoted *ḥadīṯ* makes the meaning of *al-taġannī* in these particular contexts subject to some debate. Two of these *ḥadīṯ* are:

> There is none among us who does not sing [*taġannā*] the Qur'an.
>
> God does not listen to anything as He listens to a Prophet sing [*taġannā bi*] the Qur'an [in some versions: . . . a Prophet, beautiful of voice, sing the Qur'an and lift his voice with it].[50]

One or both of these statements of the Prophet are cited in every work on Qur'anic recitation, and in many of the *samā'* works as well.[51] Most of these works include a discussion of the interpretations given *taġannā* in the context of these *ḥadīṯ*. The most complete discussion is in *Al-Jāmi' li-Aḥkām al-Qur'ān* (al-Qurṭubī 1968: 1/11–17). Al-Qurṭubī begins with the most common argument against a musical interpretation of the term, citing a number of authorities, lines of poetry, and other examples of linguistic usage to show that *taġannā* means "to become rich" (more commonly, *istaġnā*). According to this interpretation the *ḥadīṯ* would read: "There is none among us who does not enrich himself [spiritually] with the Qur'an." Al-Qurṭubī also presents other interpretations, none of which points to any sort of melodic recitation. For example, the reference to singing in the statement of Ibn al-Aᶜrābī (see note 48 for variant), "The Arabs were given to singing [*ġinā'*] and reciting [*našīd*] as regards most of their words, and when the Qur'an was revealed they desired that it be their passion and practice instead of singing," in its reference to "singing" is taken to mean that the Arabs abandoned their love of singing in favor of the (nonmelodic) recitation of the Qur'an, rather than that they substituted a musical recitation of the Qur'an for their songs (al-Qurṭubī 1968: 1/13).[52]

Al-Qurṭubī follows this with a full account of the arguments in favor of the musical sense of the term. This author stands out both for his detailed discussion of the two sides of the issue (most of the scholars mention the one interpretation, "to become rich," giving most of their attention to its rebuttal) and for his conviction that none of the *ḥadīṯ* so often quoted in support of melodic recitation can in fact be so interpreted.[53]

Most scholars, however, seem to accept a musical interpretation of *taġannā*. The author of *Lisān al-ᶜArab* (Ibn al-Manḏūr 1966: 373) cites Abū lᶜAbbās' judgment that *taġannā* (in the *ḥadīṯ* beginning "God does not listen . . .") can be interpreted to mean both enrichment (*istiġnā'*) and making music (*taṭrīb*). Al-Šāfiᶜī is widely quoted in his defense of the musical sense. In *Lisān al-ᶜArab* it is reported that his proof that *taġannā* means *taḥsīn al-ṣawt* is in the Prophet's recommendation to "Embellish the Qur'an with your voices" (Ibn al-Manḏūr 1966: 373). Elsewhere it is reported by al-Ṭabarī that al-Šāfiᶜī says that if the Prophet had meant to say "enrich" he would have used the word *yastaġnī* (in some versions, *yataġānā*, e.g., al-Saᶜīd 1967: 314, footnote 3), and would have left out the modifier "beautiful of voice."[54] Al-Ṭabarī is further cited, "It is known in the speech of the Arabs that *taġannī* is *ġinā'*, *ḥusn al-ṣawt bi l-tarjīᶜ*."[55]

Tarjīᶜ (plural *tarjīᶜāt*)

This is another term with musical connotations which is used to describe Qur'anic recitation. It is difficult to define, as it is not part of current musical vocabulary. From the literature, we can deduce that *tarjīʿ* describes a vocal quality or technique associated with singing. Such definitions as "reiteration of the voice [*tardīd al-ṣawt*] in the throat,"[56] "an act of quavering, trilling" (Lane 1863–93: 3/1039), and the use of the term to describe the sound of the (released) bow string [*rajʿat al-qaws*], Lane 1863–93: 3/1039) would seem to apply to the throat trill, an ornamental vocal technique heard in Iranian, Syrian, and Iraqi music today. In one source we read that *tarjīʿ* is the sound that could be produced by a rider whose mount sways to the extent that his voice is (repeatedly) interrupted (al-Jawziyyah 1970: 1/165).[57]

The term also seems to carry a sense of prolonging and raising the voice: "ʿAbd Allāh ibn Muġaffal, in his *tarjīʿ*, by the prolonging of the voice, in reading or reciting, imitated the like of āh, āh, āh" (Lane 1863–93: 3/1039, quoting Tāj al-ʿArūs). This seems to be a confusion with ʿAbd Allāh ibn Muġaffal's report of the Prophet's reciting (see below). In *Al-Muḥīṭ* (al-Fīrūzabādī 1913: 3/28) we read that *tarjīʿ* in the call to prayer is the repeating of the profession of faith (*šahādah*) in a raised voice (and possibly in a higher-pitched voice). Al-Qurṭubī defines *tarjīʿ* as "raising the voice [in terms of audibility], and making music with it [*taṭrīb*]" (al-Qurṭubī 1968: 1/11).

Descriptions of the Prophet's recitation invariably mention both *tarjīʿ* and *madd* (prolongation): "It [his reciting] was [characterized by] *madd*";[58] "and he would do *tarjīʿ* [*yurajjiʿū*]."[59] In a *ḥadīṯ* Anas ibn Malik (cited by Ismāʿīl 1978: 50) describes the Prophet's prolonging the long syllables of the *basmalah*, "*bi smi **llāhi** ṛ-ṛaḥ**mā**ni ṛ-ṛa**ḥī**m*." In *Al-Ṭabaqāt al-Kubrā* we read that the Prophet did not do *tarjīʿ*, "but he did prolong some of the durations" (Ibn Saʿd 1960: 376).

> Many descriptions of the Prophet's reciting refer to the report of ʿAbd Allāh ibn Muġaffal. We read, for example, that: he [the Prophet] would sing (*taġannā bi*) the Qur'an and make his voice do *tarjīʿ* in it sometimes, as he did the day of victory [over Mecca] in his reciting, "Verily We have given thee a mani-

fest victory" [*innā fataḥnā laka fatḥam͠ mubīnā*] [Qur. 48/1],
and ʿAbd Allāh ibn Muġaffal related that his *tarjīʿ* [consisted
of] āh, āh, āh three times.

(al-Jawziyyah 1970: 1/165)

This report is somewhat baffling unless we apply the rules of
tajwīd to the text. It then becomes clear that there are in fact
three prolonged "āhs" in the Qur'anic verse: "*innā fataḥnā laka
fatḥam͠ mubīnā.*" The implication is that *tarjīʿ* in this context denotes a prolongation, rather than a reiteration, though it is indeed
possible for the long vowel to be "prolonged" in another sense by
reiteration, as is evidenced by Ibn Qayyim al-Jawziyyah's statement:

> The Prophet used to recite with *madd* but not *tarjīʿ* for these
> (with *tatrīb*) give the glottal stop where there is none and pro-
> longation where there is none, and the reverberation of the
> long vowels *several times over*, and that is excessive and not
> permitted.
>
> (al-Jawziyyah 1970: 1/168; emphasis mine)

This same report is also the focus of a debate as to whether the
tarjīʿ of the Prophet was intentional or was the result of his being
shaken by the swaying of his riding camel:

> [The *tarjīʿ* of the Prophet] can be ascribed to the lengthening
> of the vowels in the right places, and it is conceivable that it is
> a report of his voice [as it was affected by] the swayings of the
> female riding camel.[60]

Ibn Qayyim al-Jawziyyah argues that if all the Prophet's utterances
regarding Qur'anic recitation were collected (and he cites most of
those quoted in this chapter) it would become clear that his *tarjīʿ*
"was a matter of choice, and not imposed by his camel's swaying"
(al-Jawziyyah 1970: 1/165). Moreover, he adds that if it were not a
matter of choice, Ibn Muġaffal would not have mentioned it. Ibn al-
Ḥājj agrees that there is no evidence for the *tarjīʿ* being other than
intentional, but points out that it must have been the sort of reciting that "does not obscure the meaning of the Qur'an with reitera-
tions of voices and a plethora of *tarjīʿāt*, for were it to come to the
point where one did not know the meaning, well, that is forbidden
by consensus" (Ibn al-Ḥājj 1929: 53).

The resistance to associating *tarjīʿ* with Qur'anic recitation lies, of course, in its use as ornament in singing. We read in the histories of Arabic music that the caravan song was the first example of *tarjīʿ* among the Arabs.[61] In two sources the type of singing in pre-Islamic Arabia called *sinad* is associated with *tarjīʿ* and "many notes and pitches."[62]

Al-Qurṭubī, rejecting the musical connotations of *taġannā*, says "there is nothing in them [the various interpretations so far given] which indicates a recitation with tunes and *tarjīʿ*" (al-Qurṭubī 1968: 1/13). And yet another interpretation rejects those who would see *taġannā* as *tarjīʿ* and *taṭrīb* (al-Qurṭubī 1968: 1/13). In fact, a number of scholars who reject the musical sense of *taġannā* make a point of disassociating the term from *tarjīʿ*.[63]

In the same context, but with an opposite opinion, Ibn Qayyim al-Jawziyyah says, "It is known that in the speech of the Arabs *al-taġannī* is *ġinā'* which is *ḥusn al-ṣawt* by means of *tarjīʿ*" (al-Jawziyyah 1970: 1/166).

Tarannum and *Tarnīm*

These are near synonyms and are not used to designate any particular style of Qur'anic recitation, but are associated with recitation in general. The dictionaries equate *tarannum* with the sound of the dove, the locust, and the (released) bow.[64] Several sources equate it with *tarjīʿ* (Lane 1863–93: 3/1166). In any case it seems to be a technique of heightened speech, closely bound to the text it supports, and distinct from the vocal elaborations of singing.

There is some indication in the literature that it has a close association with *ġinā'*. Lane cites a definition of *tarnīm* as *taṭrīb al-ṣawt* (Lane 1863–93: 3/1166). Labīb al-Saʿīd makes the same definition, and he distinguishes the recitation rendered with *tarannum* (*al-muṣḥaf al-murannam, al-muṣḥaf al-tarnīmī*) from the less melodic and more speech-bound style (al-Saʿīd 1970: 61).

A variant of a well-known *ḥadīṯ* substitutes *yatarannamu* for *yataġannā*:

> God does not listen to anything as He listens to a Prophet beautiful of voice reciting the Qur'an with *tarannum* [variant: . . . a Prophet beautiful of *tarannum* with the Qur'an].[65]

It is in fact difficult to judge if this signals a more musically elaborate sense of *tarannum*, or a less musically elaborate sense of *taġannī*. I would opt for the former, as this variant is mentioned in only one of the many discussions of melodic recitation I have read, a fact which seems to indicate that it is probably not considered a particularly strong piece of evidence in support of melodic recitation. Still, Ibn Qayyim al-Jawziyyah, commenting on this version, says that *tarannum* can only be executed with vocal artistry, *taḥsīn* and *taṭrīb* (1970: 1/166). And Labīb al-Saʿīd quotes Sibawayhī to indicate that *tarannum* implies a more elaborate chanting by means of prolonging the long vowels: "When they do *tarannum* they cling to the *ʾalif*, *waw*, and *yāʾ* [/ā/, /ū/, and /ī/] because they desire to draw out the voice" (1970: 64).

But the concept of simplicity and lack of artifice in *tarannum* prevails. It is strongly associated with the singing of the Arabs of pre- and early Islamic Arabia, and Arab and Western sources seem to agree that this music was "little else than unpretentious psalming" (Farmer 1973: 13, citing Perron), or "simple" or "natural" airs (Talbi 1958: 185). *Tarannum* is variously translated into English as "cantillation" (Farmer 1942: 4), "simple humming or singing" (al-Faruqi 1979: 107), or "humming" (Rosenthal 1958: 2/403). Al-ʿAllāf writes that the Arabs were inspired by the rhythm of the camel and began to recite with *tarannum* the poetry which was natural to it, and "they called the *tarannum* of that poetry *ġināʾ*."[66] But Muḥmūd Kāmil writes: "The Arabs in pre-Islamic times were devoted to poetry and took great pride in it and delighted [*ṭaraba*] in its recitation [*tilāwah*] without *tarnīm* or *ġināʾ*" (Kāmil 1973: 10). He adds, however, that this was the first step toward music, and that it was when the camel-driving song appeared that the Arabs took up *tarnīm* (Kāmil 1973: 11). At this point there were two kinds of *ġināʾ*—that with poetry as text, called *tarnīm al-šiʿr*, and that of nonpoetic texts, *tarnīm al-qirāʾah li-ġayr al-šiʿr*, which Ibn Xaldūn calls *taġbīr*.[67]

This association of *tarnīm* with text brings up the speech-bound aspect of *tarannum*, an aspect which characterizes the chanting of Urdu poetry, called *tarannum*, today. In an excellent article on this subject, Regula Qureshi points out that *tarannum* in this context does not exist apart from the text it supports, and that although recognizable tunes are used, it is not perceived melodically (Qureshi 1969: 445–46). She writes: "The overall speech rhythm is maintained and syllables are neither prolonged nor shortened" because "recitation is essentially a linguistic communication" (Qureshi 1969: 443).

It is the sense of *tarannum* as a melodic performative mode in which the text is primary which prevails in the contemporary definition of the term, and which makes it totally acceptable in the context of Qur'anic recitation. Labīb al-Saʿīd concludes that the references to David's melodious reciting of the psalms "indicates overwhelmingly that *tarannum* is in general demand for the recitation of religious texts" (al-Saʿīd 1970: 40).

Tartīl (Verbal Noun of *Rattala*)

Like *qirā'ah* and *tilāwah*, *tartīl* denotes recitation. Unlike the other two terms, however, *tartīl* bears the whole weight of what has been considered the ideal Qur'anic recitation since the revelation of the Qur'an. Not only was the Qur'an transmitted to Muhammad in this mode ("*wa rattalnāhu tartīlan*," Qur. 25/32), but Muhammad was directed to recite it in the same manner ("*wa rattili l-qur'ānā tartīlan*," Qur. 73/4).

It is significant that in the dictionaries examples illustrating the meaning of *tartīl* as recitation are overwhelmingly drawn from references to Qur'anic recitation, and not from the recitation of other texts. The term was, however, used in pre-Islamic times in connection with the oral rendering of a text.[68]

Tartīl, in its original sense, relates to well-spaced teeth;[69] thus, applied to speech, it denotes clear enunciation, distinct articulation: for example, "And chant the Qur'an very distinctly," "And recite the Qur'an in slow measured rhythmic tones" (Arberry's [1955] and ʿAlī's [1946] respective interpretations of the verse "*wa rattili l-qur'ānā tartīlan*," Qur. 74/3). In other words, "*tartīl* in recitation is . . . the making of consonants and vowels clear, like the mouth with well-shaped teeth" (al-Qurṭubī 1968: 17).[70]

Another sense derived from the original is the clear spacing and consecutive ordering of the parts recited. In Lane we read that the term *tarsīl* ("easy utterance; without haste") denotes *tartīl*, some say, "with the consecution of the parts" (Lane 1863–93: 3/1081). Šayx ʿĀmir ʿUṯmān says *tartīl* is "when part follows part with deliberation and understanding and without rushing."[71] ʿAlī's interpretation of the verse "*wa rattalnāhu tartīlan*" (Qur. 25/32) is "We have rehearsed it to thee in slow, well-arranged stages, gradually" (ʿAlī 1946: 933).

Because *tajwīd* reflects and preserves the clear sound of the sacred text as it was revealed to Muhammad, it is an integral component of *tartīl*. Just as it is obligatory for a Muslim to recite the Qur'an according to the rules of *tajwīd*, it is "the duty of each Muslim who recites the Qur'an . . . to recite it with *tartīl*" (al-Zarkaši 1957: 449). And the justification of this duty is the same as that for *tajwīd*: "Verily God desires that the Qur'an be recited as He sent it down."[72] It is significant that the authors of most works on *tajwīd* give prominence to the scriptural directive to *tartīl* (Qur. 73/4). And they elaborate:

> Know that God Most Blessed and Almighty sent down the Qur'an with *tajwīd* inasmuch as He said, "*wa rattil l-qur'āna tartīlan*," that is to say, "We sent it down with *tartīl*, which is *tajwīd*."
>
> (Naṣr 1930: 22)

> [*tartīl*] is the *tajwīd* of the letters and the knowledge of the pauses.[73]

> . . . and the aim of this *tajwīd* is the *tartīl* of the Blessed Qur'an as God Most High sent it down.
>
> (Muḥaysin 1970: 3)

The quality of deliberate and clear enunciation seems to be what characterizes the reciting of the Prophet: "a reciting made clear letter by letter [*qirā'ah mufassarah ḥarfan ḥarfan*]."[74] Šayx Ibrāhīm al-Šaʿšāʿī described his father's recitation in these terms:

> My father recited the Qur'ān *mufassar* so that listeners would understand what is intended, piece by piece, not long phrases. Even the religious scholars said, "You have made us understand what we did not know before."
>
> (Šayx al-Šaʿšāʿī)

Another component of *tartīl* is its slow tempo:

> . . . and *tartīl* in recitation is unhurriedness in it and slowness.
> (al-Qurṭubī 1968: 1/17)

> . . . and [the verb] *rattil* means reciting, and the *tartīl* of the Qur'an is slowness in it, and enunciation of the consonants and vowels.
> (al-Ḥuṣarī 1966: 25)

> . . . and the foreigner who does not understand the meaning of the Qur'an, *tartīl* and slowness are recommended for him too, because that is closer to reverence and respect and more affecting of hearts than babbling and speed.[75]

The virtue of a slow and deliberate recitation is threefold: an increased likelihood of clear and correct execution; encouragement of attentive contemplation of the meaning of the text; and, consequently, an enhancement of the overall effect of the recitation. Al-Suyūṭī quotes Ibn Masʿūd on this issue: "Do not scatter [recitation] about like the scattering of dates, nor babble it deliriously as is done in poetry, but attend to its wonders and move hearts with it."[76] Scholars unanimously agree that it is better to recite a few verses of the Qur'an with *tartīl* than to read the whole of the text in the same length of time without *tartīl*,[77] for "reciting with contemplation and understanding is the greatest aim and the most important requirement, and thus are breasts gladdened and hearts enlightened" (Ibn ʿAbbās, cited in Naṣr 1932: 240).

Al-Suyūṭī relates that when a man boasted to the Prophet that he could recite a large portion of the Qur'an in a short time, the Prophet warned against such glibness, alluding to a people whose recitation "does not go further than their throats,[78] but if it [recitation] fell on the heart then benefit would be rooted there" (on the authority of Ibn Masʿūd in al-Suyūṭī 1910: 1/107–8). Al-Qāri' adds, "The people whose reciting goes no further than their throats are those who do not contemplate it or act according to it" (al-Qāri' 1948: 22). Al-Zarkašī says of the reciter that "his heart must be occupied in contemplating the meaning of what his tongue expresses, for he must know the meaning of each verse" (al-Zarkašī 1957: 450).[79] Al-Zarkašī continues with an account of the various meanings and moods of the Qur'anic text, recommending that the reciter be aware of them and responsive to them, concluding, "and if he does this then he has achieved complete *tartīl*" (al-Zarkašī 1957: 452).

In summary, *tartīl*, with regard to speech, denotes clear articulation and well-spaced presentation of the parts. With regard to recitation of the Qur'an (and it is almost totally restricted in usage to the Qur'an), it is a slow and deliberate recitation according to the rules of *tajwīd* (which ensure correctness and clarity), done in a spirit of reverence, and with contemplation and expression of the meaning. All this increases understanding of the text, and because of the divine command to recite with *tartīl*, it is the preferred mode of recitation.

Tartīl may or may not be melodic. In *Kitāb al-Lumaʿ* the author underlines the nonmelodic character of *tartīl* when he says that "putting tunes on the Qur'an is not allowed" and cites the verse, "*wa rattili l-qur'ānā tartīlan*" (Qur. 73/4) in support of this view (al-Sarrāj 1960: 357). In the older sources, in general, the consensus seems to be in favor of a nonmelodic *tartīl*. The only example I found to the contrary was al-Qurṭubī's version of Abū Mūsā l-Ašʿarī's response to the Prophet's praise of his voice (see above): "Had I known you were listening, I would have beautified my voice with the Qur'an and embellished it and made it *tartīl*."[80]

It is difficult to pin down modern Egyptian usage of the term *tartīl*, because, with the exception of Qur'anic scholars and those in a position to know its more specific requirements,[81] it is rarely used, and then rather vaguely applied. I have heard it equated with both of the main styles of recitation in Egypt. Although both styles fulfill the requirements of scholarly usage of the term (i.e., application of the rules of *tajwīd*, leisurely tempo, attention to meaning, etc.), they differ as to sound, context, and intent. *Tartīl*, when it specifies the style of recitation called *murattal* (past participle of *rattala*), denotes a recitation used in prayer, devotion, and learning in which "there is no *mūsīqā*, *taġannī*, or *tanġīm*" (Šayx Aḥmad al-Ruzayqī). But *tartīl* may also denote the slow melodic style of public recitation called *mujawwad*. A contemporary scholar cites the same Qur'anic verse cited by al-Sarrāj al-Ṭūsī to support his view of a nonmelodic interpretation of *tartīl* to conclude a discussion of the necessity of melodic and vocal technique in bringing out the meanings of the Qur'an (Anonymous 1974: 29). Labīb al-Saʿīd states that *tartīl* "is not usually free of *tarnīm*" (al-Saʿīd 1970:

62). And one informant distinguished *tartīl* from *ḥadr* and *tadwīr* (see chapter 3) not in terms of tempo or application of *tajwīd* but in terms of melody (Šayx Rašād Rušdī). Šayx Muṣṭafā Ismāʿīl was referring to the *mujawwad* style of recitation when he stated that "Šayx Rifʿat, Šayx al-Šaʿšāʿī, Šayx Muḥammad al-Sīsī are all good, but each one has a particular atmosphere in his *tartīl*" (Šayx Muṣ ṭafā Ismāʿīl).

Tajwīd al-Qur'ān

The sense of beautifying (*taḥsīn*) and embellishing (*tazyīn*) inherent in the basic meaning of the root J W D ("to do well" as opposed to "to do correctly") appears in such definitions of *tajwīd al-qur'ān* as "the ornament of *tilāwah* and the adornment of *qirā'ah*, and it is the giving of the letters full value . . ." (Ibn al-Jazarī 1908: 6) and "an excellence free of error in pronunciation . . . and its [the Qur'an's] beautification" (Ibn al-Jazarī 1908: 5). In his commentary on Ibn al-Jazarī's work, al-Qārī' cites other commentary to the effect that what is meant by *taḥsīn* and *tazyīn al-ṣawt* is in accordance with the science of *tajwīd*, and the two *ḥadīṯ* "Embellish your voices with the Qur'an" and "Embellish the Qur'an with your voices" are interpreted as a reference to qualities inherent in the rules of *tajwīd*.[82]

In modern Egyptian usage, the rules governing recitation are *aḥkām* (or *qawāʿid*) *al-tajwīd* (the rules of *tajwīd*), while *tajwīd al-qur'ān* more commonly denotes the melodic and performative style, *qur'ān mujawwad*.[83] "The technical term most widespread and most appropriate to the Qur'an [for melodic recitation] is '*tajwīd*,' and it is, in fact, the authorized melodic rendering [*al-talḥīn al-muxtass*] of the Qur'an" (al-Saʿīd 1970: 56). The verb *jawwada*, is also employed in the sense of reciting with melody and vocal artistry (*ṣōt*):

> They used to recite melodically [*jawwada*] with *ṣōt* in the time of the Prophet.
>
> (Šayx Aḥmad al-Ruzayqī)

> I would recite [*qara'a*] *qur'ān mujawwad* with *ṣōt*.
>
> (Šayx Fatḥī Qandīl)

Another clear example of *tajwīd* in the melodic sense is: "There are people who reject *tajwīd*, saying that reciters play with their voices in the Qur'an, and that the Qur'an says, "*wa rattili l-qur'ānā tartīlan*, so why *mujawwad* at all? Keep it *murattal*" (Šayx Aḥmad al-Ruzayqī). The dominance of the melodic sense of *tajwīd* and its related forms was perhaps best demonstrated by the statement of one reciter in defense of the practice of *mujawwad*: "The Prophet said, 'Whoever does not recite the Qur'an with *tajwīd* [*jawwada*] is a sinner'" (Šayx Aḥmad al-Ruzayqī). This statement is in fact a reference to the rules of *tajwīd*, and is not attributed to the Prophet but is taken from Ibn al-Jazarī's versified manual on *tajwīd*.[84] Ibn al-Jazarī is greatly respected as a scholar, and his works on *tajwīd* and *qirā'āt* are considered classics. The line quoted above is the one most widely quoted in support of correct (and not necessarily melodic) recitation. It is significant, therefore, that the statement should be applied to melodic recitation and given the force of the Prophet's authority.

Scholarly usage of this term is generally restricted to a recitation according to the body of rules which comprise the science of *tajwīd* and does not denote a melodically enhanced recitation.

In conclusion, usage of all these terms can perhaps best be demonstrated by grouping them according to the connotation polarities of less melodic/more melodic (fig. 1). However, we should keep in mind that a major difference between scholarly usage and modern Egyptian usage is that, according to the former, the terms are not necessarily defined in reference to melody, whereas we could deduce from modern Egyptian usage that there are basically two kinds of recitation: the melodic and the nonmelodic. The generic terms for recitation of the Qur'an are *qirā'ah* and *tilāwah* in scholarly and modern usage, and *tartīl* in scholarly usage.

Finally, the following two passages demonstrate both the density and the interchangeability of some of this vocabulary in scholarly usage:

> . . . and *luḥūn* is the plural of *laḥn* and it is *taṭrīb* and *tarjī'* of the voice, and its *taḥsīn* in the *qur'ān* and in poetry and in singing.
>
> (al-Qurṭubī 1968: 1/17)

Older scholarly usage:

Less melodic	*More melodic*
taḥqīq (see chapter 2)	*talḥīn al-qur'ān*
tartīl	*al-qirā'ah bi l-alḥān*
tajwīd	*al-taġannī bi l-qur'ān*
	al-tarannum bi l-qur'ān
	al-qirā'ah bi l-taṭrīb
	taḥsīn al-ṣawt bi l-qur'ān
	tazyīn al-ṣawt bi l-qur'ān
	tarjī' al-ṣawt bi l-qur'ān

Modern Egyptian usage:

al-qur'ān (or *al-muṣḥaf*) *al-muḥaqqaq* or *mu'allim* (see chapter 2)	*al-qur'ān* (or *al-muṣḥaf*) *al-mujawwad*
al-qur'*ān* (or *al-muṣḥaf*) *al-murattal*	*al-qur'ān bi ṣ-ṣōt* (*bi l-ṣawt*)
tartīl al-qur'ān	*al-qiṛạ'a bi ṣ-ṣōt* (*bi l-ṣawt*)
	tajwīd al-qur'ān
	tartīl al-qur'ān
	al-qiṛạ'ạ bi n-naġamah
	al-qirā'a bi t-tanġīm
	al-qirā'a bi l-alḥān
	al-taġannī bi l-qur'ān

Figure 1

> *al-taġannī bi l-qur'ān* is *taḥsīn al-ṣawt* with it, and *tarjī'* in its *qirā'ah*, and *taġannī* with whatever one desires of *aṣwāt* and *luḥūn*.
>
> (al-Jawziyyah 1970: 1/166)

Ḥuzn

An appropriate summary to this chapter is a clarification of the term *ḥuzn* and its related forms. The concept of *ḥuzn* embraces all of the qualities of the ideal recitation and can be considered a key to our understanding of the significance of the total experience of recitation.[85]

Ḥuzn is most generally translated as "sorrow" or "grief," and this definition does fit some contexts:

> Ibn Hurayrah used to recite "When the sun shall be darkened" (Qur. 81/1), making it so full of *ḥuzn* [*yuḥazzinuha*] that it resembled a dirge.
>
> (Ibn al-Jazarī 1932: 1/370)

> Verily the meaning of *yataġannā bihi* [see above] is *yataḥazzanū bihi*, that is, he demonstrates *ḥuzn* in his reciting, which is the opposite of joy.
>
> (al-Qurṭubī 1968: 1/13)[86]

> Where there is in it [the Qur'anic text] intimidation, threat . . . weeping and *ḥuzn* are necessary.
>
> (al-Makkī 1961: 99)

> You never saw Ḥasan al-Baṣarī except you would think he was on the brink of disaster.
>
> (al-Qušayrī 1959: 71, from a section on the virtues of *ḥuzn*)

H. G. Farmer translates Ibn Qutaybah's statement "*kāna qirā'ātuhu ḥazanan*" as "his reciting was a dirge-like cantillation."[87] One modern Arab scholar accepts the sense of sorrow and grief when he writes that, since the earlier songs of the Arabs were improvised, sad, and without artifice, "the conservatism of the legal scholars, solicitous of recovering the purity of the first age of Islam, insisted therefore, that the Qur'an necessarily be recited with a sad voice [*voix triste/bi-ḥazanin*]" (Talbi 1958: 185). However, one feels uneasy about such a statement, and one feels doubly so if the words "sorrow" or "grief" are inserted into some of the following *ḥadīṯ*:

> Recite the Qur'an with sorrow [*ḥuzn*]. Verily the best reciter is he who when he recites the Qur'an stimulates grief [*yataḥazzanu*].
>
> (al-Suyūṭī 1910: 1/109)[88]

> Recite the Qur'an with sorrow [*ḥuzn*] for verily it was revealed in sorrow [*ḥuzn*].
>
> (al-Suyūṭī 1910: 1/109)

Although the emotion of sorrow is definitely present in the concept of *ḥuzn*, it is clear that a definition of *ḥuzn* as "sorrow" is inadequate in this context.

Discussions of *ḥuzn* are found in the context of *ādāb al-tilāwah* (the code of behavior in recitation), and there is no doubt that *ḥuzn* is desired in reciting and listening to the Qur'an. *Bukāʾ*, or weeping, is also discussed in the same context, for it is the physical correlative to *ḥuzn*. Scholars refer to a number of *ḥadīṯ* and other authoritative statements, in addition to those given above, to substantiate the recommendation of *ḥuzn* and *bukāʾ*:

> Verily the Qur'an was sent down with *ḥuzn* so when you recite it feign *ḥuzn* [*taḥāzanū*].
>
> (al-Makkī 1961: 99; al-Ġazālī n.d.: 3/502 [*ḥadīṯ*])

> Verily this Qur'an was sent down with *ḥuzn* and grief [*kaʾābah*], so when you recite it weep, and if you do not weep then feign weeping [*tabākaw*].[89]

> If you recite . . . weep, and if the eyes of any one of you do not weep, then let his heart weep, for from *ḥuzn* springs weeping.[90]

> Recite the Qur'an with *ḥuzn* for verily it was revealed with *ḥuzn*.
>
> (al-Suyūṭī 1910: 1/109 [*ḥadīṯ*])

> I recited the Qur'an to the Messenger of God (peace be upon him) . . . and he said to me, "Oh righteous one, this is reciting! So where is the weeping?"[91]

In a discussion of the appropriateness of melodic recitation of the Qur'an, Ibn Qayyim al-Jawziyyah quotes the eminent jurist Aḥmad ibn Ḥanbal: "Melodic recitation does not please me unless it be *ḥazanan* and recited with *ḥuzn* like the voice of Abū Mūsā" (al-Jawziyyah 1970: 1/165).

From this last we deduce that *ḥuzn* is not only some sort of emotional state which is expressed through weeping, but a quality, or perhaps even a technique, of reciting which reflects that state.

Some scholars see *ḥuzn* not as a state or emotion, but as a vocal quality. The editor of *al-Maʿārif* (Ibn Qutaybah 1935) explains the statement "his reciting was *ḥazanan* [replete with *ḥuzn*]" as, "that is, there is *riqqah* in his voice."[92] We also find this association in the statement "He was a *raqīq* man: when he recited the Qur'an he caused weeping."[93] The dictionaries do show a correlation between *riqqah* (variously translated as "softness," "slenderness," and "delicacy") and *ḥuzn*. In the *Qāmūs* (al-Fīrūzabādī 1913: 4/213) we read that to recite with *taḥzīn* is to put *riqqah* in the voice (*yuraqqiq al-ṣawt*). Lane translates the phrase "he recites with *taḥzīn*" as ". . . with a slender (and plaintive) voice" (Lane 1863–93: 2/562). And he renders the expression *ṣawt ḥazīn* as "a soft or gentle, easy slender, plaintive and melodious voice" (1863–93: 2/562). In both dictionaries a certain gracefulness and elegance is attributed to *riqqah* as well: Lane translates *tarqīq al-kalām* as "the making of speech to be . . . elegant, graceful, ornate, adorned, embellished" (1863–93: 3/1131). This accords with the usage as it is applied to the more elaborate and rhythmically complex music which developed in the early days of Islam, the *ġinā' raqīq* (Ibn ʿAbd Rabbih 1968: 6/27), and to what might be seen as its poetic equivalent, the elegantly graceful poetry of the sophisticated urban centers, the *šhiʿr madanī raqīq* (Ibn ʿAbd Rabbih 1968: 33), *riqqat šiʿr madaniyyīn* (Ibn ʿAbd Rabbih 1968: 33).

The importance of the aesthetic dimension in the concept of *ḥuzn* is further indicated by the association of *ḥuzn* with the term *šajā*. The literal meaning of *šajā* is "a thing in the throat or fauces that [chokes one or] prevents from swallowing" (Lane 1863–93: 4/1510). The term also connotes grief and sorrow, but, when referring to music, it is the state of being moved, gripped emotionally, that is, "all choked up."

In the following example, in which the author re-creates the context of pre-Islamic singing, *ḥazīn* and *šajī* seem to be (near) synonyms: "the Arab would keep to himself and seek to drown in his contemplations, until his thoughts boiled over and he would repeat what was pressing on his heart with a *ḥazīn* and *šajī* tune" (al-Ixtiyār 1953: 8). Another modern scholar, writing on melodic recitation, indicates that melodies which stir the emotions (*naġamat mušjiyah*) are necessary to bring out and communicate the meaning of the text (Anonymous 1974: 29). This ties in very well with the concept of the most effective recitation being that which stirs the heart of the listener through artistry sensitive to meaning.

The concept of "softening the heart," that is, making it tender and vulnerable to being touched, is associated with this ideal in the sources (the quality of softness, *riqqah*, is the same soft and graceful quality of voice which may evoke that state): "He finds no softness [*riqqah*] in his heart when [he hears] reciting, and if the recitation were done with beautiful voice, or pleasant and touching melodies [*naġamāt ṭayyibah šajiyyah*], he would find *riqqah* and would take pleasure in listening" (al-Sarrāj al-Ṭūsī 1960: 356).

There are many examples that link *ḥuzn* directly to musical artistry and its effect. For example, a number of scholars equate the "singing" or "artistry" sense of *taġannā* with the equivalent verbal form of *ḥuzn*, *taḥazzana*.[94]

> The proof that the meaning of the *ḥadīṯ* is beautification of the voice and appropriate music is that the reciter's reciting affects the listeners with *ḥuzn* just as the appropriate music in poetry is that which enchants and stirs [*ṭaraba*] its listener.
>
> (al-Jawziyyah 1970: 1/166)

> He means by *taġannī* that the reciter [should] beautify his voice in the place where the singer beautifies his voice in his singing, except that, by means of *taḥsīn al-ṣawt*, he indicates *taḥazzun* without *taṭrīb*.
>
> (Ibn al-Hājj 1929: 54, citing al-Ḥalīmī)

The association of *taġannā* with *taḥazzana* explains the otherwise baffling passage in al-Ġazālī's section on weeping (*bukā'*): "Weeping is desirable in recitation. . . . and he [the Prophet] said, "He is not one of us who does not sing [*taġanna*] the Qur'an" (al-Ġazālī n.d.: 3/502). Al-Šāfi'ī writes, as proof that *taġannā* carries the sense of singing rather than enriching, that the reciter "stimulates *ḥuzn* and does *tarannum* with the Qur'an, and recites with *ḥadr* [quickly] and *ḥuzn*" (al-Sa'īd 1967: 312, footnote 3, quoting al-Subkī).

The association of *bukā'* with *ḥuzn* is another clue to the meaning of *ḥuzn*, for it is a response to spiritual and aesthetic stimuli (truth and beauty, if you will). It is clear that *bukā'* in this context is not the weeping triggered by grief.

As regards the aesthetic stimuli, it is well documented in the sources with which we have dealt that art, especially music and poetry, can move listeners to tears. A contemporary Egyptian scholar describes the extreme effect music has on the senses, feelings, and emotions, and finds an explanation for the fact that recitation has an even greater effect in the innate music and artistry of the text itself, over and above the actual sense of the words:

> How many eyes have filled with tears and hearts with awe and apprehension when the Qur'an flowed over these hearts. . . . from whence does the Qur'an derive this magic which dazzles the mind and shakes the heart? From its phrases? its meanings? from both? . . . the nerve which touches it all . . . is the apparent and hidden music in the verses of the Qur'an.
>
> (Abū l-ʿAynayn 1974: 25)

Many of the reports of David's beautiful singing and reciting mention that "he wept and caused weeping" (al-Jawziyyah 1970: 1/167). The following anecdote is of the same class as those which attribute various persons' conversion to Islam to their having been stirred by the beauty of a recitation of the Qur'an:

> Al-Ṭayyib al-Baṣrī, a Jew, wept on hearing the recitation of Abū l-Xawx, and was asked, how is it that you wept on hearing the Book of God, and you don't believe its truth? He said, verily the heart-rending emotion [*šajā*] of it made me weep.
>
> (al-Saʿīd 1970: 323, quoting al-Jāḥiḍ)

One of several such stories which were told to me is that of an American who, hearing a five-minute excerpt of Šayx Rifʿat's reciting over the radio, was so moved that he came to Egypt, took instruction, and became a Muslim. There are stories in both the older and the modern sources which refer to Christians and Jews converting to Islam "because of hearing his reciting and the beauty of his voice."[95] A clear acknowledgment of the role of artistry in evoking tears is the statement made by a participant in a weekly listening session (*nadwah*): "Šayx Rifʿat recites the Qur'an for the Qur'an and not for art. Still, there is art, because he was able to make people weep."

As regards the former stimulus, that is, that weeping is a response to truth, the following verses from the Qur'an are cited to support the recommendation to *bukāʾ*:

When the signs of the All-Merciful were recited to them [the Prophets] they fell down prostrate, weeping.

(Qur. 19/58, al-Saʿīd 1967: 320)

. . . and when they hear what has been sent down to the Messenger, thou seest their eyes overflow with tears because of the truth they recognize.

(Qur. 5/86, in al-Ġazālī n.d.: 8/1169)

Weeping is one of the manifestations of the ecstatic state, and if we read descriptions of that state, we see that there are many parallels with *ḥuzn*. Indeed *ḥuzn* is a sort of ecstasy of the kind sought by the Sufis by means of *samāʿ* and *ḍikr*;[96] it is the same vulnerability (softening of the heart) to the religious truth of the particular experience, in this case reciting:

Ecstasy is Truth. It is what grows up out of the abundance of the love of God Most High and out of sincerity in desiring Him and in longing to meet Him. That is stirred up by hearing the Qur'an also. . . . The saying of God Most High, "In the remembrance of God do hearts find rest" [Qur. 13/28], indicates that, as does his saying, "Whereat shiver the skins of those who fear their Lord; then their skins and their hearts soften to the remembrance of God" [Qur. 39/24]. And everything that is experienced as a consequence of *samāʿ* (because of *samāʿ* in the soul) is ecstasy.

(al-Ġazālī n.d.: 8/1168–69)

It is in this context that al-Ġazālī describes the effect of hearing the Qur'an recited, and the signs of the effect are weeping, swooning, and even dying (al-Ġazālī n.d.: 8/1169; see also chapter 3).

There are a number of reports which testify to the Prophet and his companions weeping on hearing the Qur'an recited,[97] and these reflect, not only the power of the Qur'an, but the spirituality of the listeners, for vulnerability of the heart is a quality of the religious person:

Verily I recite to you a *sūrah* and whoever weeps, he has paradise, and if you do not weep, then feign it.

(al-Suyūṭī 1910: 1/109, quoting ʿAbd al-Malik Ibn ʿUmayr)

> Weeping is the mark of those intimate with God [ʿārifīn] and the sign of the devout worshipers of God.
> (al-Saʿīd 1970: 106–7, quoting al-Nawawī)

Although *ḥuzn* does not seem to be a part of the modern Egyptian lexicon for ideal recitation, weeping is very much so (I often saw the eyes of listeners fill with tears), and it carries the same association with the religious ideal. One of the qualities for which the reciter Šayx Muḥammad Rifʿat is praised is that he wept a lot (*kān kitīr il-bukāʾ*), and the spirituality of Šayx Muḥammad Ṣiddīq al-Minšāwī's reciting was pointed out to me with the phrase, "Listen to how he weeps here." Both Šayx Rifʿat and Šayx al-Minšāwī are singled out for the *rūḥāniyyah* (spirituality) and *taṣawwuf* (Sufi-like quality) of their character and their recitation.

Of course, any act of piety, whether it be praying, reciting, or weeping, can become an empty gesture, and scholars warn against the danger of hypocrisy:

> And he stipulates, regarding *taḥzīn*, that the reciter in his reciting be clothed in *ḥuzn* of the heart . . . and let him be on guard against showing with his tongue what is not in his heart.
> (Ibn al-Ḥājj 1929: 55, quoting al-Qurṭubī)

In two sources we read of the various scandalous innovations which were introduced into recitation, among them a practice called *taḥzīn*:

> . . . and it is that the reciter abandons the natural and the customary in reciting and performs it differently as if he were grieving, almost weeping from fear of God and humility. However, this has been rejected because of the hypocrisy in it.[98]

Al-Ġazālī makes careful distinction between affecting ecstasy for purposes of show, and affecting it in order to invoke the desired state and explains, thereby, the recommendation to feign *ḥuzn* and *bukāʾ*:

> Of this feigned ecstasy [*tawājud*] there is that which is blameworthy, and it is what aims at hypocrisy and at the manifesting of the exalted states in spite of being quite destitute of them. And there is that [of feigned ecstasy] which is praiseworthy, and it leads to the invoking of the exalted states and the gaining of

> them for oneself, and bringing them to oneself by means of a ruse . . . and therefore the Messenger of God commanded him who did not weep at the reciting of the Qur'an that he should feign *bukā'* and *ḥuzn*, for, while the beginning of these states may be forced, their ends are true.
>
> (al-Ġazālī n.d.: 8/1167)[99]

The final key to understanding *ḥuzn* is in its association with *xušūʿ* and *xašyah* (verbs *xašaʿa* and *xašā*, respectively). *Xušūʿ* indicates humility, awe, and submission, and *xašyah* indicates fear of God and apprehension (of His judgment), and both are widely recommended in the sources for both reciter and listener, for

> the Qur'an is a place of *xušūʿ* as it is a reminder of death and what comes after it. It is not an occasion to give pleasure in the perception of beautiful sounds.
>
> (Ibn Xaldūn n.d.: 426)

Al-Suyūṭī introduces his section on *ḥuzn* and *bukā'* with the statement: "Weeping, pretending to weep for he who cannot, as well as *ḥuzn* and *xušūʿ* are desirable in recitation" (1910: 1/109). Al-Qurṭubī summarizes a concept of the ideal recitation when he writes that what is meant by *taġannā bi-* in the controversial *ḥadīṯ* is "the beautification of the voice, reciting by means of *xušūʿ* and *tarqīq* and *ḥuzn*" (1968: 1/15). In Egypt today *xušūʿ* is very much a part of the ideal for reciting, and the reciter who recites with *xušūʿ* manifests a gravity and dignity in accord with his understanding of the import of the text.

Al-Makkī (1961: 99) describes the ideal recitation as one in which the reciter recites promises with longing, admonition with fear, warning with severity, explanation with gentleness.[100] And he adds that some reciters, "if they recited a *sūrah* and their hearts were not in it, would repeat." He then cites, as an example of this ideal recitation, the *ḥadīṯ* "The reciter most beautiful of voice is he who when he recites you see that he fears God [*xašā l-llāh*]."[101] In other words, the most effective reciter is the one who feels intimately what he is reciting:

> I was reciting the Qur'an, but I found no beauty in it. So I said to myself, "Recite it as if you were hearing it from the Messenger of God (peace be upon him)," and its beauty came. Then

> I wanted more, so I said, "Recite it as if you were hearing it from [the Angel] Gabriel (peace be upon him)," and its beauty increased. Then I said, "Recite it as if you were hearing it from the Lord of all Being," and the whole of its beauty came forth.
>
> (al-Saʿīd 1970: 96, quoting al-Šaʿrānī ʿIzz Muslim Ibn Maymūn al-Xawāṣ)

To feel the immediacy of the message is very much akin to being affected by ecstasy, and, indeed, weeping can be a sign of *xušūʿ* and *xašyah*, as in the report that when the companions of the Prophet listened to recitation, "they wept for fear of God" (Šayx Fatḥī Qandīl). A Qur'anic verse often cited in connection with *ḥuzn* and *bukāʾ* is "They fall down upon their faces weeping; and it increases them in humility [*xušūʿ*]" (Qur. 17/109). This verse is given the following commentary by a modern scholar:

> A feeling of earnest humility comes to the man who realizes how, in spite of his own unworthiness, he is brought, by God's mercy, into touch with the most sublime Truths. Such a man is touched with the deepest emotion, which finds its outlet in tears.
>
> (ʿAlī 1946: 726)

This sensitivity or vulnerability to the truth which evokes tears is central to our definition of *ḥuzn*, as the following statements indicate:

> Verily the reciter contemplates what is in it [the text] of threat and intimidation and convenant and contract, then he considers his own shortcomings in his affairs, and his limitations, so that, without a doubt, it affects him with *ḥuzn* and he weeps.
>
> (al-Ġazālī n.d.: 3/502)

> [variant of the above] . . . and if *ḥuzn* and weeping don't attend him in that state, then let him weep for lack of it.[102]

> . . . and they recommended the pretense of *ḥuzn* and weeping so that the cares of the worshiper would be focused on what was recited so he would contemplate the words so that his heart would be with their meaning. For *taḥāzun* and *tabākī*

> [feigning *ḥuzn* and *bukā'*] lead to focusing one's cares and emptying the heart [of distraction].
>
> (al-Makkī 1961: 99)

> They [the Ixwān al-Ṣafā'], in their reciting and supplication, used "melodies from music called *al-muḥzin*, and they are those which soften [*raqqaq*] hearts when heard, and cause eyes to weep, and impart to souls regret for past sins, sincerity of soul, and renewed peace of conscience."
>
> (al-Saᶜīd 1967: 332, quoting from al-Rasā'il)

Al-Qušayrī devotes a section of his text to a number of epigrams in praise of the state of *ḥuzn*. These become more comprehensible in light of the above:

> Verily God loves the *ḥazīn*.
> It is said that *ḥuzn* prevents greed, fear, and fault.
> *Ḥuzn* is one of the qualities of the people of manners.
> When virtue dies, *ḥuzn* leaves the earth [as well].
>
> (al-Qušayrī 1959: 71)

It should be obvious that the terms "sorrow," "grief," "plaintive," and so forth, which are variously used to define *ḥuzn*, are inadequate in conveying the full sense of this concept. It should be equally obvious that a single-word definition of *ḥuzn*, in the context of recitation, is impossible. *Ḥuzn* is the awareness of the human state vis-à-vis the creator. With *ḥuzn* one knows true humility, awe of the divine, human fraility and mortality. This awareness, and the emotion it stirs on the part of the reciter, is communicated through the reciter's voice and artistry, heightening the listeners' sensitivity and awareness and moving them to tears.

All of the requirements for the ideal recitation point toward the same end: recitation of the Qur'an should be an engrossing religious experience and not simply a transmission of information, entertainment, or an automatic means of acquiring merit. Thus the command to recite the Qur'an as it was revealed has as much to do with evoking the moment of revelation and reaffirming its significance as it does with preserving the text. Likewise, both reciter and listener should approach recitation with sincere intent to open themselves up to the experience. The role of the reciter is not only to transmit the meanings of the text, but to stir the hearts of listeners with those meanings. It is recognized that the use of musical skills plays an important role in communicating not only the meaning of the text, but the significance of the recitation experience by capturing the emotions, affecting the senses, and engaging the total attention and focusing it on the significance of the Qur'an.

5. The Sound of Qur'anic Recitation

Introduction

We have discussed how the recitation of the Qur'an should sound according to theory, as well as the convergence of scholarship and belief in forming that ideal. We now move to a discussion of how it actually sounds. At the very basis of this discussion, and of the study as a whole, is the understanding that the sound of Qur'anic recitation is recognizably unique. Its characteristic sound is reproducible and therefore necessarily organized according to a set of underlying principles. The system of organization has certain special features that distinguish Qur'anic recitation from other cultural forms such as music. I assume, however, that the organizational system is not self-contained, but shares patterning principles, such as cultural values and aesthetic orientation, with other modes and forms of Egyptian society.

In order to understand the significance and effect of the sound, that is, how it works on the listener and why it works the way it does, we must describe and then account for it in terms of the ideals, expectations, and responses of those who practice the tradition. In other words, we must attempt to relate the actual sound and perception of it to the material discussed earlier—*tajwīd*, the *samāʿ* polemic, and the nature of the Qur'anic text. We must also take into account more concrete factors, such as the expectations and responses generated by the overlap of recitation with music, by economic considerations, and by the factors of artistic choice, through which the individual reciter establishes personal style. The list is not complete;[1] the variables are endless. It will suffice to say that determining the sound of recitation, ideal and actual, is

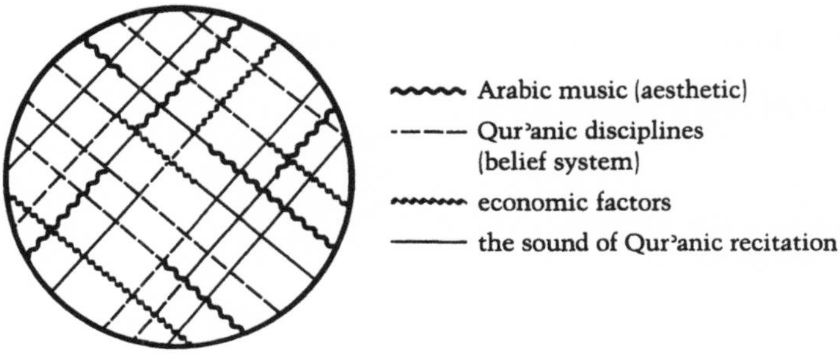

Figure 2

not an exercise in simple cause-and-effect logic; that is, the sound should not be considered the final product of a one-directional chain of ideals and values that begins with perception of the nature of the Qur'an and ends with a particular melodic cadence, vocal quality, or tempo. Rather, the relationships are multidirectional, for the sound is to be considered one manifestation (the most obvious and accessible) of a complex and dynamic system of values which is shaped by the intersections of a number of regulative factors, including the sound itself, as seen in figures 2 and 3.

There are, in fact, two distinct styles of Qur'anic recitation in the Egyptian tradition: *murattal* and *mujawwad*. They are alike in that they share the same basis—knowledge of the text and adherence to the rules of *tajwīd*—but they differ in that they fulfill different sets of expectations and thus are evaluated according to different criteria. The *murattal* style is characteristically relaxed, quiet, speech-bound, and, above all, is generally used to communicate the content of the Qur'an. Whether recited in pedagogical or devotional contexts, the aim of the *murattal* style is the clear and accurate presentation of the text. The *mujawwad* reciter, on the other hand, adds to this basis a command of the Arabic melodic system and a conscious manipulation of the parameters of recitation with the intent to affect listeners. The characteristics of the *mujawwad* style are intended to produce an emotional and religious effect on listeners; its contexts are public and performative.

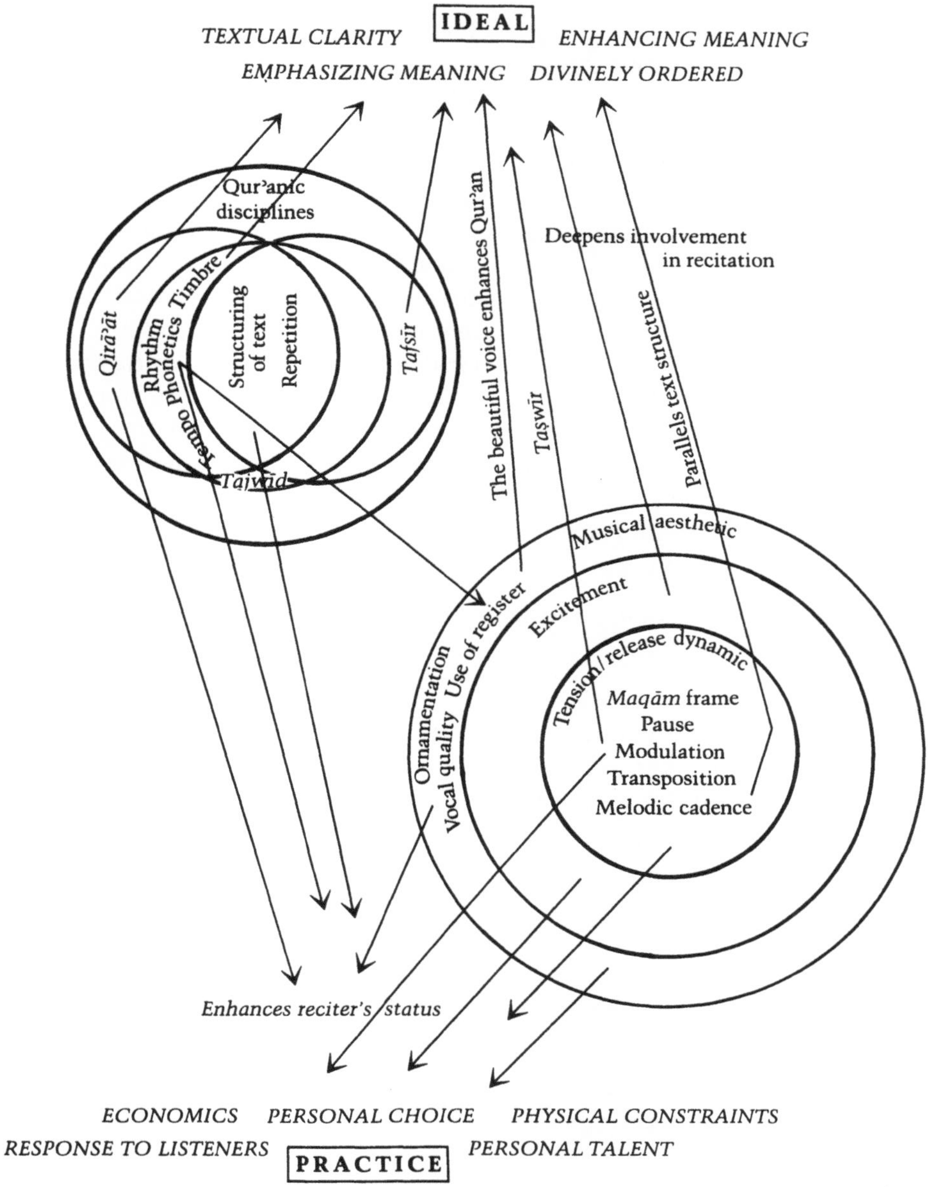
IDEAL
TEXTUAL CLARITY
ENHANCING MEANING
EMPHASIZING MEANING
DIVINELY ORDERED
Qur'anic disciplines
Qirā'āt
Rhythm
Phonetics
Timbre
Tempo
Structuring of text
Repetition
Tafsīr
Tajwīd
The beautiful voice enhances Qur'an
Taṣwīr
Deepens involvement in recitation
Parallels text structure
Musical aesthetic
Excitement
Ornamentation
Vocal quality
Use of register
Tension/release dynamic
Maqām frame
Pause
Modulation
Transposition
Melodic cadence
Enhances reciter's status
ECONOMICS
PERSONAL CHOICE
PHYSICAL CONSTRAINTS
RESPONSE TO LISTENERS
PERSONAL TALENT
PRACTICE

Figure 3

Its aim is to convey not only the text itself, but an artistic elucidation of its significance through the manipulation of the sound. The heightened, dramatic, and artistically focused performance of *mujawwad* recitation reflects this intent.

It is expected that *murattal* recitation will be correct according to the rules of *tajwīd*, and it is evaluated according to this expectation. However, in *mujawwad*, correct *tajwīd* is taken for granted, and it is expected that the recitation will be affecting in its beauty. Whereas one is refreshed spiritually by the *murattal* recitation, one experiences (ideally) through *mujawwad* an overt emotional involvement as well. When the two styles are evaluated, learning and worship are positive characteristics invariably mentioned in connection with *murattal*, while the aesthetic effects and artistic choices of the reciter figure prominently in any discussion of *mujawwad*. When asked to characterize the difference between the two styles, most informants, listeners and reciters alike, described *mujawwad* as having artistry and *murattal* as having none:

> *Mujawwad* is the same as *murattal* except with vocal artistry [*bi-ṣōt*].
>
> (Šayx Muṣṭafā Ismāʿīl)

> *Mujawwad* is called thus because there is artistry in it . . . those who want to listen to vocal artistry and melody won't listen to *murattal*. . . . the one has something of music [*mūsīqā*] in it and the other a great deal of worship [*ʿibādah*].
>
> (Šayx Muḥammad al-Ṭablāwī)

> There is no vocal-artistic effort [*ijtihād ṣōtī*] in *murattal*.
>
> (Šayx Aḥmad al-Ruzayqī)

> *Murattal* is a standard recitation without melodic artistry.
>
> (Š. ʿAbd al-Bāsiṭ ʿAbd al-Ṣamad)

> There is no melodizing [*tanġīm*] in *murattal*, the reciter recites to people straightforwardly.
>
> (Šayx ʿAbd al-Ḥakam)

The terms "artistry" and "vocal artistry/voice" are important to the distinction between the two styles, because informants do admit to the presence of musical elements such as the *maqāmāt* in the *murattal* style: for example, "Murattal doesn't have complete vocal artistry, but there is melody [*nağam*]" (Šayx Saᶜīd al-Saḫḫār). But, although "music gets into everything, even ordinary speech," it is a question of degree (Šayx Ibrāhīm al-Šaᶜšāᶜī). Since both styles may, therefore, form a continuum of musicality, a more significant distinction between them would be the reciter's intent with regard to that musicality. Thus, whereas in the *murattal* style melody has its basis in the given rhythm of the text (Suleiman Gamil), in the *mujawwad* style melody arises out of the reciter's manipulation of musical materials for effect, whether spiritual or aesthetic.

Although not so generally and explicitly stated by informants, another distinguishing factor between the two styles is the nature of the contexts (public or private) and of their general intent. Because one does hear *murattal* in the context of corporate prayer—that is, in public and on the religious radio stations—and because the public style of some professional reciters is subdued and close to the *murattal* style, it is perhaps an oversimplification to distinguish *murattal* from *mujawwad* strictly in terms of private versus public context. However, one can say that more people *recite murattal* in private context, and more people *listen* to *mujawwad* in public context. Since expectations of *murattal* and *mujawwad* recitations differ within the culture, I apply different criteria to the analyses of the two styles. Thus, the sound of the *murattal* recitation is related most directly to its private context and private devotional as well as pedagogical intents. Because the *mujawwad* style is generally considered the model of recitation, it is related to the expectations and intent of the ideal recitation as it is described in scholarly works, as well as to the elements of artistry which figure so prominently in any reference to this style.

Murattal

The sound of the *murattal* style of recitation is in accord with its instructional and devotional practices; thus, the principle underlying the production of its sound is maximum clarity of text. The text is recited straight through, with no part emphasized over any other. The basic structural unit, the phrase, is defined by the text (usually the verse line), or (in longer verses) by breath capacity. Each

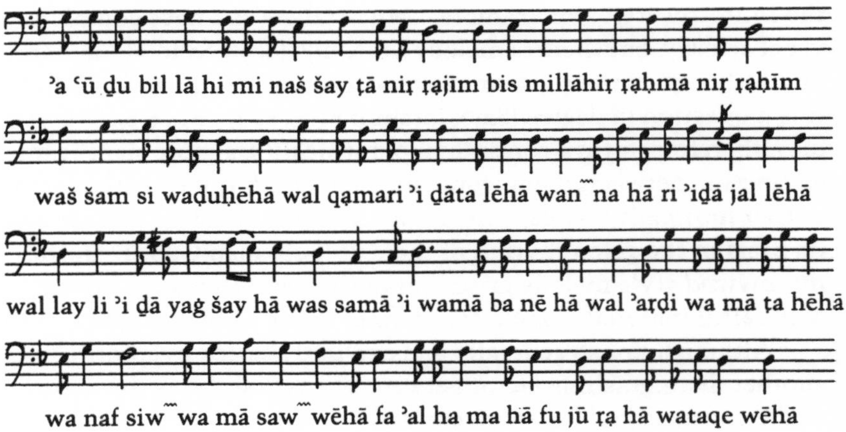

Figure 4. Šayx ʿAbd al-Mutaʿāl Manṣūr ʿArafah, Qur. 91/1–8

Figure 5. A student in Š. ʿĀmir's *maqraʾah*, Qur. 2, from v. 61

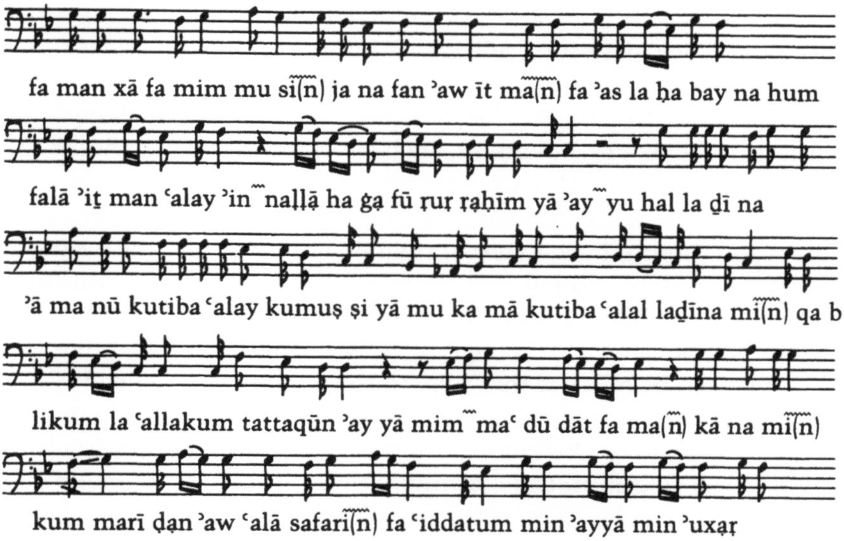

Figure 6. Š. Maḥmūd Xalīl al-Ḥuṣarī, Qur. 2/182–84

phrase is performed in a single breath and followed by a pause. The pause between phrases is only long enough for the reciter to draw breath. The voice is relaxed, and, although it may be pitched slightly higher than the normal speaking-voice register, the volume is that of ordinary conversation, or quieter. Melodic movement is contiguous and kept to a range of a fourth or fifth, although the register may be extended by gradual stepwise motion. The tempo is quick. Maximum clarity is ensured by giving each syllable only one pitch or, at most, two pitches for longer syllables. Delivery, in general, is text-bound; vibrato and other vocal ornamentation is rare. There is no mixing of the *qirāʾāt*. Differences in personal style are largely a matter of melodic contour, pitch reiteration, and intonation (figs. 4, 5, and 6),[2] but these are not consciously cultivated: they can be likened to differences in handwriting styles or subphonemic differences in language in that they are not significant to the style. The still, relaxed posture of the *murattal* reciter, as well as the absence of gesture, reflects its self-contained and private nature.

Although the *murattal* style is text-bound to a great degree in terms of delivery and intent, such a recitation is by no means reduced to a dry didactic exercise, nor is it a poor cousin to the *mujawwad* style in terms of its aesthetic appeal. The rhythm, alliteration, internal and external rhyme of the text, and the elegance of its expression, combined with the relaxed but clear murmuring of its delivery, make a sound both soothing and refreshing, one which has wide appeal among Muslims and non-Muslims alike.

The accessibility of this style to the nonprofessional and its particular suitability for instruction, due to its clarity, make *murattal* the standard of Qur'anic recitation. The basic requirements for anyone learning *murattal* are simply those of learning to recite according to the rules of *tajwīd*, namely, mastery of the text itself and knowledge of the rules of *tajwīd*.[3] The more of the Qur'anic disciplines one has mastered, the more intelligently one can recite, but a beautiful voice and an artistic sensibility are not considered essential to the *murattal* style.

The sound of *murattal* can be further explained in terms of the project initiated by the scholar and teacher Dr. Labīb al-Saʿīd, in conjunction with the Ministry of Religious Endowments. The project, begun in 1960, was to record and broadcast this style.[4] Dr. al-Saʿīd undertook to have the recited Qur'an recorded as a response to what he considered a decline in the oral tradition of the Qur'an. The recording would provide an authoritative and correct model for learning and memorizing the text according to the rules of *tajwīd*, would be a reference in those cases where orthography differs or is confusing, and would be a protection against distortion and error. As the oral equivalent of the ʿUṯmānī text, it would also further Muslim unity. The style best suited to these aims, according to Dr. al-Saʿīd, is *murattal*.

The *murattal* style was widely employed in prayer and instruction; but, according to Dr. al-Saʿīd, this style, lacking an authoritative and prestigious model, was in danger of being overshadowed by the more popular (and yet more inaccessible, due to its requirements) *mujawwad* style. Throughout his book on the project Dr.

al-Saʿīd contrasts the accessibility and intent of *murattal* with that of *mujawwad*:

> It was the purpose of the committee [supervising the project] to provide for the public a model of a style of chanting which could be easily mastered by the average person. al-Mushaf al-Murattal (the Qur'anic text recited in Murattal) was not to be a teacher of professionals; it was to be a teacher of laymen, a help to all those who wished to recite the Koran correctly and thus, accomplish what is for Muslims, a meritorious religious act. . . . Accordingly, the Tartil style was adopted. Our desire was to disseminate this style on as wide a scale as possible in order to counter-balance the influence of the more elaborate and difficult styles which were the special preserve of the professionals. It seemed to us that if these highly complicated styles were allowed eventually to monopolize the scene, as they might very well do if alone used in recording and broadcasting, the learning of the Koran by the average man would actually be obstructed, and Koranic recitation as such would become a jealously guarded craft.
>
> (Weiss, Berger, and Rauf 1975: 113–14)[5]

In his proposal to the Ministry for the project, al-Saʿīd wrote:

> It is true that some broadcasting stations have records of certain portions of the Sacred book, recited by various readers; but the records we have in mind would be of a different nature. The musical enchantment [*taṭrīb*] of the listeners, for example, would not be among its purposes; its primary purpose, rather, would be instruction. Obviously the ordinary individual caught among the pressing affairs of everyday life cannot and should not attempt to recite the Koran in the melodic manner [*al-tarīqah al-talhīniyyah*] of those readers whose recitations are heard over the broadcasting stations and at formal gatherings.

The first professional reciter to record in this project, Šayx Maḥmūd Xalīl al-Ḥuṣarī, corroborated this view in an interview when he explained that, while the *mujawwad* style is clear, it is not for those who want to memorize the text. Another reciter, Šayx Aḥmad al-Ruzayqī explained to me that while it is possible to memorize and learn the *qirā'āt* from the *murattal* style, this is not possible with the *mujawwad* style. It is significant that the criterion for those reciters selected for the first recording and broadcasting of the *murattal* style was, first and foremost, that the reciters be masters of *tajwīd* and *qirā'āt*. The only requirement regarding the voice was that it be of acceptable recording quality, a fairly arbitrary and debatable criterion. Consequently, of the first three reciters, two were respected scholars, and the one prominent professional reciter (Šayx al-Ḥuṣarī) was a well-known scholar as well.[6]

The private nature of the *murattal* style is such that, as mentioned above, it had never been recorded for broadcast. The unexpected effect of the broadcasting of this style was to create in the minds of many Egyptians the idea that this was a new and somehow distinct style, separate from that which they themselves use in prayer and instruction. I met a number of people who credit Šayx al-Ḥuṣarī with being the first to recite *murattal* style. He explained that it was only that he was the first to record and broadcast it. Dr. al-Saᶜīd relates that on June 4, 1959, he set up a public recitation of the *murattal* style, performed by Šayx al-Ḥuṣarī in a hall at al-Azhar University, to "try out the *murattal* style on the public": "The audience was generally favorable and many remarked that the style of chanting used enabled them better to concentrate on the meaning of the words."[7] In fact, the private nature and the sound of *murattal* have not been changed by its broadcast and commercial recording, because the original intent of instruction and devotion remains the same.

Mujawwad

In contrast to the *murattal* style, the *mujawwad* recitation is rendered only in a public context: it is first and foremost a performative style. At work in this style is the concept of human will within the framework of the immutable divine. Thus the unchanging and divinely ordained *tajwīd* is one context in which the *mujawwad* reciter's personal choice may function specifically, with regard to structuring, rhythm, and choice of general text system (*qirā'ah*). Another area of personal choice is the melodic parameter, and here fixity is expressly forbidden by religious authorities lest it infringe on the primacy of the text. Therefore, the ideal in the *mujawwad* style is that a spontaneously crafted melody be executed on the fixed text in the context of public performance, and that, at the same time, personal choice be executed whenever possible in order that the recitation be most responsive to the meaning, the particular occasion, and the emotions of the listeners. This issue of fixity versus freedom is basic to the *mujawwad* style and directly affects several aspects of its performance.

The professional reciter—that is, the reciter to whom an audience is an economic necessity—does not recite *mujawwad* except in public performance. He thus avoids the risk of imposing a fixed melody on the Qur'anic text. This is not to say that a reciter never repeats himself, or that he does not have a repertoire of melodic phrases characteristic of his personal style. This does happen. However, the fact that these are not consciously crafted for public presentation makes them more acceptable to the conscientious listener. Just how far-reaching in practice are the ramifications of the ideal recitation is illustrated by the incorporation of "warm-up" and rehearsal (two aspects usually excluded from the performance contexts of other traditions) into performance. This is true even in the context of recording the *mujawwad* style in a studio for broadcast (i.e., where the recitation is intended for listeners, but not actually performed in public). Šayx Muṣṭafā Ismāʿīl objected to the short time limit allowed for studio recordings (forty-five minutes at the most, as opposed to one to three hours for a live performance). He admitted that he needed fifteen to twenty minutes to warm up his voice, which left him only ten to thirty minutes of good voice.

Likewise, there is no private practicing of the melodic style. To gain expertise in manipulating melody, the *mujawwad* reciter must practice with a text other than the Qur'an. If he uses the Qur'anic text, it must be in the context of public performance. Thus, some of the repetition of text characteristic of the *mujawwad* style can be attributed to the reciter's conscious correcting of a phrase textually, or improving it melodically: "When I do a high passage and feel it is not up to its potential [lit., not ripe], I do it again—still not right—again—OK. I keep repeating until it is good. I am aware of the presence of critical listeners" (Šayx Muṣṭafā Ismaʿīl). As for review of *tajwīd*, it is done in private and in the *murattal* style.

As a performative mode *mujawwad* has a force and intensity not present in *murattal*. Maintaining fixity and freedom, *tajwīd* and melody, presents a unique challenge to the Qur'anic reciter and certainly contributes to that intensity. The stance and gestures of the reciter reflect the effort involved. It is visible to the listeners in his clenched hands, trembling, taut facial muscles, and the expression of pain on his face, particularly in the most intense and high-pitched passages. In performance, there is little casualness of movement: the hands are not flung or dropped, but deliberately placed on the knees or at the sides of the face. One of the most characteristic (and seemingly instinctive) gestures of the professional reciter is to raise the hand (or hands) to the side of the face, fingers touching the ears, elbow raised so that the palm is almost horizontal. A variation of this gesture is to move the palm along the jaw line so that the heel hovers around the mouth and the fingers around the ears. The visual effect of this is a subtle physical shaping of the sound. Some reciters speculated that this gesture may help to project the voice so that the reciter can modulate the sound in his own ears to hear himself better, but their personal reasons for doing it were varied: "It's the custom"; "I've always done it"; "The reciter can enter into it better"; "The hand pulls out the melody"; "Like rocking back and forth, it is something not felt. One isn't aware of doing it." Rocking is especially characteristic of anyone reciting a memorized text. From my personal experience it seems to be related to the memorizing process.

If we break the *mujawwad* sound down into its characteristic (and most frequently mentioned) components, we find that they fall into two general areas of reference or organizational systems. These are 1. Arabic music, in which such aspects as melodic principles (*maqām*, transposition, modulation), use of the *maqām* frame, register, melodic cadence (*qaflah*), pause, ornamentation, and voice type have their immediate reference; and 2. the Qur'anic disciplines of *tajwīd*, *qirā'āt*, and *tafsīr*, which regulate structuring of the text, rhythm, timbre, phonetics, relative tempo, and volume (see figs. 3 and 7).

The ultimate organizational principle is the ideal recitation as defined in religious scholarship according to the nature and significance of the text (chapter 4). It is due to this ideal that those aspects of Arabic music and the Qur'anic disciplines most appropriate to recitation are selected. At the same time, the ideal is itself mutable and is shaped by the sound it generates, since people's ex-

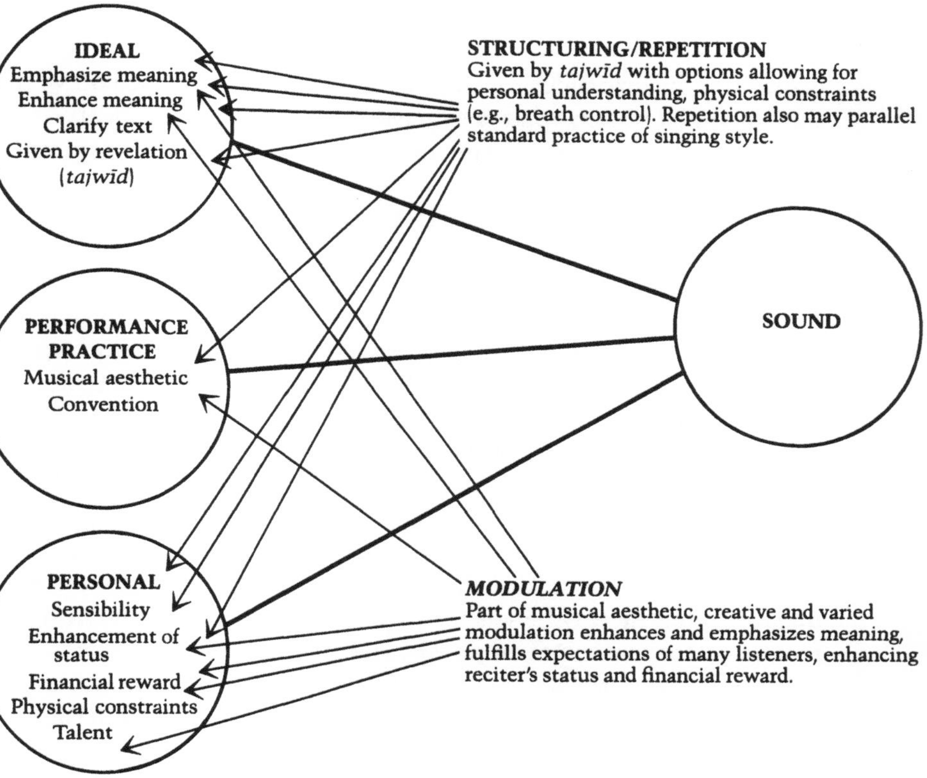
IDEAL
Emphasize meaning
Enhance meaning
Clarify text
Given by revelation
(*tajwīd*)
STRUCTURING/REPETITION
Given by *tajwīd* with options allowing for personal understanding, physical constraints (e.g., breath control). Repetition also may parallel standard practice of singing style.
PERFORMANCE PRACTICE
Musical aesthetic
Convention
SOUND
PERSONAL
Sensibility
Enhancement of status
Financial reward
Physical constraints
Talent
MODULATION
Part of musical aesthetic, creative and varied modulation enhances and emphasizes meaning, fulfills expectations of many listeners, enhancing reciter's status and financial reward.

Figure 7

pectations and attitudes toward recitation tend to be based on what they hear and not on what they have learned of abstract ideals or aesthetic principles. Thus, the use of musical elements in Qur'anic recitation is determined as much by the prestige and popularity of the Egyptian recitation style as by scholarly recommendation.

The organizational systems function as constraints on the reciter, and although each is sufficiently distinct to be considered a separate area, it is their interaction on various levels which shapes the Qur'anic recitation in theory and in performance. For example, a stylistic feature characteristic of and unique to Qur'anic recitation is the phrase rendered in a single breath. This practice is dictated by the rules regarding pause and phrase initiation of the Qur'anic discipline of *tajwīd*, and it fulfills the ideal of textual clarity. Since adherence to these rules requires that the reciter understand the text, it further fulfills the ideal of a thoughtful recitation. The reciter may also shape his phrase according to the meaning and the way he wishes to present the text, that is, through repetition for reasons of emphasis, and/or singling out of words or short phrases for the same reason. His referent here is again the ideal recitation. The *mujawwad* reciter may also determine the length of a phrase in response to audience expectations of virtuosity according to the aesthetics of Arabic music. Thus the phrase length may be dictated by the melodic pattern, that is, the textual phrase made longer to allow for melodic resolution. Attention to audience expectations is also influenced by such factors as concern for one's reputation or status as a reciter and economic reward. Finally, the reciter may be constrained for physical reasons, such as a sneeze, a cough, or shortness of breath. It is not always possible, however, to determine why a given individual recites the way he does. His choices are not always conscious, and several referents may dictate the same effect. For example, the reciter may structure the short repeated phrase for reasons of emphasis. At the same time, he may be unconsciously influenced by the characteristic style of Arabic voice music in which the singer plays with the text, singling out words and phrases not only for emphasis, but for melodic and virtuosic reasons as well. The aim here is not to link each aspect of the sound to a single determinant, but to present the range of factors and give an indication of their relationships to each other in performance (as in fig. 7).

One kind of relationship involves the type of sanction which activates a particular feature of the recitation and produces differing effects on the listener's perceptive apparatus. For example, the authority of religious scholarship which articulates the ideal of Qur'anic recitation has the greatest moral force. It dictates the use of *tajwīd*, the opening and closing formulae, the *qirā'āt*, and sectioning of the text, as well as the behavior proper to reciter and listener. It does not deal with the melodic parameter except to sanction and qualify its use.

Even within the area sanctioned by religious scholarship we see that professional conformity varies according to the degree of authority involved. For example, some scholars consider it a sin to ignore the rules of *tajwīd* in reciting the Qur'an. Mastery of the rules is a minimum requirement for the professional reciter or for any adult Muslim who recites publicly, such as the prayer leader, and is based on the divine command "*wa rattili l-qur'ānā tartīlan*" (Qur. 73/4). There is also agreement among scholars that within a single recitation, the reciter should use only one of the durational options available to him according to the rules of *tajwīd*. Thus all final long vowels within a recitation would be of the same duration, whether two, four, or six beats. But the authority for this convention is not that of divine command, and the reciter who does vary his durations does not commit a sin, but simply makes a mistake.

Oral tradition governs both textual and melodic aspects of recitation, which, while not initiated by religious authority, are consistently adhered to. For example, according to the rules of *tajwīd*, the syllable composed of a final long vowel which is followed by an initial glottal stop (e.g., *qā**lū** 'in͠na, **mā** 'a͠(n͠)zala*, i.e., *madd muttaṣil*) can take either the longer or shorter durations. However, it is inevitably given the longer durations. In fact, there is a general tendency in the more melodic style to use the longer durations, as the longer syllable allows for melodic play.[8] An example of a melodic convention is the use of the *maqām bayātī* to begin and end the recitation.

Oral tradition works through the authority of convention. Like that of religious scholarship, it can be objectively evaluated, yet it carries less moral force.

The conventions of the musical parameter are exclusively grounded in oral tradition, specifically the musical aesthetic of

Egypt. The difference between these conventions and those mentioned above is that those regulated by the musical aesthetic tradition affect the more subjective aspects of the sound, operating on the consensus of "good taste," a factor which is infinitely variable. For example, one can objectively determine whether or not a reciter has framed his recitation in *maqām bayātī*, but there will be differences of opinion as to whether a reciter uses "enough" variation in his modulation, has a "good" voice, or makes an "effective" melodic cadence. Moreover, whereas a recitation which adheres to the standards of religious authority and an equally authoritative oral scholarly tradition is "correct," one which fulfills the expectations of the musical aesthetic is "beautiful."

Ideally, of course, the correct *is* beautiful and vice versa, and indeed, the two do not seem to be distinguished in any evaluation of *murattal* recitation. Likewise, in *mujawwad*, the reciter must fulfill both expectations of beauty and correctness to satisfy his listeners and please his critics. However, such is the style and nature of the *mujawwad* recitation that often the beautiful is more compelling than the correct. I heard of one reciter who had a large following in the countryside yet scandalized the more conscientious listeners with his aberrant use of *tajwīd*. This is, admittedly, a rare case, but the opposite seems less likely, for listeners do not respond positively to a recitation that, however correct, is not considered in some way beautiful in terms of the musical aesthetic. Moreover, the consensus of those who evaluate reciters for public broadcast seems to be that beauty (in voice and melodic skill) is selectively God-given, while correctness (in *tajwīd*) can be learned by anyone. Thus, in a *mujawwad* recitation correctness is generally taken for granted, whereas beauty is linked to the musical aesthetic and is considered special. What follows is a more detailed exposition of the sound of *mujawwad* in terms of how the reciter manipulates the elements of the recitation in relation to the various regulative factors mentioned above.

Repetition/Sectioning of the Text

The basic structural unit of the recitation performance is the phrase followed by a pause. The reciter is free to end his melodic phrase at any point in the text as long as he does not obscure or distort the meaning: correct usage of the rules of pause and phrase initiation (*waqf* and *ibtidā'*) ensures this. In general, longer phrases (and the longer durational options) are characteristic of the *mujawwad* style, for they give the reciter the opportunity to exploit his melodic inventiveness, to make use of modulation skills, or simply to demonstrate the sheer physical virtuosity of long breath capacity.

One structuring technique characteristic of this style is to present the text in short clear phrases characterized by syllabic and unornamented melodies, and then to repeat the text in a single long phrase. In fact, a sequence of short phrases usually signals a melodically elaborate recapitulation of the text executed in a single long breath. This technique allows the reciter to be both clear and inventive in his art, fulfilling demands both of the ideal and of the musical aesthetic. The effect on the audience is to heighten involvement by means of delaying the resolution provided by the longer phrase: that is, the greater the sequence of short phrases, the more tension is prolonged. The tension and release experienced by the listeners, however, is evident in their response, which is restrained until it breaks like a wave in the pause following the long phrase.

Although the through-recited style of the *murattal* is also characteristic of the *mujawwad* style as done by reciters of past generations, more and more reciters are using their knowledge of pause to clarify or emphasize a part of the text. This adds a rhetorical and dramatic element to the recitation. The *mujawwad* phrase may therefore be composed of not only a verse line, but a single word, a word repeated several times, a few words, or several verses, depending on how the reciter wishes to convey the text. This kind of phrasing varies according to the reciter's understanding of the text and/or his personal style, or even the demands of the melodic line. Since the sense of a phrase may or may not be complete, one way in which the reciter builds tension and strikes emphasis is to prolong the syntactic as well as the melodic resolution of a phrase.

Two examples of sectioning are given in figures 8 and 9. In the first, the reciter isolates the word *'Aḷḷāh* in a single phrase. Since *'Aḷḷāh* is also an exclamation of wonder and delight, it not only emphasizes that God is the light of the heavens and earth, but acts as a commentary on that statement, as well as the whole section of

ʾAḷḷạ̄h
ʾAḷḷạ̄hụ nūru s-samāwāti wa l-ʾaṛḍ
God is the light of the heavens and the earth (Qur. 24/35).

Figure 8

V. 35

1. *wa mā yulaqqạ̄ha ʾillā llaḏīna ṣạbaṛū*	Yet none shall receive it except the steadfast
2. *wa mā yulaqqạ̄ha ʾillā llaḏīna ṣạbaṛū*	Yet none shall receive it except the steadfast;
wa mā yulaqqạ̄ha ʾillā ḏū ḥaẓẓin ʿaẓīm	none shall receive it except a man of mighty fortune
3. *wa mā yulaqqạ̄ha ʾillā llaḏīna ṣạbaṛū*	Yet none shall receive it except the steadfast
4. *wa mā yulaqqạ̄ha ʾillā llaḏīna ṣạbaṛū*	Yet none shall receive it except the steadfast;
wa mā yulaqqạ̄ha ʾillā ḏū ḥaẓẓin ʿaẓīm	none shall receive it except a man of mighty fortune

V. 36

5. *wa ʾim͠mā ya(n͠)zaġan͠naka min aš -šayṭạ̄ni nazʿū͠(n͠) fa staʿiḍ bi l-lāh*	If a provocation from Satan should provoke thee, seek refuge in God
6. *in͠nahū huwa s-samīʿu l-ʿalīm*	He is the All-Hearing, the All-Knowing

V. 37

7. *wa min āyātih*	And of his signs
8. *wa min āyātih*	And of his signs
9. *wa min āyātihi l-laylu wa n͠-nahāṛu wa š-šamsu wa l-qạmaṛ*	And of his signs are the night and the day, the sun and the moon
10. *wa min āyātihi l-laylu wa n͠-nahāṛu wa min āyātihi wa min āyātihi l-laylu wa n͠-nahāṛu wa š-šamsu wa l-qạmaṛ*	And of his signs are the night and the day, and of his signs, and of his signs are the night and the day, the sun and the moon
11. *la tasjudū li š-šamsi wa lā li l-qạmaṛ*	Prostrate yourselves not to the sun and the moon

V. 35

12. *wa mā yulaqqạ̄ha ʾillā llaḏīna ṣạbạṛū wa mā yulaqqạ̄ha ʾillā ḏū ḥaẓẓin ʿaẓīm*	Yet none shall receive it except the steadfast; none shall receive it except a man of mighty fortune

V. 36

13. *wa ʾim͠mā ya(n͠)zaǧan͠naka min aš-šayṭạ̄ni nazʿu(n) fa staʿiḏ bi l-lāh*	If a provocation from Satan should provoke thee, seek refuge in God
14. *in͠nahū huwa s-samīʿu l-ʿalīm*	He is the All-Hearing, the All-Knowing

V. 37

15. *wa min āyātihi l-laylu wa n͠-nahāṛu wa š-šamsu wa l-qạmaṛ*	And of his signs are the night and the day, the sun and the moon
16. *lā tasǰudū li š-šamsi wa lā li l-qạmaṛ*	Prostrate yourselves not to the sun and the moon
17. *wa sǰudū li l-lāh*	Prostrate yourselves to God
18. *wa sǰudū li l-lāh*	Prostrate yourselves to God
19. *lā tasǰudū li š-šamsi wa lā li l-qạmaṛi was ǰudū li l-lāhi llaḏī xạlaqạhun͠na ʾĩ(n) kũ(n)tumū ʾiyāhu taʿbudūn.*	Prostrate not yourselves to the sun and moon, but bow yourselves to God who created them, if Him you serve.

Figure 9. From *Sūrat* Ḥa-Mīm (Fuṣṣilat) Reciter: Šayx Kāmil Yūsuf al-Bahtīmī

text which the reciter now repeats. In the second example, the dramatic high point of the text is the command "Prostrate yourselves to God" (phrase 17), which is itself part of a longer verse. Most of the listeners know the text and anticipate this point in the text. The reciter leads them slowly up to the preceding phrase, "Prostrate yourselves not to the sun and the moon," and the silence of the pause is full of tense expectation, but instead of continuing, he returns to verse 35 (phrase 12), thus increasing the tension and sustaining it by staying in the high register. When the climactic phrase does come, after another slow ascent in pitch, it is performed as an isolated phrase, high-pitched, set apart from the rest of the text with pauses and repeated. The reciter then delivers the same phrase, a third time in the context of the whole verse.

In the classical Arabic music tradition the practice of breaking up a given text in performance is well established and very much a part of the aesthetic. A singer is expected to play with the words of the text, and single words or phrases may be repeated for emphasis, or simply to provide a structure on which the singer can display his or her voice and vocal skills. The emergence of this practice in Qur'anic recitation is probable evidence for continuing overlap between music and recitation and supports the view that recitation has become increasingly secularized since it joined the world of the mass media. The segment outlined in figure 10, for example, is from a performance which is valued by the reciter's followers for its virtuosic display of various durational options and melodic inventiveness, but denied official broadcast on the grounds that the reciter's manipulation of the rhythmic options of the text and the repetition do not enhance the meaning of the whole passage. In other words, the sound is exploited for its own sake, without reference to the significance of the text. While this is acceptable, indeed admired, in music, it violates the nature and intent of Qur'anic recitation. This is an example of the "beautiful" taking precedence over the correct.

Religious scholarly consensus regarding the breaking up of the text in recitation is that the reciter may repeat for emphasis, but may not "play" with the text for purely melodic or vocal reasons. Thus there is disapproval of the practice of single-word repetition in general; the single word is considered too small a unit to be meaningful and extensive repetition of it may obscure or interrupt the meaning and syntax of the longer phrase.

Scholarly consensus also decrees that the reciter may jump forward in the text, but not backward. If he jumps to another *sūrah*, whether to its beginning or middle, he must mark it with the opening formula (*basmalah*). However, not all reciters adhere to this latter point: there are prominent and respected reciters who do jump into the middle of a *sūrah* and omit the opening formula. Likewise, certain pairs or clusters of *suwar* are popularized as "set texts" and treated as a unit without any intervening opening formulae (e.g., *al-Fātiḥah/al-Baqarah*; *al-Duḥā/al-Inširāh/al-Tīn*, etc.). Such practice is generally not censured by the authorities unless it is compounded by the more basic aberrations such as faulty *tajwīd*.

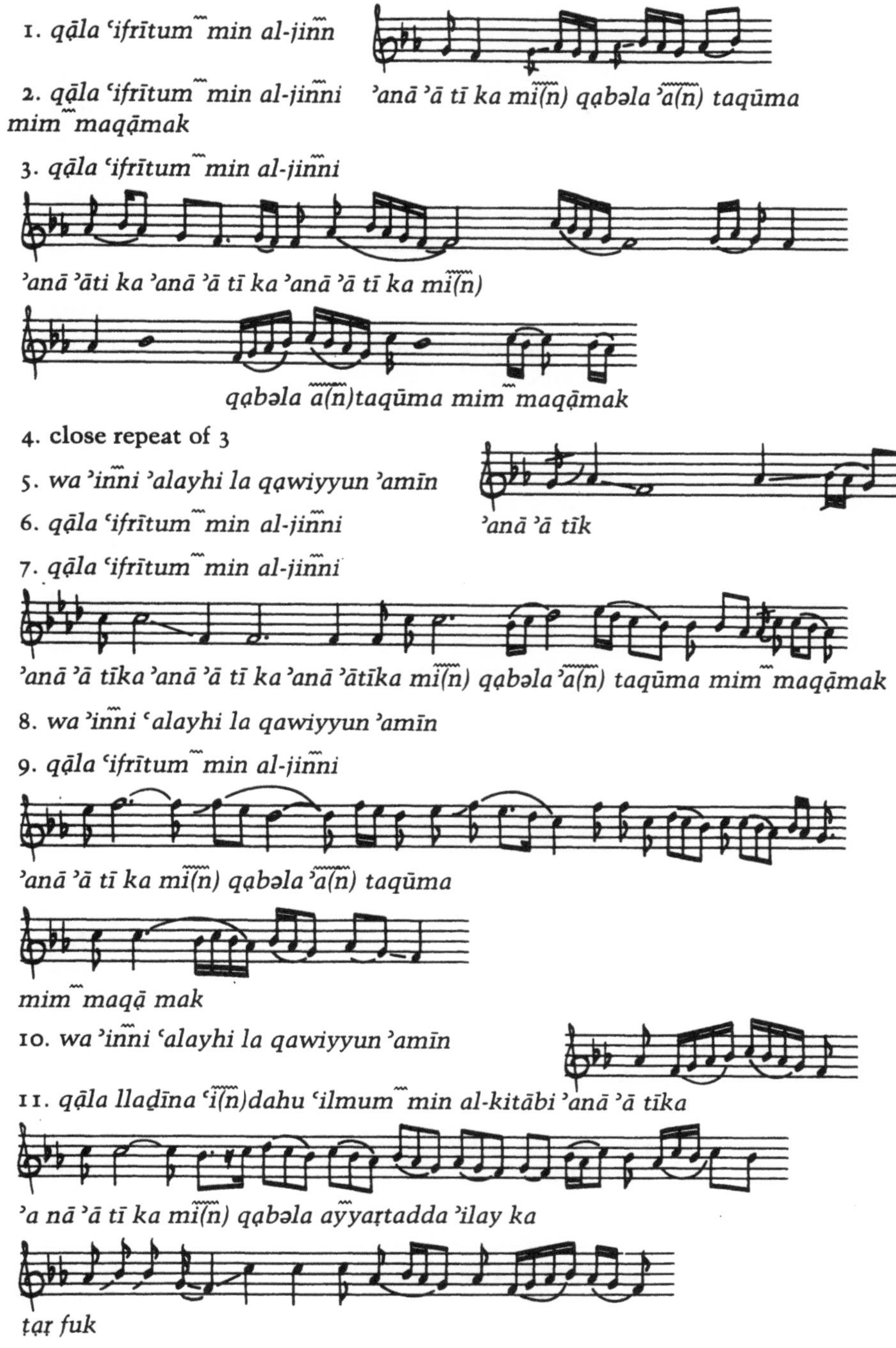
1. qạ̄la ʿifrītum͠ min al-jinn͠
2. qạ̄la ʿifrītum͠ min al-jinn͠i ʾanā ʾā tī ka mi͠(n) qạbəla ʾa͠(n) taqūma
mim͠ maqạ̄mak
3. qạ̄la ʿifrītum͠ min al-jinn͠i
ʾanā ʾāti ka ʾanā ʾā tī ka ʾanā ʾā tī ka mi͠(n)
qạbəla a͠(n)taqūma mim͠ maqạ̄mak
4. close repeat of 3
5. wa ʾinn͠i ʾalayhi la qạwiyyun ʾamīn
6. qạ̄la ʿifrītum͠ min al-jinn͠i
ʾanā ʾā tīk
7. qạ̄la ʿifrītum͠ min al-jinn͠i
ʾanā ʾā tīka ʾanā ʾā tī ka ʾanā ʾātīka mi͠(n) qạbəla ʾa͠(n) taqūma mim͠ maqạ̄mak
8. wa ʾinn͠i ʿalayhi la qawiyyun ʾamīn
9. qạ̄la ʿifrītum͠ min al-jinn͠i
ʾanā ʾā tī ka mi͠(n) qạbəla ʾa͠(n) taqūma
mim͠ maqạ̄ mak
10. wa ʾinn͠i ʿalayhi la qawiyyun ʾamīn
11. qạ̄la llaḏīna ʿi͠(n)dahu ʿilmum͠ min al-kitābi ʾanā ʾā tīka
ʾa nā ʾā tī ka mi͠(n) qạbəla ay͠yaṛtadda ʾilay ka
ṭaṛ fuk

Figure 10. Šayx Muṣṭafā Ismāʿīl, Qur. 27/39–40

The pause following each phrase and the audience's response in Qur'anic recitation are also characteristic and well-established features of the improvisatory style of Arabic music. The importance of audience response to the quality of a performance is well documented for both singing (*Kitāb al-Aġānī*, tenth century) and recitation (see chapter 7). The same dynamics of tension/release and expectation/delay/resolution operate in both music and recitation. For the reciter and singer, the pause is a time to collect energies, plan the course of the next phrase, and gauge the effect of one's performance on the listeners. The tension may or may not be relaxed during the pause, depending on whether the reciter has resolved the syntactic or melodic phrase or is carrying it over into the next phrase. For the listeners a pause following the resolution of a phrase is a tremendous relief of tension when the held breath of expectation is collectively released. At such moments the response of the listeners is particularly vocal; the pause is filled with the sound of listener response.[9] Because there is a direct correlation between the resolution of tension set up by the performer and the vocal responsiveness of listeners, the reciter must tread a fine line between stimulating an appreciative response of his success in arousing the hearts of the listeners and stirring them to the uncontrollable ecstasy which interrupts the recitation and obstructs the ultimate intent of the experience.

Voice Quality

The desirability of a beautiful voice (*ṣawt ḥasan*) in reciting the Qur'an is one of the more frequent and compelling arguments in favor of melodic recitation, and it is firmly entrenched in the definition of the ideal recitation. Voice is one of the first qualities mentioned when people talk about reciters: they are identified and characterized by their voice quality, and it figures prominently in their status as performers. Thus, Šayx ʿAbd al-Bāsiṭ is known for his light, high, "feminine" voice, Šayx al-Bahtīmī for a strong and clear voice in both registers, Šayx al-Ṭablāwī for the newness, freshness of his voice. In general, the same standards of voice quality apply to both recitation and singing: reciters are criticized for a blaring, feeble, nasal, dry, rheumy (*fī balġam*) voice, whereas a strong, clear, and flexible voice is appreciated.

Occasionally the musicality of a reciter is so effective that his reputation transcends what listeners agree is a weak or raspy voice. Šayx ʿAlī Maḥmūd was often cited to me as an example of a reciter whose voice was not compelling, but whose mastery of the *maqāmāt* made that factor negligible in establishing his reputation. Some listeners feel that the great Šayx Muḥammad Rifʿat's voice was weak and dependent on amplification, but this does not detract from the overwhelming effect of his reciting.

The low and relaxed voice of *murattal* is, in *mujawwad*, characteristic only of the low register, while a tense but full voice, one suited to maximum projection, characterizes the upper register in *mujawwad*. The use of the full voice is the clearest indication of the public nature of this style. Before the widespread use of electronic amplification, reciters were known for the carrying power of their voices, and the "strong" voice is still valued. Microphone and loudspeakers now constitute standard equipment in the performance of the *mujawwad* recitation, even in the more intimate contexts. For example, when a reciter dropped by a listening session in a home and gave a short performance, or when he recited in a suite of offices to celebrate the opening of a new business, we still listened to the voice amplified through the microphone and loudspeakers provided by the host. Similarly, reciters auditioning for radio broadcasts are judged on the quality of their "studio" or "broadcast" voice, that is, the voice as it is transmitted through microphone and loudspeaker.[10]

Register

In *mujawwad*, as in music, the use of register is unlimited except by individual voice capability. Some reciters excel in the high register (e.g., Š. ʿAbd al-Bāsit), others in the low register (e.g., Šayx al-Sindiyūnī), and some are famous for their ability to exploit both registers (e.g., Šayx Kāmil Yūsuf al-Bahtīmī, and Šayx Muḥammad Rifʿat). It is conventional in *mujawwad* recitation (and in the improvisatory style in general) to begin the performance in the lower register, gradually ascending to the upper register as the voice warms up, then, after exploring both registers, to return to the lower pitches to end the recitation. Characteristic of the *mujawwad* style, however, are the sudden shifts in register from phrase to

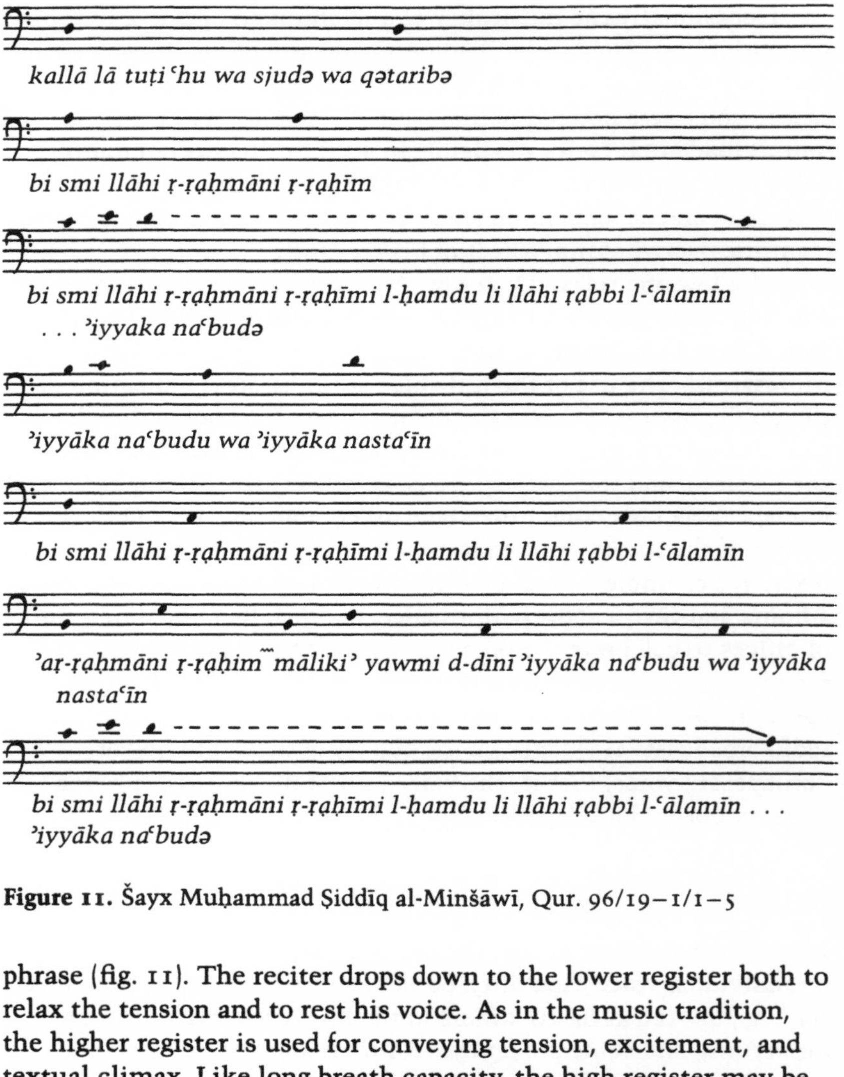

Figure 11. Šayx Muḥammad Ṣiddīq al-Minšāwī, Qur. 96/19–1/1–5

phrase (fig. 11). The reciter drops down to the lower register both to relax the tension and to rest his voice. As in the music tradition, the higher register is used for conveying tension, excitement, and textual climax. Like long breath capacity, the high register may be exploited for reasons of virtuosity and have nothing to do with proper intent or meaning. Both have the effect of heightening tension and exciting the listeners, however, and, as we have seen, this is part of the ideal if used properly. In general, the only gauge of proper intent is listener response, for which the reciter is largely responsible (see chapter 7).

Melody

With a few exceptions, melodic characteristics (e.g., melodic contour, conventions of modulation and transposition, use of melodic cadence [*qaflah*], *maqām* frame, ornamentation] are dictated in Qur'anic recitation by the aesthetics of the improvisatory style of Arabic music. Thus, in *mujawwad* the melody also proceeds generally in contiguous step-wise motion, but leaps of a fourth or more are not uncommon, and the ambitus of pitches may extend to over an octave (figs. 12 and 13). Likewise, the pitch range is extended by the technique of substituting a pitch for its octave.

The reciter's responsibility to the meaning may dictate the ac-

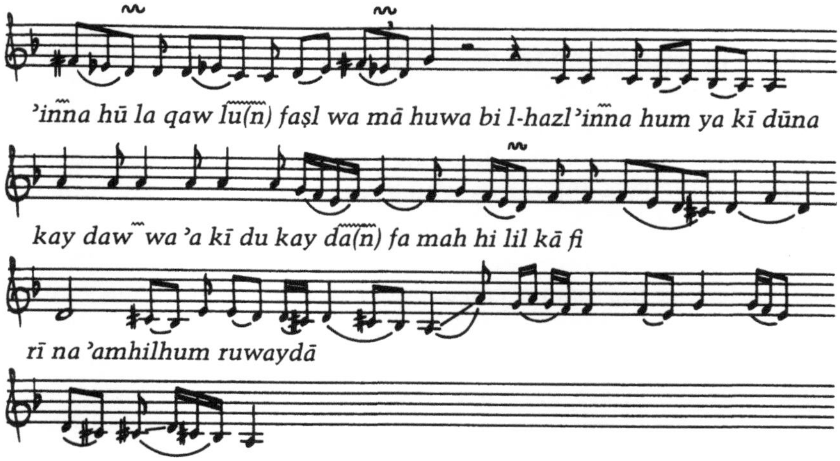

Figure 12. Šayx Muṣṭaf Ismāʿil, Qur. 86/14–17

Figure 13. Šayx ʿAlī Maḥmūd, Qur. 86/9–10

tual choice of melodic patterns of *maqāmāt*. The reciter who has mastered the *maqām* principle is more likely to be melodically responsive to the meaning: this is one justification of a reciter's musical training. His performance is also more exciting to the musically sophisticated, who expect varied and subtle use of modulation. For some listeners the number of different *maqāmāt* the reciter can present or hint at in a single phrase is a mark of his musical skill, and some reciters refer to as many as four or five in a phrase, or eighteen or nineteen during a single performance. This tends to be a virtuosic use of the skill, again, unrelated to meaning and the ideal intent, yet it seems to be considered acceptable, perhaps because only a few listeners are musically sophisticated enough to appreciate it as virtuosity.

Transposition (moving the same melodic pattern or *maqām* up or down in register), on the other hand, is considered the easy way to melodic variation. The use of transposition rather than modulation (shifting from *maqām* to *maqām*), "too much" melodic repetition, and a "blaring" voice characterize a type of recitation known as *rīfī*, *baladī*, or *šaʿbī*, terms which carry connotations of rural or lower-class urban life, that is, musical ignorance. The musically educated listener scorns this kind of reciting as boring and obvious, preferring the nuance and subtlety of a more consciously cultivated art.[11]

Absence of melodic clarity is criticized—listeners need to know where they are and where they are being led. The reciter who has not mastered the *maqām* system cannot give a clear definition of his melodic position and direction ("his voice doesn't wear the *maqām*"). Likewise, his modulations may be awkward, abrupt, and jarring; like the unpleasant voice, this interrupts or distracts from the intent of recitation. This convention may also be justified by the ideal recitation in that it involves the listeners actively in the performance.

Inventive transposition and modulation contribute to the tension and emotion of a performance, especially as it is the convention to begin and end the recitation in the same *maqām*, *bayātī*.[12] The general convention of framing a musical improvisation with a *maqām* is thus specified in the Egyptian tradition of Qur'anic recitation. A skillful reciter will spin out his melody further and further from *maqām bayātī*, leaving the audience in suspense as to how he will be able to return to base. A phrase rendered in the low register of *bayātī* is as much a signal of the end of the performance as is the closing formula (*ṣadaqah*).[13]

The real test of the reciter's (and musician's) melodic skill is the melodic cadential formula, the *qaflah* or the *waqf*. Reciters often articulate the importance of *qaflah* as an anchor point in the compositional or improvisatory process:

> Everything introduces what is next, but it is not exactly planned ahead of time. . . . [the reciter] must know ahead how he will cadence.
>
> (Šayx Muṣṭafā Ismā'īl)

> I take aim. I must know where I am going, must save back in order to end correctly. In that way you do have to know where you are going in order to prepare. Listeners wait for the *qaflah*.
>
> (Šayx Hāšim Haybah)

It is by means of the *qaflah* that the reciter demonstrates his artistic subtlety and his control of the melodic material. The *qaflah* is built on the last one or two syllables of the phrase (especially if the penultimate syllable is long) and usually involves some melismatic ornamentation. Šayx Aḥmad al-Ruzayqī distinguished two main types of *qaflah*: the "calm" one, without ornamentation or melisma (*qafla hadya*), and the "provoking" or "burning" one (*qafla ḥarrāqa, ḥarrāša*). According to Š. Aḥmad, the latter has more notes and stimulates and moves the listener (lit., shakes the listener). Šayx 'Abd al-Bāsiṭ added that this second *qaflah* has art in it.

The musical importance of the *qaflah* explains to a great extent the tendency toward long durations in the *mujawwad* style. Šayx Muḥammad al-Ṭablāwī talked about the difficulty of cadencing without a final long syllable: "some with good voice go along just fine, then the *waqf* slips from them. For example, no one can stop on [the word] *'ilm*" (not only a short syllable, but a final consonant cluster—CVCC). He then demonstrated two possible cadences on this word (fig. 14). Šayx al-Ṭablāwī judged the second cadence as more effective, "because it is artistic, it has something of art in it." Again, we see that art has the power to stir listeners (see chapter 4).

Figure 14. *Qaflah*, Šayx Muḥammad Maḥmūd al-Ṭablāwī, Qur. 7/51

It is difficult to define what comprises a "good" melodic cadence (I received ambiguous explanations—it is "what stimulates the listener's heart"). However, one can distinguish two techniques for achieving it: resolving the tension set up in the phrase melodically and/or giving an unexpected direction to the melodic line. In the first case, the cadence completes the symmetry of the melodic contour of the phrase (figs. 15 and 16). In the second case, an ambiguous pitch, one shared by two *maqāmāt*, may be introduced, or the final pitch may be secondary to the *maqām* initially defined, thus pointing the way to a new *maqām* in which it is primary (fig. 17).[14] Listeners seem to enjoy the ambiguity of a *qaflah* that lets them guess at possible melodic development. Obviously, this takes place at a musical level, and it is a further example of how, in spite of the Qurʾanic ideal, artistry for its own sake occurs in recitation.

Just as the end-rhyme pulls the listener to the end of the line by resolving the tension set up by the variation of regular rhythmic patterns, so, too, the melodic cadence is fashioned by the reciter to resolve melodic tension with a return to the starting pitch area. Furthermore, by means of melismatic ornamentation, the melodic cadence may parallel the effect of the return to the end-rhyme, in

Figure 15. Šayx Muḥammad Rifʿat, Qur. 19/7

Figure 16. Šayx Muḥammad Ṣiddīq al-Minšāwī, Qur. 1/7, 2/1

Figure 17. Šayx Muḥammad Rifʿat, Qur. 19/18

*Not part of the text here, this *hu* may be an example of careless "montage." Where there is a break in the tape, reconstructors sometimes repair it by splicing in the text from another part of the performance or from another performance altogether. Although care is taken to match pitch levels and *maqāmāt*, a syllable is treated as an independent unit and may be extracted from any word. The technique of "montage" is most often applied to a missing *basmalah* or *ṣadaqah*.

Figure 18. Šayx ʿAbd al-Bāsiṭ ʿAbd al-Ṣamad, Qur. 19/10

Figure 19. Šayx Muḥammad Ṣiddīq al-Minšāwī, Qur. 96/15–16

that attention is focused on the end of the line. These effects emphasize the final syllables of the line, a characteristic of the *mujawwad* style. The skilled professional reciter uses the *qaflah* to resolve tensions set up by his modulations, or to raise the level of tension in counterpoint to the resolving role of the end-rhyme.

Another aspect of melody is ornamentation; trills, slides, turns, and vibrato are all part of the reciter's repertoire and are derived from the singer's tradition (fig. 18). However, certain types of vocal ornamentation found in the singing style, such as exaggerated swooping or sliding to pitches, are avoided by reciters as being "too much like singing." We are again confronted with the paradox that while recitation should be musical, it must be maintained as distinct from music. Vocal ornamentation may also be criticized as being superfluous to the text. Thus Mr. Ḥusayn Rifᶜat told me his father's skill for many vocal effects often went undemonstrated because he felt it would not enhance the text, but, rather, would be an empty display of virtuosity. Some *mujawwad* reciters make effective use of ornamentation to elaborate what is basically a mono- or bi-tone melodic line (fig. 19).

The following comments demonstrate some of the various personal and aesthetic bases on which reciters make their melodic choices:

> I begin slowly and calmly, then to the middle range, then to the highest register. . . . I don't plan. If I decide on [*maqām*] *nahawand*, maybe my voice wouldn't give it. It comes according to what suits the voice. If I find myself doing well in *ṣaba* and it seems I can go on to *ḥugāz*, I do, and if it seems my voice is tired, I go back to *ṣaba* for a while and then to *sīka* or *nahawand*.
>
> (Šayx Fatḥī Qandīl)

> I make my choices on the spot, aware of what is coming in the meaning of the text, but I must return to *bayātī*.
>
> (Šayx ᶜAbd al-Bāsiṭ ᶜAbd al-Ṣamad)

> With a low beginning, little by little [the reciter] takes hold of himself. . . . I entered on *maqām ḥugāz* with *adab* [politely], not a rude awakening, but a polite knock. "Who's there?" "Muṣṭafā." "Welcome, etc." This is manners, not rushing in on an open door when madame is sleeping.
>
> (Šayx Muṣṭafā Ismāᶜīl)

> The skilled reciter holds back from the high register. The one whose voice goes high [too quickly] can't end properly . . . it's awkward.
>
> (Šayx Hāšim Haybah)

Tempo

Tempo is slowest in the *mujawwad* style, and both phrase and pause are correspondingly longer than in *murattal*. Thus, a *mujawwad* phrase may be up to forty-five seconds long, depending on the breath control of the reciter (see fig. 18), while the pause may last up to several minutes. The slow and careful articulation of the text assures its clear transmission, but it also allows for a more melismatic melody (figs. 20 and 21). Audiences enjoy the type of melody and expect it of the *mujawwad* style, but it may undermine textual clarity, and it certainly precludes any use of the *mujawwad* style as a learning model. The slower tempo also allows for the various vocal ornamentations such as slides and trills, which further complicate the sound.

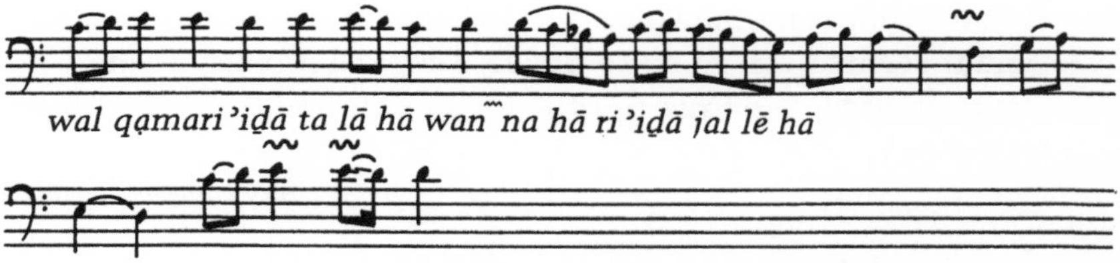

Figure 20. Šayx Muṣṭafā Ismāʿīl, Qur. 9/2–3

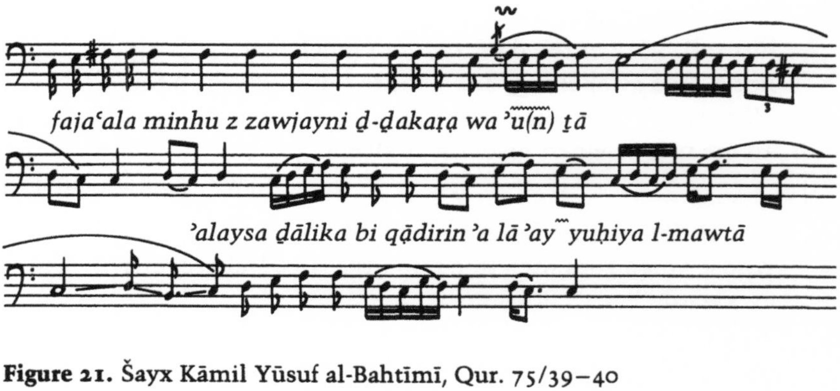

Figure 21. Šayx Kāmil Yūsuf al-Bahtīmī, Qur. 75/39–40

Qirā'āt

Within a single *mujawwad* recitation several text systems may be heard. Significantly, in Egypt, the *qirā'āt* most often heard, after the standard *Ḥafṣ ʿan ʿĀṣim*, are *Ḥamzah* and *Warš*. The characteristics of these text-systems are immediately recognizable, even to the uneducated listener. Long durations, the dropping of the glottal stop (*mūminūn* for *mu'minūn*), and *imālah* (/ā/ to /ē/)—for example, *ḍuḥēha* for *ḍuḥāha*—mark *qirā'at Warš*; *imālah* and the abrupt silence before the glottal stop—for example, *wa l*-pause-*'arḍi wa mā ṭaḥēhā* (Qur. 91/6) for *wa l-'ardi wa mā ṭaḥāhā*—are the two most obvious characteristics of *qirā'at Ḥamzah*. *Qirā'at Ḥamzah* is further marked by prefacing the phrase *'aḷḷāhu akbaṛ* to the opening formula, the *basmalah*. The particular combinations of vowels and consonants which best demonstrate the characteristics of a text-system are more concentrated in some parts of the text than in others, and listeners come to associate certain sections with various *qirā'āt*. Thus, a limited number of texts tend to be used to demonstrate the *qirā'āt* in performance.

Audience recognition is important, because when listeners hear something which differs from the standard sound, they may doubt the correctness of the reciter's delivery. Most reciters, in fact, acknowledge that their varied use of the *qirā'āt* depends on the knowledge of their listeners. The following is an edited transcription of Šayx Hāšim Haybah's statement regarding the use of *qirā'āt* in performance, and it is representative of the general policy:

> Praise to God, I have studied the seven *qirā'āt*, not ten. However, one should not recite the *qirā'āt* before people who have not studied them, because there are differences in the *qirā'āt*. For example, I come to recite before people and they are accustomed to the *qirā'ah* of the *muṣḥaf*,[15] that is, there is no one present who knows the *qirā'āt* well. But they say to us, "this verse again, *ʿammi š-Šayx*," for me to repeat it in *Ḥafṣ*—no, I couldn't. I should repeat with the *qirā'āt*. But with the condition that the [particular] *qirā'āt* not have [major] differences. For example, if I say "*yā 'ayyuhā lladīna 'āmanū 'i(n) jā'akum fāsiqu(m) bi naba'i(n) fa tabayyanū*" [Qur. 49/6]. They say, "Again, oh *šayx*." I prefer to say *fa tabayyanū*. There

> is another *qirā'ah* which says *fa-taṯabbatū*. And when I say *fa taṯabbatu* the people say, "'*Aḷḷāh*! But the *qirā'ah* is *fa tabayyanu*. The *šayx* makes a mistake." Because of this it is not right to recite the *qirā'āt* before people who don't know them . . . for example, from *surat* al-Nur [Qur. 24/34], one *qirā'ah* says, *durriyyuỹ yūqadu*, another, *durriyy'u͡(n) tūqadu*, and a third, *diriyy'u͡(n) tawāqadu*, and if I do that before some people, they say "That *šayx* is babbling nonsense," but the *šayx* is reciting correctly, they just don't understand. So you should do the *qirā'āt* before people who know the *qirā'āt*, at the very least . . . where there are differences in the *qirā'āt* it is not right to say them before people *when it makes them doubt the Qur'an*. (Emphasis mine)

The repetition of a section of text in different *qirā'āt* may be done for commentary, especially in those cases where there is a difference in vocabulary. But convention, as dictated by religious scholarship, generally, if unsuccessfully, rules against this practice. Not only does mixing the *qirā'āt* confuse the listeners and undermine the reciter's authority, it is also objectionable in that it is too easily misused by reciters who wrongly want to impress their listeners. Thus, in using different *qirā'āt* the reciter also signals mastery of a subject reserved for higher levels of education and gains added respect for his knowledge and religious authority. More often the effect is not so much instructional as aesthetic, for what is most noticeable is the change in sound. It is possible that some reciters learn specific passages according to different *qirā'āt* without having mastered the text-system as a whole in order to catch the interest and admiration of their listeners.[16]

The use of the *qirā'āt* in recitation is, therefore, a good illustration of the way in which the different regulative factors may interact. For the *qirā'āt* comprise one of the Qur'anic disciplines bearing on recitation, and their proper use is regulated by the ideal recitation and oral convention. Their inclusion in a performance, however, may be due to the more mundane considerations of professional status, economics, or the artistic demands of sound itself.

Although the ideal recitation incorporates both the religious and aesthetic principles, listeners tend to separate the organizational systems in evaluating the reciter. Thus, a reciter may be judged correct, but neither effective nor beautiful; or beautiful, but not effective or correct. In all aspects the reciter must seek to balance what are sometimes contradictory or mutually exclusive elements. The skill and tension involved in the reciter's maintaining the right balance between the correct and the beautiful contributes to the excitement and immediacy of the effect of recitation in Egypt today.

6. Maintaining the Ideal Recitation of the Qurʾan

Maintaining the separation of recitation from song performance is not solely the responsibility of the reciter. Listeners should approach Qurʾanic recitation with the proper intent and expectations, for the nature of the listeners' response depends a great deal on their perception of the experience. The perception of the art of Qurʾanic recitation as unique and distinct from musical art depends on an appreciation of the nature of the text. However, even within the Muslim sector of Egyptian society we find that this perception is not instinctively acquired—it must be learned. People who for the most part share cultural values differ as to how they approach recitation: some respond to it primarily as musical sound while others respond only to the significance of the message.

It is difficult to lead listeners away from perceiving recitation as if it were music. In Egypt today a number of institutions—in government, education, and the media—play important roles in guiding reciters and listeners toward an ideal perception and response, as well as maintaining standards separating recitation from musical entertainment. This chapter focuses on these institutions and their interplay in shaping and reproducing the sound as actually heard and experienced.

The first stage of Qurʾanic education is memorization of part or all of the text. Learning to recite according to the rules of *tajwīd* may be a second stage of learning with children; among adults, it is concomitant with memorization of the full text. Only after *tajwīd* is mastered practically are its rules learned formulaically.

Traditionally, *all* children began their education with memorization of the Qurʾan. The teaching of reading and writing followed. With the introduction of educational models from the West, the number of such traditional schools (*kuttāb*) has declined, though they continue to play a supplementary role, particularly in lower-class communities.[1] Early learning of the Qur'an is otherwise encouraged through media coverage of both the *katātīb* and national and international competitions.[2] Although the majority of participants in such activities are of lower-class origins, increasing numbers of Egyptians at all class levels are taking up Qur'anic study. For example, the move among many middle- and upper-class women toward traditional dress is accompanied by increased participation in Qur'anic study sessions.

The Ministry of Religious Endowments (Wazīrat al-Awqāf), specifically, its Office of Administration of Qur'anic Affairs (Mudīriyyat al-Awqāf, Maktab Idārat al-Šu'ūn al-Qur'āniyyah), encourages children's memorization of the Qur'an by means of an annual competition held in Cairo. Children pass an initial examination in their home provinces, and if they achieve sixty out of eighty points in memorization, and fifteen out of twenty points in execution or *adā'*,[3] they are eligible to come to Cairo to compete. The same marking system is used in Cairo as in the provinces, but the judges tend to be stricter.[4] Prizes are given according to the length of passage memorized and the quality of memorization: LE 60 (about $100 in 1978) for the whole of the Qur'an, LE 30 for half, LE 15 for a quarter with optimum scores. In fact, not much is expected at this level as regards *tajwīd*: children are not rigorously corrected on pronunciation, but many of the children do know the correct durations and nasalization. The children are examined over a period of several months, at the Mudīriyyah offices, by panels of judges composed of expert religious scholars. In 1976, 21,151 children were examined; 17,791 passed, 1,022 failed, and the sum of LE 11,758 was distributed as prize money.

Many Egyptian Muslims, as children, learn only enough of the Qur'an to use it in the obligatory prayer rituals. Children and adults who wish to increase their knowledge and learn the correct recitation have several opportunities to do so. The Sessions for Memorizing the Qur'an in the mosques (Ḥalaqāt Taḥfīḍ al-Qur'ān fi l-Masājid) and the classes in correct recitation (*maqra'ah*, plural *maqāri'*, lit., places for reciting) are public sessions sponsored by the Ministry of Religious Endowments.

In the *ḥalaqāt* the students are mostly young boys, but the class is open to all. The teachers are themselves reciters and are assigned to teach six days a week in a specific mosque. The sessions last from after the *ʿaṣr* (mid-afternoon prayer) until the *maġrib* (sunset prayer), that is, about three hours. The teachers themselves are examined for their mastery of memorization. Those already employed in the mosque as reciters for the Friday prayer session receive a salary increase of LE 5 per month. The others receive LE 3.75, and LE 1.75 is deposited in their name at the Ministry of Religious Endowments. If four or more of a teacher's students succeed in the yearly examination, the teacher receives the sum deposited in the Ministry in his name. The student is rewarded with LE .50–LE 1 per thirtieth part of the Qur'an (*juzʾ*) memorized. Thus both student and teacher are given incentive for good work. In 1976 the 210 teachers in the program received LE 2,429.

As regards the *maqraʾah*, a total of 200 reciters are appointed in Egypt (10–15 in Cairo) to hold classes in correct recitation. The teachers are acknowledged experts in reciting. They are paid weekly and according to their rank, which is determined by their expertise: for example, LE 1 for mastery of *qirāʾat Ḥafṣ* (*ʿan ʿĀṣim*), LE 1.50 for mastery of *Ḥafṣ* and any other *qirāʾah*, LE 2 for mastery of all seven of the *qirāʾāt*. The latter fee is paid to only one person, who also holds the title *šayx al-maqraʾah* and is personally appointed by the minister of religious endowments.[5] The class also begins after the *ʿaṣr* and lasts until the *maġrib* or longer. Students are of all ages and classes, from children just beginning their Qurʾanic learning to businessmen, workers, housewives, young students (both male and female), and so forth. The class procedure is flexible, but the teacher may recite for ten minutes in the *mujawwad* style, then in the *murattal* style. Each student then recites in the *murattal* style a passage he or she has prepared, either from memory or from the text. The teacher corrects the student in *tajwīd* and *qirāʾah*, and the student may be called upon to explain the meaning of the text. When a student has completed the whole Qurʾanic text according to a particular *qirāʾah*, he or she may receive a certificate of achievement from the teacher. Inspectors regularly make the rounds of the sessions to check on attendance and to provide assistance if needed.

Al-Azhar maintains institutes through the university level where a student can follow a course of increasingly advanced religious study. A number of professional reciters are graduates of some of these (see Appendix A). The institutes graduate many of Egypt's religious teachers and administrators, and the number of foreign students in the programs testifies to the prestige of the Azhari education in the Islamic world. The curriculum is determined by al-Azhar. At the Institute in Šubrā, for example, the course in *tajwīd*, theoretical (*aḥkāman*, lit., in rules) and practical (*tilāwatan*, lit., in reciting), is two years. The course in *qirāʾāt* lasts eight years.

Unless one reads specific texts in the course of religious study, most people learn the proper attitudes for recitation only indirectly, picking them up by example. It is primarily through gaining an understanding of the nature of the text itself that one learns the proper perception of recitation. Thus one is taught that the Qurʾan is to be respected as a unique and divine phenomenon. One learns to respect the material text itself by keeping it off the floor or low places and away from shoes and feet, by touching it only with clean hands, and so forth. By extension, this special understanding and treatment of the Qurʾan should carry over into the recitation context, so that it is perceived as separate from musical entertainment. One learns by observation or admonition the proper response to recitation: listeners or officials may take it upon themselves to calm the more enthusiastically vocal listener.

The professional reciter, on the other hand, is fully aware of his distinct status as a Qurʾan reciter. He has learned the Qurʾanic disciplines necessary to his art, and he may have learned some musical principles. But no one taught him to recite with melodies; it is up to him to learn to apply one to the other, calling on his skills in improvisation. Moreover, whenever he falls under the jursidiction of any official body, such as when auditioning for employment, or being officially employed, he is subject to the standards by which these bodies regulate recitation and must use his skills accordingly. He knows that what is expected of him is mastery of *tajwīd*, improvisation, and personal style. Reciters independent of any official ties are regulated in their art by economic controls, that is, the demands of listeners and patrons, which often (but not always) reflect the standards of the more prestigious and widely broadcast official reciters.

The two main official bodies which employ professional melodic reciters, exerting an important supervisory role, are the Ministry of Religious Endowments and the National Radio. The Ministry is responsible for appointing reciters to recite before the Friday prayer in mosques under its jurisdiction (approximately five hundred in Cairo). Although the reciter can choose his own text, the Friday recitation is referred to as *sūrat al-Kahf* "because it [*sūrat al-Kahf*] is well-liked and traditional."[6]

I attended an audition for such appointments at the Mudīriyyah (April 19, 1978). The candidates were not examined in *ḥifḍ* and *tajwīd*: they recited a passage of their own choosing and were judged only on their voice quality and musicality.

Friday prayers are attended by the largest crowds, so it is an important position for the reciter. In these recitations the reciter begins to build his reputation, so that his services are requested for private occasions. Some mosques are considered more important than others in that they attract larger crowds, and competition for a position in one of these mosques is great. Presently only reciters with established reputations hold positions in these mosques.[7] A reciter usually holds the position until he decides to apply for another position or until his death.

Whatever his rank, the *qāriʾ al-sūrah fil-masājid* (reciter of the *sūrah* in the mosques) receives LE 1 per recitation. He must recite in the *mujawwad* style for approximately thirty minutes before the prayer. This position is usually a reciter's only tie with a particular mosque. Occasionally a reciter may be given another mosque assignment for one Friday (e.g., if the Radio wants to broadcast a particular reciter from a particular mosque), but this is avoided as much as possible, because it necessarily involves a lot of reshuffling to ensure that every mosque has its reciter.

The Ministry is also responsible for appointing reciters to employment during the month of Ramadan. Qur'anic recitation is especially popular in Ramadan. In the old days, in the countryside, each family would hire two or three reciters to recite every night for the whole month. The reciters were paid by the month. The practice has lost its generous dimensions, and it is no longer possible for reciters to earn the bulk of their yearly income during this month. The Ministry subsidizes recitations during Ramadan in order to make up for this change.

One measure of the centrality of the Egyptian tradition is the fact that other countries send requests to the Ministry of Religious

Endowments to provide them with reciters. If a specific reciter is requested, every effort is made to comply; otherwise reciters are assigned starting with the highest ranking. If there is more than one request for the same reciter, he is given his choice, or the first request is given priority. Egyptian reciters travel to all countries of the Islamic world, and to Muslim communities as far away as England and Brazil. Usually about 100 are sent abroad, and the rest are distributed around Egypt, to the army, provincial capitals, and so forth. In Cairo, the nightly program of recitation, which is traditionally held in a large tent set up in front of Abdeen palace and sponsored by the government, is broadcast live, with the cooperation of the National Broadcasting and Television Corporation.

Every year a competition is held for Ramadan reciters seeking official sponsorship. In 1977 there were 460 competitors; well-established reciters do not, as a rule, take part, since they are in great demand abroad. The examination is held at the offices of the Mudīriyyah, and reciters are given a ranking on the basis of their performance in *hifḍ*, *tajwīd*, voice, and musicality. The Ministry pays for travel, a per diem, and a fee. The lowest fee for a reciter in Egypt is LE 75 (about $50 in 1978), and the highest fee for a reciter abroad is LE 200. Those who travel abroad receive half of the fee before leaving. The fees are further graded according to ranking. The reciter may choose his own length of performance according to his capabilities. However, he is assigned a specific program of recitations. The Embassy takes care of him, and reports to the Ministry any problems of behavior which would preclude his being sent abroad again. One problem the director mentioned was the acceptance of money over and above the given fee. This is strictly forbidden.

The role of the National Broadcasting and Television Corporation (popularly known as *il-izāʿa wa t-tilifizyūn* or just *il-izāʿa*, which I translate as "the Radio") is extremely important in setting and maintaining region-wide standards of reciting, for it is responsible for the quality of all recitations broadcast from Egypt. There are ten or so stations broadcasting from Egypt, throughout the Middle East,[8] and, except for the Western Music station (*al-Mūsīqā*), they all program recitation to a greater or lesser degree. The minimum programming is five minutes of recitation at the opening and closing of the broadcasting period.

Recitation was first broadcast in 1934, and the *mujawwad* style of reciting quickly became a regular feature of Radio programming. At first, prominent reciters, such as Šayx Muḥammad Rifʿat, were asked to recite; later, a committee was formed to screen less well known reciters for broadcasting. The effect of this broadcasting was so great that for Muslims and Christians alike the recitation of Šayx Rifʿat remains the model of the best recitation. Many Egyptians still talk about his recitations: there are many stories of how daily life came to a halt in cafes "and even in the foreign restaurants" throughout the country as everyone stopped to tune in to them. Today, the reciting of Šayx Rifʿat is still a regular feature of programming on Iḏāʿat al-Qurʾān al-Karīm and al-Šarq al-Awsaṭ.

It was not until 1964 that a station strictly devoted to the recitation of the Qurʾan was founded. The Ministry of Religious Endowments and Dr. Labīb al-Saʿīd commissioned the recording of the Qurʾan in the *murattal* style, and the station Iḏāʿat al-Qurʾān al-Karīm was set up to broadcast this in order to "counteract the attempts of the enemies of Islam to do damage to the Holy Qurʾan, and [their] efforts . . . to distort some of the text and distribute it in the African countries."[9] Programming was expanded several years later to include religious news, scriptural commentary, topical discussion, religious drama, lessons in *tajwīd*, sermons, and so forth, but it was not until 1973, at the end of Ramadan, that the first recitation in the *mujawwad* style was broadcast from this station. This was in the context of the dawn prayer (*fajr*) and was also the station's first live broadcast (Dr. Kāmil al-Buhī). Programming has expanded to twenty hours, and sixty-five percent of that is recitation. As Dr. Kāmil pointed out, much of the other programming that makes up the remaining thirty-five percent incorporates recitation, so the proportion of reciting is actually higher than sixty-five percent.

The station's programming is a mixture of studio and live recording. Live broadcasts are connected to a specific occasion, such as the memorial services mentioned above, the Friday prayers, or various religious or governmental celebrations, commemorations, and inaugurations. All acceptable recordings, whether studio or live, become part of the archives, a major source of programming.

Each week the station broadcasts the Friday prayer ritual and the recitation that precedes it (*šaʿāʾir ṣalāt al-jumʿah*) from a different mosque. This broadcast is shared by the stations al-Barnāmaj al-ʿĀmm and al-Šarq al-Awsaṭ (the latter broadcasts throughout the Middle East). It is the responsibility of the program planners to make the arrangements with the reciters and mosque personnel.[10] The usual policy is to assign these broadcasts to reciters and mosques on a rotating basis, depending on the technical feasibility for broadcast. However, a prominent reciter may be brought in for a special occasion, such as an official government visit or a celebration.

The station also sponsors *saharāt dīniyyah* (evenings of prayer and recitation and religious singing) to commemorate its greatest reciters on the anniversaries of their deaths. These are presented in a well-known mosque, are open to the public, and are broadcast live. Usually only the higher-ranking of the Radio reciters are invited to recite, and there may be as many as three top reciters in a single program.

The Radio also plays a unique role in fostering an appreciation of recitation as a unique art, not necessarily tied to a particular context. The program *Qur'ān al-Ṣahrah* (The Evening Qur'an, on Iḏaʿat al-Qur'an al-Karīm, daily, ca. 8:40–9:25 P.M.) features studio recordings from over a forty-year period. *Min Tasjīlātina*" (From among Our Recordings, on the same station, 10–11 P.M. daily) features live recordings from the same period. The early morning program *Al-Qur'ān al-Karīm* (The Holy Qur'an, on Barnāmaj al-ʿĀmm, 6–6:30 daily) also makes available to the public the best reciting of the past forty years. The Radio also cooperates with the descendants of prominent reciters by opening their archives to their collecting efforts. At present the Radio, in cooperation with the recording company Sono Cairo (Ṣawt al-Qāhirah) and Mr. Ḥusayn Rifʿat, son of Šayx Muḥammad Rifʿat, is working to make this reciter's work available to the general public. Over fifty hours of recitation have been released commercially to date.

Although it does happen that a reciter is programmed on the basis of his popularity among listeners, in general, the station personnel programs its employees according to its own ranking system and programming policy, and these reflect the standards of the ideal recitation. This is not to say that the station is unresponsive to audience demand, however, for the role the Radio plays in shaping audience expectations and popularizing reciters largely mitigates any gap there might be between official standards and public expectations. Moreover, the audience has other opportunities to hear favorite reciters, either in the context of private commissions or, for some, on commercial recordings. However, in the case of reciters no longer living, the Radio is a main source for hearing their reciting and thus is more vulnerable to public demand. In a letter to the editor of *al-Ahrām* entitled "Where is the one with the voice of angels?" the writer claims cruelty on the part of the station for withholding the recordings of Šayx Rifʿat, Šayx ʿAbd al-ʿAḏīm Zāhir, and Šayx ʿAlī Ḥuzayyin (*al-Ahrām*, July 13, 1978: 11).

One of the more significant aspects of the media, in terms of our discussion, is the role they play in imposing the standards of the ideal recitation (their role as popularizer is discussed in chapter 7).[11] Since all stations are government-supported, they are subject to the same general policy and standards. Thus, the personnel of one station, Iḏāʿat al-Qurʾān al-Karīm, are responsible for all recitations broadcast over radio and television. Technicians and staff members are occupied with such aspects as auditioning and hiring reciters, reviewing their performances, programming, training reciters (see below), and, in the context of live broadcasts, controlling the audience. It is possible to observe the efforts of the Radio personnel to bring the recitation into line with ideals in such a context: not only does the recording technician block out excessive audience noise, but it is common for officials to signal with their arms, trying to calm down overenthusiastic listeners.

The committee responsible for all recitation that is broadcast is the Lajnat al-Qurrāʾ (Reciters' Committee; for names of members see Acknowledgments). As an institution it predates the founding of the station Iḏāʿat al-Qurʾān al-Karīm. The present committee is composed of four religious scholars and administrators and two musicians, an official acknowledgment of the melodic requirement of the ideal Qurʾanic recitation.[12]

The committee meets once a week throughout the year (except during Ramadan) for a three-hour session during which it auditions reciters seeking employment with the Radio, evaluates studio and live recordings of Radio reciters, and discusses general policy.

The Radio's dictatorship of standards of Qurʾanic recitation is strengthened in that members of the committee also play a role in training reciters to their standards by coaching them in recording sessions, critically reviewing tapes with the reciter. I have heard them point out errors such as erroneous pronunciation, unsteady pitch, or weak modulation, as well as suggest specific modulation schemes: "Start with [*maqām*] *sīka*, then *rast*, and we'll tell you where to go next."

The committee conducts a biennial review for the purpose of ranking the Radio reciter. This is important, as a reciter's ranking and seniority determine his fees and the amount of exposure he receives on the Radio. For example, reciters with a score of ninety-one percent or more receive prime-time exposure once a week. This is the highest rank, the *ṭabaqah mumtāz*; in 1978 this was held by only four reciters out of the several hundred employed by the Radio. A reciter in the top rank receives a maximum of LE 45 per half hour of recording. Within each rank, however, fees may differ according to seniority.[13]

The committee's audition and evaluation sessions are also attended by the general secretary of Iḏā'at al-Qur'ān al-Karīm, Šayx 'Abd al-Ḥāfiḏ. Among his duties are the preparation of the written agenda and the writing of the evaluation in its final form. The agenda for each session lists the names of the reciters who will audition, date of previous audition, if any, and comments from previous evaluation, if any. There is also a list of tapes to be evaluated, identified on the agenda by reciter, section of text recited, and date of recording.

The audition follows a set procedure: the candidate is led into the recording booth, where he recites a section of text of his own choosing in the *mujawwad* style. This is amplified so that the committee can evaluate his recorded voice quality as well as his general musicality. The candidate is then seated before the committee, which proceeds to examine him in *ḥifḏ*, and *tajwīd*. Testing for *ḥifḏ*, Šayx Muḥammad Mursī 'Āmir or Šayx Rizq Ḥabbah will begin a phrase of the text and ask the reciter to complete it. Or they may ask him to locate a particular phrase in the text and complete it. The reciting in this context is in the *murattal* style. To test for *tajwīd*, they may ask the candidate to abstract the rules from the passage he has just recited, for example, "in [the word] '*samā'*,' what *madd* is this? How many beats does it get?" Or he may be asked, "What governs the conjunction of consonants in *jaʿala lakum*' [answer: *iḍhār mitlān kabīr*] or *qālat ṭā'if* [answer: *idġām mutajānisān*]." The candidate must achieve a total of sixty percent to pass. The breakdown of scores is as follows: *ḥifḍ*—twenty percent, knowledge of rules of *tajwīd*—twenty percent, application of rules of *tajwīd*—twenty percent, voice—twenty percent (must receive a minimum of fifteen percent), and modulation of *maqāmāt*—twenty percent. If the candidate fails only in *ḥifḍ* and *tajwīd* he is usually given a chance to repeat the audition at a later date. Whether a reciter could improve his voice and musicality was a subject of constant discussion among the members of the committee, although most of the members felt that, whereas one could improve one's knowledge of *ḥifḍ* and *tajwīd* with study and practice, no amount of practice could make an unpleasant voice pleasant or increase a reciter's basic artistic sensibility and taste, for the latter are "a gift from God." The importance of all these parameters for the effectiveness of a recitation is a basic premise of the committee's evaluations, and rarely did a committee decision split along the lines of musician/religious scholar.

The evaluations are filed, and a copy is sent to the reciter. If a reciter employed by the Radio questions the evaluation, he may be invited to go over it and the tape in question with the members of the committee.

To convey something of the atmosphere of an evaluating session, the kinds of issues considered, the vocabulary employed, the attitudes toward various aspects of recitation which are demonstrated, and the care given to the smallest detail, I include a composite report of such a session based on my notes of a number of them.

Candidate #1

[Comments on his voice as rough, dry and unsteady. However, as he warmed up his voice cleared, and the committee members became more enthusiastic.]

—He has to warm up like Šayx Muṣṭafā [Muṣṭafā Ismāʿīl].

—He should have chosen another text: he is obviously influenced by what other reciters have done with it.

—Let him record half an hour to let his personality and his independence as a reciter appear.

—We don't know what *nagama* he's doing [no clarity of the *maqāmāt*].
—He doesn't have a good sense of melody. This is halfway between *rast* and *ḥugāz.*
—Let's give him a chance to learn the *qafalāt* and *maqāmāt*. He's still young and has a future.
—But where is he going to get expertise in *maqāmāt*? He wants to play with them, but doesn't know how. "Wearing the *maqāmāt*" is a talent which can't be improved by practice.
[The evaluation, which contained a recommendation that he be given six months to free himself of imitation and to work on his melodic modulation and "musical cadences" before returning to a second audition, prompted the following exchange:]
—No, don't use the word "musical" [*musīqiyyah*]. Say "artistic," or . . . "vocal"? But he won't understand what is meant!
—Let him ask!
—We just can't have the word *mūsīqiyyah* here. Use any of the others to avoid the problem, so that this word isn't applied to the Qur'an.
[Dr. Ḥasan al-Šāfiʿī, responding to my report of the above, said that musical aspects of recitation are officially recognized, but that the terminology is avoided because it might be misunderstood. It seems to be a difference between official and unofficial contexts.]

Candidate #2
—Wrong use of *tafxīm* [pharyngealization].
—His *ʿayn* and *ḥāʾ* are too much [overpronounced so that the *ʿayn* came out with a growl].
—There's an old-style melodic pattern [*ḥaraka ʾadīma*]!
—His *dāl* after *ṣād* and *ḍād* sound like *ḍād.*
—*Ḥaraka baladī*! [Speaking the end of an *qaflah*, letting the voice slide down in pitch.]
—How shall we express this heaviness in the report? [I heard a lot of slides, and I think that this and the slow tempo account for the "heaviness," as his voice could barely carry him from note to note.]
—There is mucous in his throat [lit., in his voice].
—Yes, he needs a plumber's wire! [Laughter—in the evaluation they mentioned this quality, but substituted the word "fatigue" (*taʿb*) for mucous (*balgam*).]

[The evaluation also recommended that he "free himself from the heaviness and slowness and the lack of stability in the melodic execution, as well as from straining in the execution of some verses.]

Candidate #3

—He blares like a calf!
—Like a street vendor selling tomatoes!
—This cannot be called Qur'an! [Almost wailing, extremes of voice, abrupt change of *maqāmāt*—still, the musicians are enthusiastic, calling out the *maqāmāt* and identifying the source of the *qafalāt*: "There is Šaʿšāʿī, there is something of Rifʿat."]
—He must play the *ʿūd* [lute].
—He's correct, but I don't really like it in general. I find it tiring.
—What's this, *ibtihālāt*? [I.e., using lots of melisma.]
[Evaluation was, in fact, not difficult. For all their enthusiasm, those who enjoyed the music agreed it was not quite appropriate, would have to be toned down, and so forth.]
[Waiting for the next reciter to enter.]
—By the way, the tape we rejected last week because of the reciter's pronouncing *ʾiḏā* for *ʾilā* [this is a mistake in the essentials, the *jawhar*, of the text] . . . well, apparently it is possible to fix that up technically, so we needn't reject the whole tape, after all (tears up written evaluation].
—We'll have to hear the revised tape, of course.

Candidate #4

[Didn't show up. This was rare, as reciters wait for months, even years, for an audition that brings them the chance of recognition, regular employment, and increased fees.]

Tape #1

—Not consistent in durations.
—How many times have I told him, "Open your mouth!" [Reciter swallows or mumbles some syllables.]
[Lots of echo, which they seem to like as an effect.]
[They spent ten minutes listening over and over again to a short passage, trying to determine if the glottal stop in *wa ʾan* . . . had been dropped. It was difficult to tell. In the end, they agreed to accept it.]
[The same verse was recited three times. The first and second time

had the wrong duration—*ʾay . . . dīkum, ʾaydī . . . kum*. One of the musicians held the ending pitch of the previous verse and had the engineer skip to the third version of the verse in question to see if the pitches were compatible. The *maqām* of the two verses was the same, only an octave higher the second time, so the engineer was instructed to splice out the wrong durations and make a direct transition to the correct version (*aydīkum*, the three syllables should all be of equal length).]
[Audience noise too loud. Engineer instructed to tone it down.]
[Tape accepted.]

Tape #2
—"*Šaytānu ṛ-ṛạjīm*" [should be *Šayṭāni ṛ-ṛạjīm*].
—*Munfaṣil* too long.
—*Muttaṣil* too short.
—Mixes his *qirāʾāt*. [From *Ḥafṣ* to *Warš* and back to *Ḥafṣ* again in just a few lines. Some discussion on the acceptability of such mixing; finally, agreement that consensus is against it.]
—Wrong *waqf*. [Elaborate explanation, the essence of which was that the reciter stopped after the first half of a conditional sentence; explanation for musicians' benefit—whereas some of the religious scholars know music, neither of the musicians knows *tajwīd*.]
—The *zā* of Zakariyyāʾ pronounced *ḍā*.
[Tape rejected. Evaluation worded: "In spite of vocal excellence . . ."—i.e., too many unrepairable mistakes in *tajwīd*.]

Tape #3
—Lacks the *istiʿāḏah*.
—Could be added on by means of montage.
[Overall reaction was extremely enthusiastic. They all really enjoyed the tape, settling back with smiles, admiring comments. The musicians predicted the next *maqām* with great satisfaction—seems to reflect skill in use of *maqāmāt*, i.e., understanding of how they work together. However, they had to reject the tape, because the recording quality was bad: the recording engineer, in an effort to cut down audience response, had turned the volume down in the pauses between phrases and didn't always turn it up in time to catch the vocal line, so volume was erratic.]

There is also supervision of reciters who contract with commercial recording companies in that the recordings are made in the presence of an expert in *tajwīd* and *qirā'āt*. This not only guarantees the basic requirements of recitation, but also protects the reciter's (and the company's) reputation. In the case of officially sponsored recordings such supervision is to be expected.[14] However, even reciters who record for private companies in Egypt and abroad seek the supervision of a qualified scholar, although they are under no obligation to do so.

Not all reciters are under the jurisdiction of a supervisory body, of course. There are numerous mosques built by private persons or companies, which are administered independently of the Ministry of Religious Endowments, whose policies and reciters are in no way accountable to the religious authorities. These constitute half of the mosques of Cairo. Even reciters who are accountable to the authorities by reason of official employment are held to the official standards only in the official contexts. For example, a Radio reciter performing in the context of a private commission is free of official supervision and not subject to regulation other than that of the demands of patrons and listeners. Perhaps this explains why the gap between the ideals of recitation, according to official standards, and its practice is largest in the context of the private commission.

It is in this context that the proper attitude of the listener becomes crucial, since listener response can guide the reciter in his reciting. Although the listeners, in general, may know the text, their knowledge of *tajwīd*, and especially of the *qirā'āt*, may be faulty. Good enunciation may mask a reciter's ignorance of the rules of *tajwīd*, so that many listeners do not notice any lack. People complain that listening skills have greatly declined, so that reciters not only are not kept up to standard, but are deprived of subtle interaction and communication with their listeners, and the finer points of recitation are unappreciated. It is certainly true that a reciter's reputation is built first on the quality of his voice, second on his ability to stir the listener, and not on his mastery of *tajwīd*, or even the finer points of melody. Finally, the reciter's authority is such that the bulk of listeners grant him an automatic mastery of the basic skills without questioning their actual execution.

That the listeners are more lenient, or that they judge according to different standards, is demonstrated by the fact that qualified scholars among the authorities do criticize reciters for such practices as incorrect durations and pharyngealization, skipping around in the text, sectioning to show off breath control with no regard for meaning, playing with single words, regardless of meaning, mixing *qirā'āt* in a single recitation, and so forth, and that these reciters are among the most popular! Al-Ḥuṣarī writes:

> I have observed that some of the reciters of this century deviate from what is intended and turn away from the main path, and digress from what is right in *tilāwah* of the Qur'an when they recite from the verses whatever suits them without regard for sequence . . . and depend on the repetition of verses with different *riwāyāt* [of the *qirā'āt*], and various *qirā'āt* in a single recitation.
>
> (al-Ḥuṣarī 1967: 14–15)

The following example clearly demonstrates the impotence of the authorities to enforce their standards on anyone not under their immediate supervision: while I was in Cairo (1977–78) I heard of a man known as Šayx ʿAnṭar who began to gain widespread popularity for his reciting among people in the region near Ṭanṭa (1½ hours north of Cairo). He was, however, blatantly indifferent to the rules of *tajwīd*, to the point that some conscientious listeners made a tape of his reciting and conveyed it to the Lajnat al-Qurrā' at the Radio, asking them if something couldn't be done to stop him. Unfortunately, even in such an extreme case there was nothing the authorities could do: his continuing career was dependent only on his popular support.

The establishing of a Reciters' Union (Niqābah l il-Qurrā') represents an attempt to exert more widespread control over reciters' performances. The Union was in the planning stage while I was in Cairo, and notice of its proposed aims was published in the newspaper *al-Ahrām*:

> The Committee of Correction and Supervision of Qur'anic texts of the Union of Islamic Research [Majmaʿ al-Buḥūṯ al-Islamiyyah] of al-Azhar submitted a report to the Šayx of al-Azhar, warning of the danger of distortion as regards the Holy Qur'an recorded on tapes now displayed in the market which comprise many errors in the essentials of the Holy Qur'an and

> in the manner of its reciting according to the rules of recitings agreed upon by Islamic law.
>
> (al-Baʿṭī and al-Bārī 1978: 11)

Such improprieties were noted as adding text to the middle of *suwar* in the form of *takbīr*, *tamḥīd* (formulae of praise), tremors in the reciters' voices, prolonging of syllables and the "*talḥīn* of verses," leading to "the outburst of listeners in exciting their cries and acclaim and cheering" (al-Baʿṭī and al-Bārī 1978: 11). Such practices were noted to be especially prevalent in the *layālī* (evening recitation programs) and in the cassette industry. The editors also reported on the exorbitantly high fees which reciters command and the fact that the art of *tartīl* is dying out because there are fewer reciters and the level of recitation is qualitatively lower. It is hoped that the Reciters' Union might have some say in establishing fees or at least require that a portion of the fee earned in private commission be paid into the Union. Advocates of the Union also recommend that part of its activity be to subsidize reciters who could not make a living by means of reciting, thus recognizing both the value of dedicating one's life to the Qur'an and the economic reality of a profession which depends on popular support. All of this, say the authors, justifies a call for serious and quick work in establishing a Reciters' Union.

As finally established (according to a report in *al-Ahrām*, Sāmī 1979: 13) a year later, the Union is for Muslims over the age of twenty-one who have memorized the whole Qur'an and whose sole income comes from reciting. No one who is not an active member of the Union is permitted to recite "in government or nongovernment context." It is this clause which makes possible the enforcement of uniform standards of recitation, for the Union has the right to discipline a member "who is infringing on the rights and duties stipulated in the law of the Union, or bringing any work incompatible with the *ādāb* [code of behavior] of the profession. Such a member may be fined LE 20 [about $30] or expelled from the roster, or forbidden to practice his profession throughout the period of his censure" (Sāmī 1979: 13). It remains to be seen how such enforcement by the Union will affect the sound of Qur'anic recitation in Egypt.

7. Overlap and Separation: The Dynamics of Perception and Response

Introduction

It is clear that the ideal recitation is conceived of as something quite different from vocal musical entertainment. But, more than that, it is not music at all. Qur'anic recitation may share a number of parameters with music, most obviously, melodic and vocal artistry, but the nature of the text and the intent of its performance require its separate and unique categorization (as was clearly demonstrated, for example, in the evaluation of the Reciters' Committee—see chapter 6). This perception of the melodic recitation of the Qur'an has a great deal to do with the issues of the *samāʿ* polemic and stems from the nature of the text itself. The Egyptian tradition of recitation practice is a perfect case in point. Although the issue of the propriety of music in an Islamic society has never been resolved with any authority, acceptance of that art is firmly established in Egypt. Still, many Egyptian Muslims who do not question the propriety of music do have reservations regarding a melodic recitation of the Qur'an, and many more, if not personally convinced of this censure, render lip service to it, for the association of the Qur'an with music threatens a tenet of Muslim belief—namely, the divine uniqueness and completeness of the Qur'an. In other words, even if music were deemed completely acceptable in an Islamic context, it does not necessarily follow that a musical rendition of the Qur'an is acceptable, for the Qur'an is much more than just a beautiful text.

At the same time, the Egyptian style of recitation is well known and widely imitated all over the Islamic world. For many, this elaborately melodic style epitomizes Qur'anic recitation. Ultimately, then, the effect of resistance to associating the Qur'an with music has been not to preclude the widespread practice of melodic recitation, but to shape perception of the reality of that practice, resulting in the apparent contradiction of perception and response so fundamental to the Qur'anic recitation tradition in Egypt.

The dichotomy of the perception of Qur'anic recitation as a unique art and response to it as music could perhaps be more easily explained if the two operated in mutually exclusive arenas. For example, it would be clear enough if we could identify those who respond to Qur'anic recitation as music as those who are unaware of the nature of the text or those unequivocably seeking only aesthetic stimulation. But even Muslims who insist that Qur'anic recitation is not music and who participate in recitation with correct appreciation and sincere intent are also able to regard it as the highest example of vocal improvisation in the Arabic music tradition and may often find themselves responding to it as they would to music.

It is this obvious and (apparently) effortless mutual accommodation of perception and response which is difficult to grasp. Certainly scholars outside the tradition perceive a baffling contradiction in the fact that a performance which not only incorporates elements of music per se but draws on aspects of musical performance contexts is not—indeed, must not be—considered music. A number of Western or Western-trained scholars, in attempting to make sense of this apparent contradiction, have resorted to the convenient classifications of sacred and secular musics to define the recitation tradition in Islam.[1] Such a classification does recognize the need for some sort of disassociation of recitation from music:

> H. G. Farmer (1952) maintains that the idea of an inherent difference between secular music and sacred chant is a fiction craftily created in Islamic times in order to condone the use of musical aspects in the chant in a society where music itself was condemned from time to time by puritan individuals or movements. These conservative elements, he maintains, needed a way of separating religious chant from associations with the forbidden pleasures (malāhī), i.e., wine, women and song. It seems unwise to put so much emphasis on this idea being a new creation since the two types of music had existed

> from the Jāhiliyyah period. Secular song and religious chant were distinguished from each other before Islam. It remained a problem for Islamic culture, not to invent, but to maintain that separation throughout the centuries.
>
> (al-Faruqi 1978: 111)

But the classification of Qur'anic recitation as sacred (as distinct from secular) music is not generally accepted within the tradition. In fact, the separation of society into sacred and secular arenas is not really an Islamic concept at all, for ideally all aspects of society should share the Islamic vision. This can be seen in the very existence of the *samā'* polemic, an attempt to account for the presence of music in, or to dismiss it from, the Islamic context.[2]

Within the Islamic tradition, the fundamental distinction is between Qur'anic recitation and all music, whether sacred or secular. Such a classification upholds the absolute uniqueness of the Qur'anic text, recognizing that its divine source, marked and preserved by the rules of *tajwīd*, sets it apart from other religious texts such as the Call to Prayer, invocations, or praises for the Prophet Muhammad. This perception of the Qur'an as a unique text whose musical recitation is therefore separate from music is upheld by guidelines that do indeed give recitation a characteristic sound and effect: few people, whatever their perception of the Qur'anic text, would fail to recognize the sound of Qur'anic recitation or be unable to distinguish it from music.

To grasp fully the implications of this separation in terms of the dichotomy of perception and response, and how the actual sound and practice of Qur'anic recitation are affected, we must consider the extent to which music and recitation overlap as art and profession, as well as the extent to which they are actually separate.

Although the overlap of music and recitation so highly visible in Egypt today is often attributed by critics to the pernicious effects of modern life, the association of music with recitation is not a recent development. There is evidence that in the early period of Islam the recitation of the Qur'an was associated with the caravan songs (*rukbānī*) and with what one scholar terms the "natural" airs of the Arabs.[3]

In the *Lisān al-'Arab*, for example, we read that, according to

Ibn al-Aʿrābī (d. ca. 844), the Arabs used to sing the caravan songs not only mounted on camels, but in many different contexts, and that it was the Prophet's wish that the Qurʾan replace their passion for the caravan song (Ibn al-Manḍūr 1966: 19/373–74). In the same text, a commentator alluded to the well-known *ḥadīṯ* "He is not one of us who does not sing the Qurʾan" with the following version: "He is not one of us who has not put the Qurʾan in the place of the caravan song as regards his passion for it and his enchantment with it" (Ibn al-Manḍūr 1966: 19/373, footnote 3). One scholar sees this as evidence that the earliest recitation of the Qurʾan was adapted to the same "very simple airs" with which the Arabs clothed their verses (Talbi 1958: 185).

However, the term *al-qirāʾah bi l-alḥān* (reciting with tunes) seems not to have been applied to this recitation. In a much-quoted reference from al-Maʿārif we read that the first to recite with tunes was a certain ʿUbayd Allāh ibn Abī Bakrah (d. ca. 676).[4] According to Ibn Qutaybah, this style was neither the camel song (*hudāʾ*) nor the tunes of art music (*alḥān al-ġināʾ*). But it is obvious that this was the beginning of the association of recitation with art music, for Ibn Qutaybah speaks of this tradition in terms of a professional elite learning from a master, and passing on to students, the elements of a style of Qurʾanic recitation which was rewarded by the patronage of the elite.[5]

What little mention there is in the sources about this style of recitation places it in an elite context. Talbi thinks that in the eleventh century the style of recitation known as *al-qirāʾah bi l-alḥān* was restricted to this context because of the high standards of artistry and musical culture it required—in other words, because of what it shared with the art music tradition. According to Talbi, these standards were maintained only in the aristocracy, because the lower classes were more subject to the guidance of the religious legal scholars, who were by and large suspicious, if not hostile, to *samāʿ* in general (Talbi 1958: 188–89).

One could posit other reasons for the limited diffusion of melodic recitation. Like art music, it was dependent on the system of patronage, maintained largely by the aristocracy, as most of the reciters were also professional singers of art music. For example, we read in several sources (*Al-ʿIqd al-Farīd, Kitāb al-Aġānī*) that Qurʾanic recitation was part of the repertoire of the professional musicians, that even the *qaynah* "recited the Qur'an, recited poems, and learned Arabic."[6]

In fact, having evolved with and been subjected to the same influences as secular song, melodic recitation seems to have lost its religious sensibility at times and to have been treated as entertainment and diversion. Ibn Qutaybah mentions that the Qur'an was recited to the tunes of particular songs: "and all the reciters . . . used to insert in recitation the tunes of *ġinā'* and *hudā'* and the incantations of monks." He even cites an example of a song text, the tune of which was applied to Qur'anic verse (Ibn Qutaybah 1935: 232).[7] In the context of the *samā'* polemic another author states that, if melodies are to be disapproved of, then one should look first to freeing them from the Qur'an and the Call to Prayer (Ibn 'Abd Rabbih 1968: 6/7). And Talbi cites, as an example of the complete confusion of recitation and music, the report that professional entertainers danced to the melodic recitation of the Qur'an (Talbi 1958: 89).

In discussing the extent of which this confusion and overlap is present in the modern Egyptian tradition of Qur'anic recitation, it is important to remember that many Muslims do find such confusion objectionable, and, however visible it may be, it cannot be considered the norm.

The Overlap of Music and Recitation

I have not been able to document the history of the tradition of melodic recitation specifically in Egypt, but there is consensus among my informants that the first melodic recitation was reported some 400 years ago and that for at least 300 years Egypt has been the acknowledged leader of melodic recitation.[7] No one could satisfactorily account for the prominent role Egyptian reciters have played in this tradition: one reciter explained it simply as "a gift from God, a natural resource, like oil" (al-Suwaysī).

To reconstruct the sound of Egyptian recitation before the earliest recordings (ca. 1932), one can only glean clues from verbal accounts and posit some sort of parallel with singing styles. For example, Šayx Sa'īd al-Saḥḥār remembers his father speaking of reciters of one generation or two before the great Šayx Muḥammad Rif'at (d. 1950) who were "ninety-nine percent better than

Šayx Rifʿat." The earliest recordings available to me were those of Šayx Rifʿat, dating from the early 1930s. A contemporary of Š. Rifʿat, Šayx ʿAlī Maḥmūd (d. 1946), also made some recordings, but these date from the late 1930s and early 1940s. However, there are earlier recordings of the singing style of Šayx ʿAlī Maḥmūd which date from the late 1920s and early 1930s. A comparison of his singing style with the style of his reciting shows that they share the same melodic patterning and modulation structures, as well as the general aesthetic of the music of those decades. Reciters themselves acknowledge a shared aesthetic. I asked my informants if they felt that there has been a development or change in the style of melodic recitation from generation to generation. Although most insisted that change is impossible since the Qurʾan is fixed and immutable, Šayx ʿAbd al-Bāsiṭ ʿAbd al-Ṣamad acknowledged that there has indeed been a change, because the reciter shares the same musical background ("musical sea" was his precise phrase), and there is no denying that musical styles have changed. Šayx Muḥammad Salāmah commented that, like the famous singer of the 1930s and 1940s Ṣāliḥ ʿAbd al-Ḥāyy, he has no audience today: "Each generation has its own taste, each performer, his audience. Mine is gone, and there is no point in trying to renew it."

If we can assume that personal style and general aesthetic are indeed a shared basis for the arts of singing and Qurʾanic recitation, we can make use of the greater number of early recordings of songs from reciters' repertoires to reconstruct something of the earlier recitation style. Some of these early recordings, such as those of Šayx Yūsuf al-Manyalāwī (d. 1911), are available in private collections and take us back to the beginning of this century. Such a reconstruction is still, at best, only a guess, but it highlights the existence of an overlap in the two professions of singing and reciting that is well established in Egypt and often alluded to. A number of famous Egyptian singers began their careers as Qurʾanic reciters or were equally active in both arts. In addition to Šayx ʿAlī Maḥmūd and Šayx Yūsuf al-Manyalāwī, mentioned above, we can name Šayx Salāmah Ḥijāzī (d. 1918), Šayx Ṭāhā l-Fašnī (d. 1950s or early 1960s?), Šayx Sayyid Darwīš (d. 1923), Umm Kalṯūm (d. 1975), and many others. Both the singing and reciting of Šayx ʿAlī Maḥmūd and Šayx Ṭāhā l-Fašnī can be heard on Egyptian radio. Of those reciters who became singers exclusively, many retained the religious garb and title of the reciter long after they stopped reciting.[8] Šayx al-Ṭablāwī, a popular reciter of Cairo today, actually gave reciters credit for the very existence of the musical art when he noted that the portraits of Šayxs ʿAlī Maḥmūd, Sayyid Darwīš, and Zakariyā Aḥmad hang in the Music Institute in Cairo, adding, "the [musical] art didn't emerge except by way of the reciters."

The bridge from recitation to secular singing is in the religious songs, the *tawāšīḥ* and the *ibtihālāt*. The *ibtihālāt* are free-rhythmic solo vocal improvisations on a poetic text and given melody. The *tawāšīḥ* are also composed of solo passages of improvisation, but these are alternated with metered choral refrains. The similarity to recitation is in the religious mood, the extent of vocal improvisation, and the lack of any instrumental accompaniment. The songlike qualities lie in the metered texts and the use of chorus, set rhythmic patterns, and given melody. Moreover, unlike the reciter, the singer of *tawāšīḥ* and *ibtihālāt* is free to play with the text and to make use of the whole range of vocal ornamentation. These songs are heard in many of the same contexts as recitation, that is, during the various religious celebrations and holidays, such as the birth of the Prophet, Ramadan, and so forth. They also have a place in the programs celebrating special events, such as the *saharāt dīniyyah*, the religious evening gatherings which follow the evening prayer and commemorate events such as the death of a prominent person, the opening of a mosque, or the visit of an official.

I was told that it was the practice of the last generation of reciters (and before) to end an evening's recitation with religious *tawāšīḥ*. Some reciters had their own chorus (*biṭāna*), some depended on an impromptu chorus. Šayx Hāšim Haybah, one of the few prominent reciters practicing today who also sings in public, explained to me that listening to and singing *tawāšīḥ* "nourishes [lit., irrigates] the reciter's talent." Other reciters explained that the advantage of singing is that the reciter is free to exercise his voice and to practice his improvisatory skills without risking distortions of the holy text of the Qurʾan.[9]

The image of the reciter as singer is, however, a further confusion of the overlap of music and recitation, and this image is sometimes perpetrated by the media. For example, the magazine *al-Kawākib*, a popular publication of the entertainment industry, includes an article on professional Qur'anic reciters. In one article on the cassette industry in Egypt, there was a reference to Šayx Muḥammad al-Ṭablāwī as "one of the stars of song" (*min nujum al-ġinā'*, Anonymous 1979: 61).

To be fair, objections to extreme examples of overlap also get media coverage, such as the article published by the editors of the religious page of *al-Ahrām* on the controversy surrounding the melodic recitation of the Qur'an (Diyāb 1977: 11). This article was a response to the objections of a number of readers to the reciting of the Qur'an in the manner of singing "to the extent that there is no great difference between this type of reciting and music making."

Šayx ʿAlī Ḥajjāj al-Suwaysī's comment that before there was melodic recitation in Egypt "there were no reputations or fees" pinpoints those aspects of melodic recitation which generate most of the opposition to it, namely, a perceived overlap between recitation and the entertainment business. The fees which reciters can command, the bases of their reputations, interaction and professional rivalry among reciters, protocol governing performance structure, as well as audience expectation and response—all have a great deal in common with the entertainment industry. The objection to these practices is that they tend to subvert the intent of recitation and threaten to reduce it to just another form of entertainment or show business.

The very professionalism of the reciter contributes to his image as popular performer. This professionalism is unique to the Egyptian tradition of Qur'anic recitation, and there is some objection, especially outside of Egypt, to the profession of reciting per se. In Egypt, however, the professional reciter is taken for granted. Not only is there a large group of reciters whose primary or only means of support is their reciting, but a large number of civil servants moonlight as reciters. These part-time reciters can earn LE 5–10 (approximately \$8–\$12 in 1978) in a single evening.[10]

It is clear that one of the reasons reciters acquire musical skills is economic. Most reciters are aware that mastery of musical skills, whether by training or by instinct, is important to their economic success. The most concrete evidence of this is the role of the Radio in the career of the professional reciter. A reciter employed by the Radio can lay claim to official recognition of a certain standard of excellence which encompasses memorization of the Qur'an, knowledge of the rules of *tajwīd*, and musical artistry. The reciter may automatically raise his fees by virtue of this official recognition, and there is a general feeling that the best reciters are those hired by the Radio. It is known that there are two musicians on the committee which auditions candidates for Radio employment and that reciters who are otherwise acceptable may be told to come back after they have worked on improving their musical skills. My music teacher told me of a reciter who was doing well professionally and was encouraged to try out for Radio employment. Before sending in an application, however, he spent some time systematically learning the *maqāmāt*.

The matter of reciters' fees is a subject of some discussion among those concerned with the propriety of melodic recitation. To some extent, tradition legislates against making money off the Qur'an at all, although, like the issue of *samāʿ*, this has by no means been authoritatively resolved. In an article regarding the establishment of a Reciters' Union in Cairo, it is clear that there is concern about various abuses of recitation, among them the extravagant fees paid to some reciters. In the same article Šayx al-Ḥuṣarī states that his objection is to the exaggerated fees and not to the principle of reciters taking fees in general. But his statement is followed by that of another *šayx* who cites several *ḥadīṯ* against the principle:

> Recite the Qur'an. Do not go too far with it, nor shun it. Do not seek sustenance or material gain by means of it.
> . . . we are not permitted to charge a fee for: calling to prayer, reciting the Qur'an . . .
>
> (al-Baʿṯī and al-Bārī 1978: 11)

It is also a comment on the popularity of melodic recitation and the extent of its overlap with music that, of all the professionals dealing with the Qur'an, the melodic reciters are the ones who profit the most. The standard fee for a Qur'anic tutor in 1978 was LE 1 per hour (ca. $1.50 at that time). The highly trained teachers of the public recitation classes receive from the Ministry of Religious Endowments only token payment of LE 1–2 per three-hour session, depending on the extent of their knowledge. Reciters employed by the Ministry to recite in the context of the Friday prayer receive LE 1, and reciters officially hired to recite during the month of Ramadan earn LE 75–200 for thirty days' reciting.

However, reciters who contract with private persons for reciting are not subject to any fee limitation other than that of demand. Fees vary according to popular support for the reciter, and one "superstar" reciter can earn LE 1,000 in a single evening. Most reciters who are employed by the Radio can command LE 100–800 for a private commission of recitation. The melodic reciters are, then, paid the most extravagantly, and one may presume that it is the association of the reciter with the highly paid performer of the entertainment world, as much as the more general and traditional objection, that colors the unease felt about payment for recitation.

The extent to which the recitation tradition has absorbed attitudes and expectations of the entertainment industry can be further seen in the image of the reciter as performer, artist, and public personality. The group of listeners at any given session or public recitation is likely to comprise not only those who have come to hear the Qur'an, or to celebrate the occasions, but those who are music lovers and fans of the reciter himself.[11] Like singing stars, reciters acquire a loyal following based on personal as well as professional appeal. A few Qur'anic reciters are celebrated in the media with interviews and photo displays. A radio interview with Šayx Muṣṭafā Ismāʿīl, for example, featured the reciter at home, chatting and singing with his close friends.[12] Šayx Muṣṭafa also made a guest appearance on the television show *Nigmak al-Mufaḍḍal* (Your Favorite Star), which features interviews with popular actors, singers, and so forth. A pamphlet on Šayx ʿAbd al Bāsiṭ ʿAbd al-Ṣamad, written in English by a lecturer at al-Azhar University, includes information about his professional career, personality, family life, ideals, and even advice to aspiring reciters. For example: "Sheikh Basit is a very simple soft-hearted man. He never forgets his friends, however rich or poor they be. When sitting in his chauffer-driven limousine he loves to sit next to his driver whom he calls 'Akh Masood' Brother Masood" (Razack 1966: 6). Although the specific content may differ, reciters are subject to the same curiosity and personal comment as other public figures.

Intense rivalry may exist between the followers of different reciters. Al-Najmī cites an attempt by the followers of Šayx ʿAlī Maḥmūd to stop Šayx Rifʿat from reciting (al-Najmī 1968: 172), and their objections to the title given him (Imām of Reciters) in the radio introduction to his reciting.[13] An extreme example of the loyalty which reciters can inspire is the report that, during a public recitation, one faction found fault with the voice of the reciter. This roused his fans, and the two factions came to blows, leaving four dead and more than ten taken to hospitals (al-Saʿīd 1970: 102).

Another aspect of the reputations of reciters which parallels that of singing stars is manifested in the protocol governing their participation in a program of recitation. For example, from two to twenty reciters may participate in the same evening's program, and the order of their reciting is determined by their reputation and rank. Reputations are judged by fees, which reflect popularity, and, in the case of those reciters employed by the Radio, by an official ranking. Since the Radio reciter's rank determines how much exposure he gets on the air, and which stations broadcast his reciting,[14] it is an easily discernible criterion. If there are no radio reciters on the program, the order of reciting seems to be less strictly observed.

Just as in many nightclub programs, the younger and relatively unknown performers precede the stars. These young reciters may or may not have been hired by the patron, but it is accepted that this is the way a young reciter begins to build his reputation.

When a number of reciters are participating, everyone usually gets one turn, but when two reciters of similar rank are reciting, they may have several turns, and it is the senior one who determines the end of the reciting. This is signaled by his announcing the *Fātiḥah* (the opening prayer of the Qur'an) and leading the audience in its straightforward recital. I was present at one public recitation where the senior-ranking reciter ended the evening with his partner having had only one turn. This was considered a calculated insult to the younger reciter, as it was only about 11:30 P.M. and such evening performances normally last until well after midnight.

Reciters rarely determine who their associates may be in a public recitation, although a prominent reciter may bring along his protégé. Reciters acknowledge, and it seems to be taken for granted among listeners, that the skill of a fellow performer can enhance their own performance. One of the famous recordings in private collections in Cairo is an evening's recitation by two well-known reciters, Šayx Kāmil Yūsuf al-Bahtīmī and Šayx Muṣṭafā Ismāʿīl. Each gave what is considered a superb performance, and the feeling is that it was a spirit of competition that inspired them both. It is commonly said that when a lesser is paired with a great reciter he excels. Word gets around, and listeners with an ear for the best art find out who is reciting with whom. Some patrons may have this in mind when hiring reciters, for there is an acknowledged element of personal pride and prestige in drawing a large crowd. There is no denying that the public image of the reciter affects the expectations of listeners, in that many come to hear a particular reciter first and the recitation of the Qurʾan only second.

Etiquette also requires that reciters listen to each others' recitations, especially the younger to the older, and reciters are generally supportive of each other.

Still, I heard a number of complaints about the decline of good manners and the increase of the sort of rivalry which has led to an abuse of polite behavior. One of these well-circulated stories of rivalry concerns reciter A, an up-and-coming young star, who recited two hours and then prepared to leave. He was rebuked into staying and listening by reciter B, who was his senior, but whose reputation was on the wane. Reciter B then took his turn, reciting for three hours until dawn the very same text that reciter A had performed. Such stories of one-upmanship are relished and circulated by followers and fans, but there may still be some ambivalence as to whether these contribute positively or negatively to a reciter's image.

We can also see the overlap between music and recitation in the expectations and response of the listeners to the performance itself and to the performer. Some audiences are indistinguishable in their behavior from a music concert audience. In fact, one of the major objections to melodic recitation is that it elicits an inappropriate response on the part of the listeners. The code of behavior governing the reciter and listener (*ādāb al-tilāwah*) is very specific, and it helps to keep Qurʾanic recitation separate from the entertainment aspect of music. Although the appropriately subdued response is the norm, and reciters may be criticized for stirring up an overexcited response, it cannot be denied that the most popular reciters have an extremely vocal, even boisterous, following.

One can sort out the same sort of flattering homage given to musicians in the roar of approval and shrieks of delight with which listeners punctuate some reciters' phrases. Among the standard exclamations are, "O prayer of the Prophet" (*yā ṣalāt in-nabī*), "May God pour His blessings upon you" (*Allāh yiftaḥ ʿalēk*), "Well done" (*Aḥsant*), "God is great" (*Allāhu akbar*), and so forth. I also heard "O nightingale of the Nile" (*yā bulbul in-nīl*), "O perfection" (*yā kāmil*, a play on the name of the reciter, Kāmil Yūsuf al-Bahtīmī), "Do it again so we can memorize it" (*tāni, ʿašān niḥfazu*), and the very common exclamation *yā fitiwwa! yā fatwana!* (very approximately "Attaboy! That's the stuff!"). People would lovingly quote to me bits of specific performances they particularly liked. One man sang me a single word from one of Šayx Rifʿat's recitations which he heard years ago. A response from a more subdued audience (and one apparently more common in the past) is the pronouncing of the name of God, *Allāh*, one or more times, on the same pitch with which the reciter ended his phrase. Other phrases may be pronounced on this pitch as well, so it is not totally in unison; nevertheless, the effect is that of a choral response.

The audience also calls for repeats, shouting up suggestions to the reciter such as "We'd like to hear the same in the high register, how about it?" and special requests for *maqāmāt*, "Give us *šuri*!" or "How about some *ṣaba*? By the Prophet, we're waiting for the *ṣaba*!" There may also be some musical references to other reciters, and the knowledgeable audience will shout out its delighted recognition with the name of the reciter quoted, or such comments as "He's taken us back thirty years!"

Al-Saʿīd, in his criticism of such audience response, notes that "people are stimulated by the melody, over and above their stimulation by the meaning" (al-Saʿīd 1970: 106). This is a commonly voiced criticism. Šayx al-Ḥuṣarī told me that reciting with melodies is permissible "except for the singing and abuse of it that results in listeners following the melody and not the meaning, and this takes it far from what is intended for recitation, so people shout." Šayx Aḥmad al-Ruzayqī criticized the noisy audience which "likes the voice and the melodic cadence, but doesn't apply its mind to the meaning," and he gave as an example people who shout their delight and call for repeats when he recites about hell and punishment. Al-Saʿīd cites another criticism of listeners: that they rock and shout "as they do when listening to *ġinā'* with absolutely no difference" (al-Sa'īd 1970: 102).

Many reciters have come to depend on this audience response, saying it encourages them and inspires them to excel. Many of the reciters I talked with mentioned the importance of *tajāwub*, vocal response, and I heard such comments as:

> The studio [context] makes you feel constrained, but people encourage, and there is *tajāwub*, and things come out better than you imagined they could.
>
> The more people there are, the more enthusiasm I have, and all this encourages me, and gives me [the right] spirit.
>
> In studio recordings the *insigām* [harmony] is missing. In order to make a recording of a quality acceptable to the Radio, I imagine that I am in front of a crowd.

This last comment comes from a reciter whose reputation is limited because his studio recordings (which have the wider audience) are not as appreciated as his live recitations. There is a consensus among collectors, in general, that studio recordings tend to be inferior to those of live performances: they would agree with the reciter who said that live performances are "where the great art happens" (Šayx Muṣṭafā Ismā'īl).[15]

The objection to this attitude is that reciters who depend on audience response subvert the ideal intent of recitation and seek only to please their listeners. Šayx al-Ḥuṣarī, one of those who denies any difference in his reciting in a studio or before a crowd, dismisses those whose reciting does differ as not having the proper intent in their recitation. There is, in fact, a thin line between making the recitation meaningful to the listeners and wooing them with one's skill, as the following comments illustrate:

> The response of the listeners is also important, because the reciter can bring them back if their attention wanders.
>
> The alert reciter is aware of the listeners . . . is able to know their response to everything, and if they don't like something he can change. Even the blind reciter can tell [response] from the sound. The audience doesn't have to be hysterical; the re-

citer can sense the mood and encouragement of a calmer audience.

I like to interact with the crowd, and to do that you have to do what they want.

I can recite for an hour or two and you won't get bored. I change the melody as I see response. [If] I see you like *ṣaba*, I'll give you a lot of it.[16]

The *nadwah* is a context of recitation in which less objectionable aspects of audience response and appreciation of Qur'anic recitation are exhibited. The *nadwah* is a listening session for Qur'anic recitation; although common among music lovers, it is unique among Qur'anic contexts in that there is no occasion or event to be commemorated; rather the art itself is celebrated. Members of the *nadwah* gather to hear tapes, exchange copies of them, discuss particular performances, and share photographs and anecdotes of the reciters. I regularly attended two such sessions. The host of the first, Mr. Maḥmūd Muṣṭafā, opens his house once a week to any persons who wish to listen to his collection of taped recordings of recitation. The regular members of this gathering are devoted to collecting the works of three reciters, Šayx Kāmil Yūsuf al-Bahtīmī, Šayx Muḥammad Ṣiddīq al-Minšāwī, and their mentor, Šayx Muḥammad Salāmah. Since all are deceased, whatever recordings are in existence are of special value. Mr. Maḥmūd has a network of contacts spreading north to Alexandria and south to Luxor helping him to track down recordings made from the Radio or at public performances.

Although the basis of it all, the Qur'an, is never forgotten, and discussion of a recitation includes the meaning of the text and the reciter's skill in bringing it out, his spirituality, and so forth, a great deal of the discussion does center on voice quality, register, and use of melodic material. Many listeners, both in these sessions and in public recitations, like to follow the modulations, anticipate them, and test each other's knowledge of the *maqāmāt* with them. A particularly inspiring phrase will stimulate the listeners to stop the machine, rewind, and play it again, several times over.[17] Because these sessions are by no means limited to avowed supporters of the reciters involved, opinions differ and the discussion is lively.

I attended another weekly session at the home of Ḥājj Ḥusayn Faraj, who is not only a host and collector, but a patron of reciters. Mr. Faraj's collection is not limited by personal preference; he explained that, just as different foods please the palate in different ways, so there is something different to appreciate in each reciter. The group that gathers here is equally eclectic in its tastes, although one man who refuses to listen to anyone but Šayx Muṣṭafā Ismāʿīl is a frequent and welcome guest. Because of his more influential family background and economic position as well as his long-standing contacts with reciters and media officials, Ḥājj Ḥusayn's *nadwah* is known throughout the city, and both young and established reciters often drop by, sometimes favoring guests with a recitation.

It is important to realize that a majority of the listeners at the *nadwah* have acquired their musical knowledge only by way of their interest in the recitation and not vice versa. Moreover, this knowledge tends to comprise only those principles of music which are applicable to recitation, namely, melodic—as opposed to rhythmic—principles.

The specifically musical qualities of the art of recitation are appreciated by professional musicians as well. They point to reciters as expert performers of the "classical" art of music, and feel that the standards of this music are being preserved by reciters. The following is taken from an Iraqi newspaper, but the idea expressed could just as well be Egyptian:

> The research concluded that the music of "al-Tilawah," the way the Holy Qurʾan is recited, stands for the best-known form of Arab Classical music for it has retained within its structure the genuine characteristics of the Arab music, and hence it forms the best possible basis for solving the theoretical problems of Iraqi music.
>
> (H. Husseini 1979)

What is specifically singled out for praise in recitation by musicians and others is the improvisatory skill which has characterized music performance of preceding generations and which in Egypt is being undermined by the use of Western notation and set pieces for large ensemble. Improvisation in recitation, however, is not only still highly valued but essential to the style and spirit of recitation of the Qur'an.[18]

I heard one prominent musician, listening to a tape of Šayx Ramaḍān, exclaim with delight, "Is there a singer who does that? No, not a single one!" And the musical skill of Šayx Šaᶜbān al-Ṣayyād elicited the comment, "If Umm Kalṯūm were alive to hear him, she would go crazy over this!" It was reported to me that a musician, listening to a recording of Šayx Rifᶜat in a shop where he was doing some business, exclaimed, "Now, that's how [*maqām*] *ṣaba* should be. No one can do *ṣaba* like Šayx Rifᶜat!" (Salwa El-Shawan).[19]

Many reciters excel in a particular *maqām*, and this is part of their reputation. Everyone waits to hear *ṣabā* from Šayx ᶜAlī Ḥajjāj al-Suwaysī, and Šayx Kāmil Yūsuf al-Bahtīmī, *ṣabā* and *rast* from Šayx Rifᶜat, *rast* and *nawa* from Šayx Muṣṭafā Ismāᶜīl, and *kurd* from Šayx Ramaḍān. Reciters are aware of these expectations and recognitions of their particular skills: when I asked Šayx Ramaḍān about his use of *kurd*, he told me that he always used to listen to Indian, Pakistani, and Iranian singing on the radio and that it gave him a taste for the more rarely used *maqāmāt*. He feels that other reciters do use *kurd*, but that no one can sustain it as long as he can.

The resolution of the phrase, the melodic cadence (most commonly, *qaflah* [plural *qafalāt*], but also *rabṭa*, *lamma*, *farmal*, and *waqfa*), is considered the mark of the reciter's (and singer's) skill: "If you can't do *qafalāt* you can't do Arabic music," Suleiman Gamil, music critic and scholar, said to me. These cadences are very much a mark of personal style, and a reciter may refer to another reciter by "quoting" his melodic cadence. They are immediately recognizable to the more knowledgeable listeners, many of whom have memorized their favorites.

The terminology used by reciters and listeners in discussing Qur'anic recitation is quite revealing of the musical expectations of those involved, and these expectations, of course, play an important role in defining the aesthetic of Qur'anic recitation. The musical aesthetic of recitation has been discussed in detail in chapter 5, but some of the more common terminology shared by music and recitation may again be mentioned here.

Listeners discuss the voice quality of the reciter (*maʿdan iṣ-ṣōt*), and a reciter is classified by listeners according to whether he is best in the high register (*gawāb*), the low register (*qarār*), or excels in both, in which case he has a "wide" or "complete" voice (*ṣōt kāmil, ʿarīḍ*). The voice which is "fresh" (*ṭari*), "soft" (*layyin*), "light" (*xafīf*), and "deep" (*agašš*) is preferred over the voice that is "nasal" (*anfi*), "weak" (*ḍaʿīf*), or "tired" (*taʿbān*). An element of voice quality admired in both reciters and singers is *baḥḥa*, and the voice of Umm Kalṯūm is considered the best example of this among singers. This quality can be variously described as that of a thick, husky, sobbing, or even neighing voice, and it is considered most effective if natural to the voice and not inserted as an ornament.

It is important that a reciter keep on pitch (*ṭạbaqạ̄t* or *dạrạgāt iṣ-ṣōt*). Varied, suspenseful, and complex modulation (*talwīn*) is admired, as are the extremes of register (*gawāb ig-gawāb, qarār il-qarār*). One reciter has been admiringly dubbed *iš-šayx il-muṣawwir* (the transposing *šayx*) for his extensive use of transposition (*taṣwīr*) in his improvisation.

Another term with musical connotations I heard applied to recitation, and to wide leaps and wide-ranging runs in particular, was *sinfuniyya*. Although this may have been a usage particular to the group in which I heard it, its sense of virtuosity would be generally understood.

Such examples of overlap demonstrate that the Egyptian tradition of Qur'anic recitation is bound up with a musical sensibility which contributes to its popularity. The more extreme examples of overlap do meet with severe censure both privately and in the press, but they only highlight the risks of accepting musicality into the recitation tradition. They do not minimize its real benefits to the fulfillment of the ideal intent of recitation. And reciters are aware that this musical sensibility is sanctioned by the ideals of recitation, in which the concepts of beauty and effectiveness in Qur'anic recitation are definitely linked to musical artistry.

Thus, although all of the professional reciters I interviewed are aware of the controversy surrounding the use of melody in recitation, they not only acknowledged its widespread practice and links with the musical art, but insisted on the importance of it to their art. The late Šayx Muṣṭafā Ismāʿīl (d. December 19, 1978) told me in an interview that "the art of recitation is *mūsīqā*, and the better one can use the *maqāmāt*, the more effective the recitation." Another reciter, Šayx Hāšim Haybah, said, "Recitation is a matter of melodies and their ordering." Šayx Fatḥī Qandīl put it very bluntly: "Those [who study Qur'an] who are without good voice [*ṣawt*] will be teachers only."[20]

There is the feeling that the reciter has a responsibility to develop his talent, including musical skill, to the fullest. I was present when a prominent Egyptian composer chided a popular reciter for not studying music, saying he had a responsibility to his listeners to give them the very best. The "very best" in this case was more variation in the *maqāmāt*, and more subtle artistry in general. Šayx Fatḥī Qandīl told me, "If the voice is capable of executing the *maqāmāt*, and if the reciter is talented, he should go on and learn more by listening or attending the [Music] Institute." And Šayx ʿAlī Ḥajjāj al-Suwaysī (who did study music at the Higher Institute of Music) said, "He who does not have artistry must strive to learn and improve."

In fact, most professional reciters seek to master the principles of Arabic music. Of the eleven professional reciters employed by the Radio I interviewed (among them the most popular and highest-ranking of the Egyptian reciters), two had studied music privately, three had studied at the Higher Institute of Music, four had learned the traditional way (namely, by conscious listening and imitation), and only two made no mention of formal or conscious musical training, although they acknowledged the importance of melody per se to recitation. Perhaps more indicative of the trend of the times is the fact that of the four younger reciters, three had studied at the Music Institute.

Because most reciters carry the sound of music and recitation in their ears from birth, many can intuitively produce a melodic recitation which conforms to the principles of Arabic music. Although not able to articulate verbally what they are doing, they are aware of what sounds right because, as members of the culture, they have internalized the aesthetic which underlies music and Qur'anic recitation. In fact, most reciters I talked with insisted on the necessity of a good ear or a "sensitive" or "clean" ear (*widn ḥassāsa, widn niḍīfa*) to a successful reciter.

The traditional way of picking up musical skills was described to me by a reciter of the older generation, one most admired by musicians, the late Šayx Muṣṭafā Ismāʿīl:

> Among the listeners were a number of musicians and artists [*fannanīn*—the term can apply to knowledgeable listeners, as well as performers]. They remark, "Oh, he's doing [*maqām*] *bayāti*," "How did you do this [*maqām*] *ṣaba*," and so forth. That's how I learned. I listened to their comments. I used to recite every night, and they were always there.
>
> (Šayx Muṣṭafā Ismāʿīl)

Šayx Muṣṭafā also explained that he would listen to tapes of his own recitings, "and I listen to myself and take note of the good and the bad." Even in a live performance, he would listen critically and train himself. Šayx al-Ṭablāwī, a reciter of the younger generation who learned the same way, explained that he knows the musical conventions not from study, but from listening: "People reveal it in their comments, for example, 'give us this bit of [*maqām*] *nahawand* again'" (Šayx Muḥammad al-Ṭablāwī). Šayx Hāšim Haybah insisted that listening is the best way to learn: "When there are notes in front of you, you get lost, but if it is in the head, it never leaves."[21]

Šayx Ibrāhīm al-Šaʿšāʿī's more formal training was supervised by his father, the late Šayx ʿAbd al-Fattāḥ al-Šaʿšāʿī, himself a prominent reciter: when he had memorized the Qurʾan and mastered the rules of *tajwīd* and the *qirāʾāt*, his father took him to study with Šayx Darwīš al-Ḥarīrī, a famous singer, and the teacher of such well-regarded singers as Umm Kalṯūm and ʿAbd al-Wahhāb. Šayx Ibrāhīm spent three years with this teacher studying the principles of *mūsīqā*, the *tawāšīh*, and the *maqāmāt*. Only then did he begin to recite in public. In making the connection between his musical training and the demands of the Qurʾanic text, the reciter must depend on his ear, his talent, and his mastery of all the various skills to find the right balance that makes his art recitation and not music.

Reciters were very specific in articulating the benefits of mastering the principles of music. Šayx Muṣṭafā Ismāʿīl explained that at first he recited instinctively and, indeed, was even then very popular among the musically sophisticated. But with more artistic training he became better; he understood what he was doing and was more unerring. "I have traveled all over the world, and I'm used to travel now. When I arrive at an airport, I know what to do. Knowing the *nagama* [i.e., *maqām*] is like that. I can take control. I understand the situation." Later he added, "You must know the road so as not to get lost." Both Šayx Ibrāhīm and Šayx Aḥmad al-Ruzayqī expressed the feeling that knowledge of music helps the reciter to convey the meaning, that the reciter can be more precise in suiting the melody to the meaning.[22]

The advantage of an awareness of the principles of music seems to be the capability of playing with the material, resulting in a greater subtlety and increased emotional effect. And, of course, increased control of the musical material can effect a greater integration of meaning, mood, and sound, as well as reducing the possibility of error.

Although reciters and singers undergo the same process in mastering the principles of Arabic music, their training diverges precisely at the point where the reciter must confront the nature of his text and its relationship to music. Nothing in his musical training has prepared him to deal specifically with the Qur'anic text. There is no course of study in how to recite the Qur'an melodically. In other words, any formal training in music is limited to the principles and repertoire of Arabic music: it is up to the individual reciter to apply what he has learned to the art of reciting.

The Separation of Music and Recitation

Mastery of music is considered essential to a reciter's effectiveness. Yet, at the same time, musical training is not included in the rigorous and closely supervised curriculum which regulates other aspects of recitation such as understanding of the text (*tafsīr*), correct reproduction of timbre, duration, and so forth. That the acquiring of musical skills is left up to the individual reciter clearly reflects perception of the Qur'anic text as unique and is one way to effect a concrete separation of recitation from music. In fact, this training process demonstrates that the given perception of Qur'anic recitation is more than a mental juggling designed to justify the status quo of melodic recitation. There are real differences between music and recitation in terms of training, use of material, and the sound itself. In discussions of melodic recitation, in the various objections to it, as well as in the definitions given to the various terms denoting music, we can deduce some basic guidelines which work to maintain the separation. 1. Given the unique nature and divine source of the text, its primacy must be respected above and beyond any considerations of audience involvement, emotional effect, or personal prestige. 2. Thus any music should arise out of the inspiration of the text itself. 3. The proper intent of recitation should be to bring people closer to the Qur'an and to involve them in its significance. At this point in the discussion, it should be apparent that certain forces and motivations which differ from, and at times conflict with, these ideals of Qur'anic recitation have an important impact on the sound. It must be stressed, however, that the Qur'anic ideal remains fundamental in shaping the sound, both in and of itself and in its interaction with the conflicting forces described above. Here we return to the level of the Qur'anic ideal.

In practical terms, the first guideline, maintaining the primacy of the text, means that the basis of the reciter's art should be mastery of the rules of *tajwīd*. Preserving the text from distortion, recalling the moment of revelation, acknowledging the divine beauty of the language of the text, and ensuring an absolute clarity of pronunciation are all reasons given for the obligation to recite with *tajwīd*. In addition, Muslims cite the verse "And recite the Qur'an with *tartīl*" (Qur. 73/4) and a number of *ḥadīṯ* as the authority behind the obligation to recite with *tajwīd*. One of these *ḥadīṯ* is the following:

> Recite the Qur'an in the tunes and songs of the Arabs, and beware the tunes of the corrupt and of the People of the Two Books. There will come after me a people who will trill the Qur'an, the same trilling of singing, and of the monasteries and of the laments, and [their reciting] will go no further than their throats, their hearts seduced like the hearts of those whom their affair [i.e., reciting] pleases.[23]

It is often interpreted to mean, "Recite the Qur'an with *tajwīd*, and do not deviate from the rules applying to it" (al-Suyūṭī 1910: 1/109; Šayx Ramaḍān).

Reciters, scholars, and listeners all insist on the priority of *tajwīd* over the musical elements of recitation:

> One can benefit from the study of music, but what is important is that it not exceed the rules [of *tajwīd*].
>
> (Šayx Ramaḍān/reciter)

> The Qur'an is the word of God, and the skillful and clever reciter must recite the Qur'an and make melodic artistry with it, as he wishes, but on the basis of *tajwīd*.
>
> (Šayx al-Suwaysī/reciter)

> All of it [melodic cadencing, modulation, etc.] is based on the Qur'an, especially its syllabic durations [*madd*].
>
> (Šayx Haybah/reciter)

> The melody must not dominate *tajwīd*.
>
> (Šayx al-Ruzayqī/reciter)

> The melody must not take the reciting out of the rules.
>
> (Šayx al-Ḥuṣarī/reciter-scholar)

> The reciter must subjugate the melody to the rules of *tajwīd*.
>
> (Šayx al-Saḥḥār/scholar)

> I am free as regards the melody, but I am tied to the rules of *tajwīd*.
>
> (Šayx ʿAbd al-Bāsiṭ ʿAbd al-Ṣamad/reciter)

> He [the reciter] fits the voice to the Qur'an, not vice versa.
>
> (Ḥājj Faṛaj/contractor)

> Music is necessary, as long as *tajwīd* is the basis.
>
> (Šayx al-Šaʿšāʿī/reciter)

The late Šayx Muṣṭafā Ismāʿīl was considered suspect as a reciter by many Muslims because of his extreme musicality. But one devout scholar told me that, although he used to think that Šayx Muṣṭafā was "too musical," he had come to accept him because he realized that Šayx Muṣṭafā knew his *tajwīd*: "There is no denying the musicality of the religious text, and as long as *tajwīd* is used, and music does not distort *tajwīd* or distract from the text, it is acceptable" (Dr. Ḥasan al-Šāfiʿī).

Šayx Muṣṭafā himself told me that when asked about the reluctance to associate Qur'anic recitation with music, he responded, "As long as the rules of *tajwīd* are adhered to, the pauses are correct, the reciter can recite with music however he wishes." This statement was broadcast over national television on the program "Your Favorite Star," "with the imām of al-Azhar, the president of the republic, and countless others listening," and Šayx Muṣṭafā said he challenged anyone to disagree, but never heard a word of rebuttal.

Reciters are praised for their mastery of the rules of *tajwīd*: "he is faithful to the rules," "he doesn't swallow his letters," and so forth. More often, however, this mastery is taken for granted as the most basic requirement of a reciter and is not mentioned.

That music distorts *tajwīd* seems to be a primary objection to melodic recitation. Throughout the sources we read that in recitation, "the tune which imposes change is forbidden" (al-Qāriʾ 1948: 23), that "*tarjīʿ* and *taṭrīb* lead to [pronouncing a] glottal stop where there is none, and the trilling and prolonging of a single long vowel so that it becomes many, and this leads to excess in the Qurʾan and is not permitted" (al-Jawzīyyah 1970: 1/168; al-Qurṭubī 1968: 1/16). We read that melodic recitation distorts *tajwīd*, making a short vowel long, and assimilation where there is none, "and if it does not reach this extreme, then there is no disapproval [of melodic recitation]" (al-Rāfiʿī, cited in Naṣr 1930: 18–19).

Scholars explain the report of al-Šāfiʿī's acceptance of reciting with tunes.[24] Al-Suyūṭī (1910: 1/109) distinguishes beautifying the voice with the Qurʾan from reciting with tunes, saying that it is the latter which is risky, but as long as there is no extension or distortion of the durations, even reciting with tunes is acceptable, "and this is what al-Šāfiʿī must have meant." Naṣr (1930: 19) reports al-Nawawī's interpretation of al-Šāfiʿī's acceptance: "All acceptance [of reciting with tunes] is conditional on the absence of abuse, excess, lengthened vowels"; elsewhere he states, "There is no objection to reciting with tunes as long as the reciter does not exceed the limits of the Qurʾan" (Naṣr 1930: 18).[25]

A number of sources list objectionable and innovative practices in Qurʾanic recitation, including those which violate the rhythm of *tajwīd*, such as the practice of "those who put a long vowel in the wrong place and extend the long vowel for the sake of *taṭrīb*" (Ibn al-Jazarī 1908: 4), or of "the person who makes his voice dance with the Qurʾan, thus making long vowels overlong."[26] Al-Qurṭubī writes (1968: 1/16, 17), "And if the matter increases to the point that the meaning of the Qur'an is not understood, well, that is absolutely forbidden . . . and [the people who do this] seek to make acceptable the changing of the Book of God." Ibn Qayyim al-Jawziyyah produces a telling anecdote to emphasize the importance of adhering to *tajwīd*, specifically to the given durations:

> I heard a man ask Aḥmad [ibn Ḥanbal?], "What is your opinion about reciting with tunes?" He said "What is your name?" The man said, "Muḥammad." Aḥmad said, "Would you like it if it were said to you, 'Moooḥammad'?"
>
> (al-Jawziyyah 1970: 1/166)

An examination of what is meant by *mūsīqā* or *alḥān* in the context of discussions of the acceptability of melodic recitation (and this applies to the various terms denoting music, e.g., *ġinā'*, *talḥīn*, *taṭrīb*, *ṣawt*, *naġam*, etc.) should demonstrate that the objection to reciting with tunes is not to the use of music per se, but only to those elements in music, sacred or secular, which risk distorting the precise rhythmic and phonetic patterns of the divine text, that is, the elements of rhythm.

The term *al-mūsīqā* is used in both a general and a specific sense. The general sense denotes an ordered fluency of sound and has been applied to the Qur'anic text itself: "The Qur'an has its own music, which no one who recites it can fail to realize" (al-Saʿīd 1967: 324, and 1970: 68). This *mūsīqā* is described in various sources in terms of rhyme, rhythm, alliteration, correspondence of frequency of consonants to meaning, timbre, meter, symmetry, and so forth.[27] The more specific usage denotes the rhythmic and pitch organization that characterizes Arabic art music in both theory and practice.[28]

It was the development of a music theory, as well as the introduction of *īqāʿ*, the rhythmic pattern separate from the prosody of the text, which distinguished the imperial art music of the Arabs from the music of pre- and early Islamic Arabia. The two types of music are distinguished in the sources not so much by terminology as by context and by the characterization of the former as crafted, studied, metered, and mannered, and of the latter as instinctive, natural, and innate. And "what is disapproved of and forbidden" as regards recitation of the Qur'an is:

> what is arrived at only by means of manneredness, craft, and rehearsal, as the songs [*aṣwāt*] of *ġinā'* are learned with those various tunes, which are simple and complex according to particular rhythms and composed meters, and which do not occur except by instruction and manneredness. . . . And whoever has knowledge of the affairs of the forebears knows absolutely that they are innocent of reciting with the studied tunes of *mūsīqā*, which are *īqā'* and set, numbered movements.[29]

The reasons for rejecting this music are clear. Certainly the association of *īqā'* with a life-style of indulgent wealth may be one reason. But the more widely expressed reason is that the Qur'anic text has its own rhythms which have nothing to do with the musical rhythms of *īqā'*. When a melody, bound up with and characterized by a particular rhythm, independent of any text, is imposed on a text, it is the rhythm of the text which tends to be adapted to the melody and not vice versa. For the Qur'anic text to adapt to a melody denies not only its primacy over any external embellishment, but its very nature and identity, which is characterized in part by its own fixed rhythms. Thus, we read, "The Qur'an, by its nature and style, has a compelling force over minds and souls, and it is a power which absolutely does not require external *mūsīqā*" (al-Sa'īd 1970: 65). And ". . . the voice is beautified in reciting it, and the melody is made excellent, because the Qur'an is the word of God, uncreated, and cannot be embellished by a created voice or a melody extrinsic to it" (al-Sarrāj al-Ṭūsī 1960: 339). Šayx al-Ruzayqī explained that adapting song tunes to recitation is impossible, "because the Qur'an has its own *mūsīqā*, and you cannot clothe the Qur'an in any other *mūsīqā*." Šayx al-Ḥuṣarī makes clear that it is the rhythmic patterns and not the pitch patterns (*maqāmāt*) which distort *tajwīd*, when he says that the study of *mūsīqā* is not necessary to the reciter: ". . . since the rules of *mūsīqā* are different, what use are they? If the reciter learns *mūsīqā* especially, he sins when he recites with the rules of *mūsīqā*. However, if it is there naturally in his voice, it is all right."

The danger of fixed melodies to the durations of syllables in *tajwīd* is very real: it is generally accepted that the parameter in which most mistakes are made in the melodic recitation of the

Qur'an is duration. This was borne out by my own observation: a list I made of mistakes noted by the Reciters' Committee in its evaluations of auditioning reciters and recorded tapes demonstrated that the most common mistake was the lengthening of a syllable beyond its given duration. It is difficult enough to preserve the given textual rhythm while improvising a melodic line. The dangers of losing it altogether to a melodic line which is conceived rhythmically apart from the text are even greater.

The second guideline regulating Qur'anic recitation—namely, that music should arise out of the inspiration of the text—further exploits the distinction made between the "natural" music of the early Arabs and the "mannered" music which appeared with the conquests. A great deal is made of this natural music, for the disapproval of the use of metered, set tunes in recitation is balanced by the recommendation to musical spontaneity in recitation. In practice, the second guideline is interpreted to mean that music in recitation should be improvised in response to the immediacy of the text. Thus, "what is meant by *alḥān* in all these cases [which accept melodic recitation] is tunes which originate from the natural voice of the reciter" (al-Ḥuṣarī, cited in Diyāb 1977: 11).

Ibn Xaldūn describes this "natural" music:

> Many people are gifted to achieve it by nature. They do not need any special instruction or craft for it. . . . Many Qur'an readers belong in this category. In reciting the Qur'an they excel in modulating their voices as if they were the *mizmār*, and they inspire emotion through the beauty of their performance and the harmony of their melodies.
>
> (Ibn Xaldūn n.d.: 425)

"Natural music" is also described as:

> without affectedness or rehearsal or learning, rather it is free and natural, and *taṭrīb* and *talḥīn* come to it naturally in the course of it . . . and souls accept it gladly and find it delightful for its being in harmony with nature and the lack of artifice and craft, for it is innate, not assumed, and this is what our forebears practiced and listened to.[30]
>
> (al-Jawziyyah 1970: 1/169)

Ibn Xaldūn insists on separating the two kinds of music:

> Mālik disapproved of reciting with tunes and al-Šāfiʿī permitted it. Here it is not a question of crafted musical melodies. There can be no difference of opinion about the fact that they are forbidden. The art of singing is something entirely unconnected with the Qurʾan. . . .
>
> The precedence [given to] the correct oral rendering of the Qurʾan [over a melodic rendering] is obvious from [the danger of music] changing the transmitted recitation. Thus melody [*talḥīn*] and correct Qurʾanic recitation can in no way be combined. Rather, what they [the authorities] have in mind is the simple music to which nature guides the naturally musical person.
>
> (Ibn Xaldūn n.d.: 426)

The distinction made between the spontaneous and natural music of the early and pre–Islamic Arabs and the self-conscious and studied art of the later Islamic empire clarifies the otherwise puzzling objection to melodic recitation on the grounds that it is an innovation, given the early association of recitation with the camel songs and tunes of the Arabs.[31] A qualitative distinction is thus made between that "pure" art of the early Arabs and the art contaminated by exposure to an influence of the decadent civilizations conquered by them.

Ideally, the recitation is new every time, with no imitation or memorization.[32] For example, Šayx al-Šaʿšaʿī said that if a reciter recites the same verse the same way every time, "some would call that '*talḥīn*' and that is forbidden. You must not [even] use the same *maqām* for every mention of hell." Šayx Muṣṭafā Ismāʿīl described a performance in Alexandria: "I had been reciting for half an hour—only fifteen lines in half an hour!—and I cadenced on *al-dunyā l-maʿrifah* [*sūrat Luqman*], and everyone went wild and asked for it again, but I could never do it again." It was not a question of his refusing to repeat it; rather, he could not reconstruct what he had spontaneously performed in the throes of inspiration. One fan praised Šayx Muṣṭafā because, although contrary to the ideal, "most reciters memorize the words and tune together and cannot improvise. They would make mistakes if they had to use another melody," but Šayx Muṣṭafā "doesn't remember from time to time what he does" (Ahmad Muṣṭafā Kāmil). In fact, the best reciters are distinguished from their less-skilled colleagues by their constant renewal and development of their material. Some reciters are criticized because they have been "reciting the same thing for twenty years!"

One of the most common risks of the overlapping of singing and music is that "the reciters take from the art of singers and composers and imitate them," and critics point to specific examples, such as the reciter who "took from the art of ʿAbd al-Ḥamūlī [prominent musician, 1843–1901], and would imitate him in all his melody making" (al-Saʿīd 1970: 67–68).

Even adapting a melody from another Qurʾanic recitation is risky, and the use of set melodies and imitation in recitation is disapproved of because they have associations beyond the immediate rendering of the text. Thus we find that another objection to the uses of fixed melody and the recommendation to spontaneous melody is based not only on the possible conflict of Qurʾanic rhythm with melodic rhythm but on the transcendent and fluid nature of the Qurʾan itself. This objection would apply, for example, to the various attempts to compose music for the Qurʾan to ensure its correct and appropriate rendering;[33] such attempts do not impose a rhythm external to the text, but they are not acceptable because they fix and make humanly finite what is divinely infinite. Such a prescriptive, notated musical arrangement would fix the Qurʾan, immutable yet variously manifested, to a single, humanly created expression, precluding the spontaneous expression of its inspiration and reducing the revelation to mere text. The value of an innovative and personal style in Qurʾanic recitation is therefore very much grounded in the perception of the nature of the text, and, although the new and unexpected does, in itself, delight, the aesthetic is not necessarily parallel to the Western aesthetic of creative originality.

Reciters learn the melodic style by listening and by imitating, but it is clear that personal style is valued over imitation, that imitation is considered a learning technique, an initial stage in the professional reciter's education:

> When I came to Cairo, they asked him [a prominent musician] about me, and he said, "There is one thing: it is enough that he

> doesn't imitate. He is himself." The newspapers said the same thing, and I was proud of this testimony. I don't want people to say, "*Allāh*! That's just like Rifʿat!"
>
> (Šayx Muṣṭafā Ismāʿīl)

> What is important to me in reciting is that someone hears me from far way and says, "That's Hāšim Haybah."
>
> (Šayx Hāšim Haybah)

Šayx Ibrāhīm al-Šaʿšāʿī tried out for the Radio in 1957–58, but wasn't accepted: "They told me, 'you imitate your father—don't.' They gave me a year [to develop my own style]."

> The imitator doesn't last long . . . the excellent reciter doesn't imitate. Imitation of melodic cadences is something else.
>
> (Š. ʿAbd al-Bāsiṭ ʿAbd al-Ṣamad)

As indicated in Š. ʿAbd al-Bāsiṭ's statement above, some imitation—or, to be more precise, some quoting or borrowing—is not only acceptable but appreciated, and many reciters do use recognizable elements from each other's styles. These elements are largely the melodic cadence and the *maqām* sequence,[34] but also sectioning of the text and use of register, such as Šayx Rifʿat's slow ascent and descent, or Šayx Muṣṭafā Ismāʿīl's more abrupt changes.

A distinction is made between imitation (*taqlīd*) and influence (*taʾṯīr*). Although Šayx Muṣṭafa Ismāʿīl asserted the uniqueness of his personal style from the beginning, other reciters admit to the influence of models on their personal style. Šayx Aḥmad al-Ruzayqī made the distinction when he referred to his mentor, Šayx Muḥammad Ṣiddīq al-Minšāwī. Their voices are similar, he said, and they used to recite in the same program (they are from the same part of Upper Egypt), but he emphasized that it was not a matter of imitation, but of "inclining the ear toward him." When I asked Šayx Ramaḍān if quoting someone's *qaflah* in the middle of a recitation was *taʾṯīr* (influence) or *taqlīd* (imitation), he answered that imitation is a matter of doing a complete recitation in someone else's style. Thus, the imitation—in the sense of quoting or borrowing—of an *qaflah* here and there, can be, in fact, a feature of influence. Šayx Ramaḍān talks about the influence of Šayx ʿAlī Maḥmūd on his own style, particularly in the movement from *maqām* to *maqām*. This influence is more than a vague inspiration, for

Šayx Ramadān's listeners recognize Šayx ʿAlī Maḥmūd's style in particular phrases of Šayx Ramaḍān's recitations, and these phrases bring the name ʿAlī Maḥmūd to their lips in delight. Šayx Ramaḍān agrees that "it is important not to imitate, but to be oneself." Still, he thinks that "the reciter who is not influenced by previous reciters is not sound [*salīm*]". In addition to his own style, Šayx ʿAlī Hajjāj al-Suwaysī is known for his skillful imitation of (not influence from) Šayx Rifʿat. This is a deliberate and conscious effort to reproduce the sound of this master. Šayx al-Suwaysī says it is a matter of the particular pitches, the *maqāmāt*, and what he calls "the color of the voice." Šayx al-Suwaysī's effort is appreciated by listeners for both the sound and the talent which a successful imitation of this unsurpassed (in the opinion of the majority of listeners) style demonstrates.[35] It is clear that melodic imitation and/or influence ensure continuity and balance originality and that this is extremely important to a tradition based on the immutability of the Qurʾan.

There is, in fact, little evidence in the sources to support the popularly held assumption that religious scholars reject melodic recitation because of the association of music and singing with corrupt practices. In the sources I consulted, I found few instances of rejection of melodic recitation on this basis. Al-Qāriʾ reports that the Ḥanafī scholars do not permit *taġannī*, *tarjīʿ*, and *talḥīn* in reciting or listening to this type of recitation, because all these resemble acts of the dissolute in their corruption (al-Qāriʾ 1948: 22–23). Al-Qurṭubī (1968: 1/29) reports that it is not permitted to recite the Qurʾan with the tunes of *ġināʾ*, for these are like the tunes of corrupt people, the monks and dirge singers (another reference to the *ḥadīṯ* "Recite the Qurʾan in the tunes and songs of the Arabs . . ."). In Naṣr (1930: 18) we read that al-Mālik disapproved of reciting with tunes "because it resembles *ġināʾ*".[36] But in reading such statements it is important to keep in mind that the *ġināʾ* associated with un-Islamic practices is also the sophisticated and mannered *mūsīqā* which distorts the Qurʾanic text. Compare the following statement with the above:

> If no limits are placed on what can be done in recitation it leads to all sorts of excesses, such as trilling and variation of the various rhythms [*īqāʿāt*] and tunes resembling *ġināʾ* as

> those who practice *ġinā'* do with verse lines, and as do many reciters in the cemeteries,[37] and many of the melodic reciters [*qurrā' al-aṣwāt*] who change the Book of God and sing it in the manner of tunes and poetry and *ġinā'*. And they execute the *īqā'āt* on it like *ġinā'* exactly, making bold with God and His Book and playing with the Qur'an . . . and it is known that *taṭrīb* and *talḥīn* are a quick means to this.
>
> (al-Jawziyyah 1970: 1/168–69)

Likewise, the prejudice against the use of musical instruments to accompany recitation is complicated by the fact that improvisation is restricted by a plurality of voices.[38] The corporate recitings of the Qur'an which are part of some Sufi devotions are fixed and unison compositions, but are obviously more related to the speech-bound, participatory style than to the melodic style of professional reciters.

A great deal of discussion is devoted to the proper intent of the reciter's performance, for he may be correct in his *tajwīd*, spontaneous in his melody, yet distract his listeners from the appropriate experience because he is guided by the wrong intent. The proper intent is, briefly, to bring people in touch with the significance of the revelation. It is ultimately this intent which distinguishes Qur'anic recitation from music, however great the overlap in sound, just as it is the intent which ultimately distinguishes the reciter from the singer. Proper intent, then, is the third guideline for correct recitation practice. It is recognized that one of the dangers of using music in reciting the Qur'an lies in the overwhelming power of music over human hearts and minds. If the music does not derive its inspiration from the text itself, that text may become merely an excuse for musical showmanship.

Artistic sensibility and talent are only part of what is required of the reciter, for, unlike the singer, he carries a great responsibility for the effect of his rendition, an effect which goes beyond to the rules governing the oral rendition of the text, and it is recognized that his training in *tajwīd* and his focus on the details of articulation and pronunciation give him an expertise which the singer, who has studied only the rules of music, lacks. It is taken for granted, in fact, that the best singers have been those who were reciters or were exposed to *tajwīd*. The reciter depends on his knowledge of the *maqāmāt*, his skill in modulation, and his sensitivity to their effect to communicate the meaning of the text best, to involve his listeners more totally in the experience, stimulating their interest, understanding, and response. It is the use to which his musical skills are put that makes him a reciter and not a singer. And the ultimate regulator of his performance is the significance of the text.

Reciters are proud of the expertise and responsibility which distinguish them from singers, considering themselves reciters first and artists second (e.g., Šayx ʿAbd al-Bāsiṭ ʿAbd al-Ṣamad). That distinction is clear to those involved in reciting, and that there is confusion on the part of those who only consider the sound and not the intent of recitation, is perhaps best exemplified by an anecdote told by the late Šayx Muṣṭafā Ismāʿīl. Šayx Muṣṭafā is considered by many to have been the most musical and artistic reciter of his time. He remembered that he happened to be staying in the same hotel in Beirut as the famous musician ʿAbd al-Wahhāb. The two got together, and ʿAbd al-Wahhāb handed Šayx Muṣṭafā the *ʿūd* (lute), and, after reciting the first line of the text of a song, said, "Sing!" "I don't know how," said Šayx Muṣṭafā. "Go on," said ʿAbd al-Wahhāb, repeating the line of verse. "I don't know how to sing," said Šayx Muṣṭafā, "I only do Qurʾan." ʿAbd al-Wahhāb took back the *ʿūd* and they sat talking. And ʿAbd al-Mahhāb finally said, "How can you come out with what you do in your reciting and not be aware of what it is?" "I believe in God," said Šayx Muṣṭafā.

Thus, the reciter "must not mix singing with reciting in any old way . . . for the meaning is what drives the reciter spontaneously to the suitable melody" (Xašabah 1975: 12). Šayx al-Ḥuṣarī stated that, as regards melodic recitation, "everything is permitted except for the *taġannī* in which there is abuse, namely, that which follows melody, not meaning, and distances from what is intended in reciting." Likewise, melodic recitation is not forbidden "if there is nothing in the intent of corruption, violation, vanity, or abandonment of the limits" (al-Sarrāj al-Ṭusī 1960: 344). Šayx al-Ḥuṣarī described his own reciting: "I am accustomed not to go in the direction of music which leads to deviation, nor to repeat verses. . . . Those who do otherwise, do it to please people, and they cannot do it without the encouragement of the crowd. They recite for the masses and not for God." The Reciters' Committee (Lajnat al-Qurrāʾ) criticized the pronunciation of a certain reciter (he was making /ü/ out of /ū/) in terms of intent: "He does it for artistic reasons, to please the listener." Šayx al-Ṭablāwī talks about reciters "who take from songs, and people say it is like singing. There is nothing of God in it. The reciter just wants to enchant the crowd." There are also a number of references and criticisms in the literature regarding those reciters who use melodies in their reciting to attract monetary reward.[39]

The propriety or impropriety of a reciter's intent may be gauged by the response of the listeners, and the reciter is held responsible for the effect of his performance. Thus, it is reported that when al-Šāfiʿī recited, people wept and increased their clamor and weeping "because of the beauty of his voice . . . and when he saw this, he would stop reciting" (al-Saʿīd 1967: 315–16). The late Šayx Muṣṭafā Ismāʿīl was criticized by some Muslims in spite of his correct *tajwīd*, because listener response to his reciting was so hysterical. Such a response clearly violates the code of proper response which is set out in the various manuals on recitation behavior (*ādāb al-tilāwah*). As noted above, most professional reciters welcome a certain amount of vocal encouragement and evidence of stimulation, and, to a certain degree, the reciter's reputation is linked to his ability to stir his listeners, but there is no doubt that he must take care that the desire for popularity does not become the main intent of his effort. The successful recitation, the one that fills the listeners with *ḥuzn* and puts them in touch with their mortality, the power and mercy of God, and the beauty and significance of the Qur'an, should not stimulate an uncontrolled ecstasy and vocal hysteria. The most extreme appropriate response is quiet weeping. Shrieks and shouts and fainting only interrupt the desired experience.

To summarize, although certain aspects of the musical art are officially admitted and welcomed into Qurʾanic recitation, and there is, in fact, a confusing overlap between music and recitation, a separation between the art of Qurʾanic recitation and the art of music is carefully maintained, in terms of both regulating the sound and regulating the perception of that sound.

Qurʾanic recitation is considered a unique art. Categorizing recitation as religious music is misleading, for the music that makes use of religious text or is performed in religious contexts shares, in Egypt, all the elements of the secular music, namely, the melodic and rhythmic systems of the *maqāmāt* and the *īqāʿāt*. Qurʾanic recitation, however, draws from the melodic system only.

The uniqueness of the art is also based on the nature of the text itself. Tradition dictates that it be preserved from any change and, at the same time, from the fixity of a precomposed or repeated melody, and that it be the foundation which generates the recitation art. Thus, the reciter should adhere to the rules of *tajwīd*, his use of melody should be spontaneous and improvisatory, and both he and the listener should approach recitation with the proper intent, based on an understanding of the significance of the text. Otherwise, the recitation becomes what one informant termed "mere music," and the reciter, a "mere artist."

Conclusion

The Qur'an is central to Islam, and its immanence in Islamic society is essentially oral. The pervasive sound of recitation becomes basic to Muslims' sense of their culture and religion even before they can articulate that sense, and by listening to Qur'anic recitation they participate in an experience with meaning far beyond the immediate sound or occasion.

The recitation of the Qur'an is more than the enunciation of text and more than the literal fulfillment of a devotional exercise. As defined by generations of religious scholars, the ideal recitation of the Qur'an should involve reciter and listener in the significance of the revelation, intellectually and affectively as well as spiritually, for each moment of recitation evokes the moment of revelation. Thus the sincere participant in recitation often is, and indeed should be, moved to tears by the wonder and beauty of the event, by the awe of God, and by humility in the face of His omnipotence.

Scholars and other authorities not only sanction melodic recitation of the Qur'an, but recognize that the melodic aspect must be present if recitation is to meet the ideal of complete involvement on the part of the listener. This acknowledges the essential power of melody to engage the emotions and heighten the listener's involvement in recitation. The style of recitation that most completely realizes this ideal in terms of stated intent and elicited response is *mujawwad*, the melodic style of public performance. The prestige of this style of recitation and its dissemination throughout the Islamic world have popularized and developed the ideal of Qur'anic recitation as it has been defined by religious and scholarly consensus.

At the same time, acceptance of melodic recitation as representing a justifiable or even a legitimate Islamic ideal has been tempered by the *samāʿ* polemic, a debate concerning the appropriateness of music in an Islamic context. For, in contrast to many other religious systems, the Islamic tradition holds music to be of human origin and organization, and not of divine inspiration. One might speculate as well that it is not so much the un-Islamic associations of music (luxury and vice) that call up objection as it is music's compelling power, which makes it a rival with Islam for human souls. Thus, to the extent of its overlap with the musical arts, the melodic style of Qurʾanic recitation is also subject to questioning and censure. Such criticism is heightened by the association of some aspects of contemporary recitation practice with attitudes perhaps more appropriate to the milieu of professional entertainment than to religious practice—personality cults surrounding superstar reciters, professionalism in the ranks of reciters, and the large fees they command. Furthermore, the tendency of listeners to respond to recitation purely as music, rather than entering into the divine realm of the Qurʾan, is also seen as a risk inherent in melodic recitation.

In fact, Islamic tradition stresses the utter distinctness of Qurʾanic recitation from all forms of music, whether sacred or secular. Inherent in this position is the perception of music as a unified melodic and rhythmic system with its own performance contexts, intents, and expectations on the part of listeners, which are ideally distinct from Qurʾanic recitation. The reciter's use of only some aspects of music—specifically, the melodic system, vocal techniques, and the general musical aesthetic—do not, in this view, make his art music.

It is not enough to say that melodic recitation of the Qurʾan is not music. Such a statement provokes those outside the tradition to such dismissive comments as "it is music—they say it is not, but of course it is," implying that one is dealing with an intellectual ruse, based on convenient labeling that allows Muslims to accept what would otherwise be unacceptable. Given the overlap of music and melodic recitation in terms of sound and context, such a point of view is understandable. However, the perception of melodic recitation as other than music is more than intellectual scrambling by religious scholars faced with the fact of melodic recitation's overwhelming popularity, just as it is more than the desire to disassociate recitation from an art that has often been regarded with suspicion. Due to the absolutely unique nature and identity of the Qur'an itself, the divine source and significance of the text, Islamic culture views its recitation as a separate art, distinct from other arts with which it seemingly overlaps, that is, poetry and music. Thus it must be recognized by those outside the culture that it is the uniqueness of the Qur'an that demands a special classification for its recitation, a classification for which there may be no parallel category in non-Muslim societies.

To define Qur'anic recitation simply as a form of music would undermine this special status of the text, thus making recitation into a purely human endeavor. As we have seen, from the early days of Islam to the present, guidelines and prescriptions have served to concretize and maintain the divine identity of the recitation for reciter and listener alike. The fundamental requirement is, of course, the precise use of *tajwīd*, the system of rules codifying the sound of the revelation itself.

But in spite of these forms of regulation and guidance, actual responses to recitation may become uncontrolled, inappropriate to the occasion, and insulting to the text. The implications of this dynamic are felt in all aspects of both theory and practice of Qur'anic recitation, from formulation of the ideal model to the editing of recordings to the social organization of professional reciters.

The dynamic itself has been generated by a fundamental paradox expressing the balance and separateness of the divine and human spheres—on one hand, the Qur'an is perfect; on the other hand, the Qur'an is enhanced by melody. Egyptians expressed the two truths of the paradox separately to me many times, but no one ever attempted to explain the obvious contradiction, or even noted the paradox. As long as the supremacy of the Qur'an is maintained in performance, one need not confront the role of melody required in the ideal recitation.

But the use of melody in recitation may threaten the balance of the divine and the human spheres, for its abuse may transform the divine character of Qur'anic recitation into mere musical entertainment. Still, it is the abuse of melody, and not its presence per se, that is censured.

This concern for balancing the divine and human spheres is characteristic only of the *majawwad* style of recitation. Such a juxtaposition does not figure in the nonmelodic style of recitation, *murattal*; nor, significantly, is *murattal* considered great art. If we consider that the paradox exists by virtue of not only the separateness but the exclusivity of the divine and human spheres, then perhaps the presence and force of melody are required in spite of the attendant risks to the divine nature of the Qur'an, because melody is the means by which the divine is comprehended. At that point great art happens.

Appendix A. Consultants

PROFESSIONAL RECITERS

Šayx Maḥmūd ʿAbd al-Ḥakam (d. 1982). Born in Karnak in Upper Egypt, he came to Cairo in 1933, having established his reputation in the south. His first intention was to study at al-Azhar, as reciting was secondary to his studies. However, because of his voice, he was encouraged to become a professional reciter. He said it is the Radio which really encourages professionalism: employment by the Radio is important in establishing an audience and a wide reputation. He was with the Radio since 1944. Šayx ʿAbd al-Ḥakam cited Šayx Rifʿat as the major influence on his reciting, although he also listened to Šayx ʿAlī Maḥmūd, Šayx al-Šaʿšāʿī, and others not known generally in Cairo. He never studied music, but considered music beneficial to recitation. Šayx ʿAbd al-Ḥakam is admired for the dignity and correctness of his reciting as well as a subdued but fluent musicality.

Šayx ʿAbd al-Bāsiṭ ʿAbd al-Ṣamad (b. 1927). He came to Cairo from the city of Armant in Upper Egypt in 1950, having established his reputation in the south. He is the first reciter in his family, but his grandfather was a religious scholar of al-Azhar training. Šayx ʿAbd al-Bāsiṭ is probably the best-known of Egyptian reciters outside of Egypt, as he was the first to make commercial recordings of his reciting, and he has traveled extensively outside of Egypt. Among his recordings are the complete text of the Qurʾan in both styles, *murattal* and *mujawwad*. Šayx ʿAbd al-Bāsiṭ is one of the four top-ranking reciters in Egypt. He was the first president of the newly formed Reciters' Union (see chapter 6). Šayx ʿAbd al-Bāsiṭ is admired for breath control and his high, clear (*ḥarīmī*) voice.

Šayx Kāmil Yūsuf al-Bahtīmī (d. 1969 at the age of about forty-seven). He was a protégé of Šayx Muḥammad Salāmah, and it is said that the influence of his mentor shows in his high registers and melodic cadences. The influence of Šayx Rifʿat shows in the lower registers. Šayx Kāmil studied music with the well-known *qānūn* (type of zither) player Aḥmad Ṣabrā. He is especially admired for the quality of his voice; he is one of the few reciters whose voice is equally clear, strong, and relaxed in both the high and low registers. It is also said that he is one of the few reciters whose studio recordings are as effective as the live performance recordings.

Šayx Hāšim Haybah (b. ca. 1920). He is from a village north of Cairo, near Benha. His father was the owner of a rug factory. Šayx Hāšim says that he always wanted to be a reciter. He memorized the Qur'an and learned the *qirā'āt*. In those days (1927–34) there was no recitation on the Radio, so he learned the art by listening to reciters in person. He also learned his music by listening. He journeyed to Cairo to hear Šayx ʿAlī Maḥmūd recite, and stayed, listening to Šayx Muḥammad Rifʿat and Šayx Muḥammad Salāmah. He joined the Radio in 1951. Šayx Hāšim has also established himself as a singer of religious songs. His voice is light and high, and fluent with ornamentation.

Šayx Maḥmūd Xalīl al-Ḥuṣarī (d. 1980). He was born near Ṭanṭa (north of Cairo). When he was twenty-five years of age he went to Ṭanṭa and established himself as a reciter. He was the reciter at the well-known Aḥmadī mosque there. Ten years later he moved to Cairo, joined the Radio in 1944, and became the reciter at the Ḥusayn mosque in 1955. In Cairo Šayx al-Ḥuṣarī also studied at al-Azhar University: he was a well-known religious scholar and author of many books on various aspects of the Qur'an. He was also involved in the recent Azhari printing of the Qur'anic text. His status as reciter was somewhat official: he held the title *šayx al-maqāri'*, and his opinions were frequently solicited and quoted by the media. He also accompanied the rector of al-Azhar on his travels and was invited to participate in the World of Islam festival in London (1976). Šayx al-Ḥuṣarī's recordings are widely distributed outside Egypt. As one of the four top-ranking reciters in Egypt, he recorded the complete Qur'anic text in both styles of recitation, *murattal* and *mujawwad* and was the first to record and broadcast the *murattal* style (see chapter 5). Šayx al-Ḥuṣarī is known for the correctness of his recitation. His son also recites professionally.

Šayx Muṣṭafā Ismāʿīl (1905–1978). Born in Mīt Ghazāl, a village near Ṭanṭa (north of Cairo), Šayx Muṣṭafā learned the Qur'an, and at about the age of fifteen or sixteen he went to study at the Azhari institute in Ṭanṭa. He studied the Qur'anic sciences and planned to continue his studies at al-Azhar University in Cairo, but was encouraged to become a reciter. He began to establish his reputation in the Delta in the 1930s. Šayx Muṣṭafā first went to Cairo in response to an invitation to recite. He soon established his reputation in Cairo and was invited to recite for King Farouk during Ramadan, 1944. He joined the Radio soon after, having negotiated for longer recordings, as his voice needed a minimum of time to warm up. Šayx Muṣṭafā admired the reciting of Šayx Muḥammad Rifʿat and Šayx ʿAbd al-Fattāḥ al-Šaʿšāʿī but was proud of his own unique style. He did not study music formally, but mastered the art by listening, and from his associations with the best musicians of his day. Šayx Muṣṭafā traveled extensively and was known abroad from his personal appearances. Although as a top-ranking reciter he recorded the complete text of the Qur'an in both the *murattal* and *mujawwad* styles, his recordings are not generally available outside Egypt. Šayx Muṣṭafā was the official reciter of Anwār al-Sadāt and traveled with him to Jerusalem in 1978. Šayx Muṣṭafā is considered one of the most effective reciters of this century, extremely innovative musically, yet correct in *tajwīd*. One can count a generation of younger reciters among his imitators. At the time of his death, Šayx Muṣṭafā was reciter at the prestigious al-Azhar mosque.

Šayx Muḥammad Ṣiddīq al-Minšāwī (d. early 1970s?). He is of the same generation as Šayx Kāmil Yūsuf al-Bahtīmī, and, in fact, he was also a protégé of Šayx Muḥammad Salāmah. His father was also a well-known reciter, and his brother, Šayx Maḥmūd al-Minšāwī, has now established himself as a respected professional reciter in Cairo. Šayx al-Minšāwī was born in Upper Egypt and established himself as a reciter there before coming to Cairo. He is especially admired for the spirituality, gravity, and dignity of his style.

Šayx ʿAlī Maḥmūd (1878–1949). Also admired for his singing (he made a number of commercial recordings), Šayx ʿAlī Maḥmūd is one of the models for musical reciting. It is said that he would render the call to prayer from the Ḥusayn mosque with a different *maqām* for each day of the week. A number of reciters, such as Šayx Muḥammad Salāmah, and Šayx Maḥmūd Muḥammad Ramaḍān, show and acknowledge his influence on their own style of recitation. His style is characterized by the melodic cadences and a density of modulations.

Šayx Fatḥī Qandīl. He grew up in rural Egypt, where he was taught the Qur'an by his father. He studied at the Azhari institute in Ṭanṭa, then at al-Azhar University in Cairo, where he earned an advanced degree in Qur'anic sciences. He teaches *tajwīd* and *qirā'āt* at the Institute of Qira'at in Šubrā. Šayx Fatḥī began reciting for the Radio in 1970. He studied music at the Music Institute in Cairo.

Šayx Maḥmūd Muḥammad Ramaḍān. Šayx Ramaḍān was born (ca. 1929) in the same *baladi* area of Cairo in which he still lives. His father was a cloth merchant. He learned the Qur'an in the *kuttāb*, the traditional primary school, and continued his studies with a Šayx, from whom he also learned *tajwīd*. He learned music by listening and studying with private tutors, among them the prominent *qanūn* player Aḥmad Ṣabrā. Šayx Ramaḍān joined the ranks of Radio reciters in 1972. He is highly respected for his musicality, and he acknowledges the influence of a number of reciters on his style. He is considered to be of the "school" of Šayx ʿAlī Maḥmūd.

Šayx Muḥammad Rifʿat (1882–1950). His father was a merchant. Šayx Rifʿat is unanimously considered the best reciter of this century. He is admired for his musicality, his mastery and understanding of the art of recitation in all of its aspects, his spirituality and uprightness, and his right intent. Šayx Rifʿat was the first reciter to broadcast his recitation (1934), and his voice and style, as well as his general character, have been a model of the ideal reciter to generations of Egyptians and others ever since. Music critic and composer Suleiman Gamil specifies aspects of Šayx Rifʿat's style such as the unpredictability of the melodic line and the resonance of his voice. Others point to his mastery in correlating melody to meaning (*taṣwīr al-maʿnā*). In addition to recordings made by the Radio, there exist a great number of recordings made by Zakariyyā Muḥrān Bāšā and Muḥammad Xamīs which his son, Mr. Ḥusayn Rifʿat, is dedicated to making available to the public.

Šayx Muḥammad Salāmah (ca. 1888/1900–1982). Šayx Salāmah was a student at al-Azhar University, and at the age of nineteen was encouraged to become a reciter. He had already been reciting since the age of ten. Šayx Salāmah fought in the Saʿdist rebellion against the British in 1919 and proudly acknowledged his role in that. He is the only prominent reciter who refused to record for the Radio, one of the reasons being the latter's failure to comply with certain conditions set by him, such as not having the Qur'an broadcast into the streets and taverns and not having the female announcer present in the same room while he was recording. He participated in a conference of reciters in 1937 which resulted in the establishment of a Reciters' Association. The issue at stake was that some reciters were afraid that broadcasting recitation would harm the less prominent reciters, as their services would be less in demand. Šayx Salāmah was both extremely articulate and sincere about his faith. In performance he was restrained in his gestures, ignoring the admiring comments, even turning away from those who came up to kiss his hand or compliment him. Only in the high registers did he seem to me to interact with his listeners. When another reciter was performing, Šayx Salāmah would listen with eyes closed and head bowed. He was the acknowledged mentor of Šayx Kāmil Yūsuf al-Bahtīmī and Šayx Muḥammad Ṣiddīq al-Minšāwī, both of whom lived in his house for a period of time. Some speak of the "school" of Šayx Muḥammad Salāmah as being in a direct line from the style of Šayx ʿAlī Maḥmūd. Šayx Salāmah studied music with Šayx Darwīš al-Ḥarīrī, teacher of several prominent musicians and reciters, such as Šayx ʿAlī Maḥmūd, Šayx Sayyid Darwiš, and Šayx Zakariyyā Aḥmad. He used to sing and play the *ʿūd* until the death of his wife. Šayx Salāmah is considered to be second only to Šayx Rifʿat in correlating melody to meaning (*taṣwīr al-maʿnā*).

Šayx Aḥmad al-Ruzayqī (b. ca. 1939). One of the younger generation of reciters, he grew up in Upper Egypt in the same area as Šayx ʿAbd al-Bāsiṭ ʿAbd al-Ṣamad, and Šayx Muḥammad Ṣiddīq al-Minšāwī. Šayx Aḥmad was encouraged to become a reciter because of his beautiful voice. He recited in public at Qina, and at the age of twenty entered the Music Institute to study the art of Arabic music. He also learned from listening to Šayx Rifʿat, Šayx Muṣṭafā Ismāʿīl, and Šayx ʿAbd al-Bāsiṭ ʿAbd al-Ṣamad, but considers Šayx Muḥammad Ṣiddīq al-Minšāwī his mentor because they have similar deep voices and voice quality, are from the same area, and used to recite on the same program. Šayx Aḥmad sings and plays the *ʿūd* as well. He is president of the Reciters' Union.

Šayx Ibrāhīm al-Šaʿšāʿī (b. 1930, Cairo). He is the son of another prominent reciter, Šayx ʿAbd al-Fattāh al-Šaʿšāʿī. His grandfather was also a reciter, and now his son is beginning Qurʾanic studies. He memorized the Qurʾan, learned *tajwīd* and *qirāʾāt* in school with Šayx ʿĀmir ʿUṯmān (see below), and received a degree from the Azhari institute. He then studied for three years with Šayx Darwīš al-Ḥarīrī, a famous musician and teacher. He did not begin to recite in public until 1954–55. Šayx Ibrāhīm joined the Radio in 1968. He holds the position of reciter at the Sayyidah Zaynab mosque, a post held by his father before him. He acknowledges the influence of his father's style on his own and says that his father was influenced by Šayx Aḥmad Nadā, a reciter of the generation before Šayx Rifʿat. Šayx Ibrāhīm is admired for his deep, rich voice, his renderings of *qirā'at Warš*, his knowledge of pause and beginning (see chapter 2), and the general dignity and gravity of his recitation.

Šayx ʿAlī Ḥajjāj al-Suwaysī (b. 1926). His father was chief clerk at the Islamic court in Cairo. He studied Qur'an with Šayx Abū ʿAzīz al-Saḥḥār, a prominent Azhari scholar and father of Šayx Saʿīd al-Saḥḥār (see Acknowledgments). Šayx ʿAlī Ḥajjāj al-Suwaysī began reciting in public at an early age: he remembers reciting for a group of Yemenis at a conference when he was only seven or eight years of age. Šayx ʿAlī joined the Radio in 1946–47 and entered the Music Institute to study *ʿūd* and music theory for four years when he saw the encouragement and success of his reciting. He used to sing a great deal, but now he just recites. He impresses one with how much he enjoys reciting. Šayx ʿAlī is admired for his use of *maqām ṣaba*—his voice is considered especially suited to *ṣaba*—and for his imitation of Šayx Muḥammad Rifʿat.

Šayx Muḥammad Maḥmūd al-Ṭablāwī (b. 1936 near Cairo in Mīt ʿUqba). He studied the Qur'an in the traditional school, the *kuttāb*, and was singled out for his voice and encouraged to become a professional reciter. He learned music by listening and cites Šayx Maḥmūd ʿAlī l-Bannā, Šayx al-Bahtīmī, and Šayx Abū l-ʿAynayn al-Šaʿīšah as reciters he particularly admires. Šayx al-Ṭablāwī was the first to record on cassette tape, and his recordings are widely distributed and extremely popular in Egypt, both in Cairo and in the countryside. People attribute his popularity to his impressive breath control and the "freshness" of his voice. Šayx Muḥammad al-Ṭablāwī succeeded Šayx Muṣṭafā Ismāʿīl as reciter at the al-Azhar mosque.

SCHOLARS AND TEACHERS

Šayx ʿAbd al-Mutaʿāl Manṣūr ʿArafah. Šayx ʿAbd al-Mutaʿāl graduated from the Institute of Qirā'āt in Šubrā, became a teacher there, and, at the time I studied with him, held the position of dean of the Institute. He is presently assistant to the general director of the General Administration of Qur'anic Affairs at al-Azhar. Šayx ʿAbd al-Mutaʿal presents a daily radio lesson on the rules of *tajwīd, Al-Raḥmān ʿAllama l-Qur'an*, in conjunction with Šayx Rizq Ḥabbah (see Acknowledgments). He also participated in preparing the most recent Azhari publication of the Qur'anic text. As my teacher he was extremely organized, patient, and encouraging.

Šayx ʿĀmir al-Saʿīd ʿUtmān. One of the prominent scholars and teachers in Cairo, he has taught *tajwīd* and *qirā'āt* to many of the leading professional reciters. An expert in these sciences, he teaches three of the public recitation classes with humor, asperity, patience, and an amazing command of the material. Šayx ʿĀmir also serves on a number of panels which evaluate reciters' performances, such as the auditions for the Friday prayer reciters, the International Recitation Competition in Malaysia, and so forth. He holds the title and position of *wakīl* (deputy) *Šayx al-maqāriʾ*.

Appendix B. The Seven *Aḥruf* and the *Qirāʾāt*

The *qirāʾāt* (lit., recitings or readings) denote variant readings of single words, phrases, or passages of the Qurʾanic text. The Arabic works on the *qirāʾāt* most commonly in use in the Azhari institutions in Egypt are Ibn al-Jazarī's *Al-Durrah al-Muḍiyyah fī l-Qirāʾāt al-Ṯalāṯ al-Mutammimah li l-ʿAšar*, known as *Al-Durrah*; Abū Qāsim al-Šāṭibī's *Ḥaraz al-Amānī wa Wajh al-Tahānī*, known as *Al-Šāṭibiyyah*; and their various commentaries, among them Ibn al-Qāṣih's *Sirāj al-Qāriʾ al-Mubtadā wa Taḏkār al-Muqriʾ al-Muntahā*; ʿAbd al-Fattāḥ al-Qāḍi's *Al-Wāfī fī Šarḥ al-Šāṭibiyyah fī l-Qirāʾāt al-Sabʿ*; al-Ḍabbāʿ's *Al-Adāʾah fī Bayān Uṣūl al-Qirāʾah*. Ibn Jinnī's *Al-Muḥtasab* treats the uncanonical *qirāʾāt* (*al-qirāʾāt al-šāḏḏah*).[1] For a general introduction to the *qirāʾāt*, I refer the reader to Weiss, Berger, and Rauf (1975: chapters 1–4 and 7) and Paret (1979: 127–29). The following material is not so comprehensively treated in Western-language works.

In Islamic tradition, the basis of Qurʾanic text variation is traced back to a number of *ḥadīṯ* concerning the revelation of the Qurʾan in seven *aḥruf* (singular *ḥarf*). Some examples of these *ḥadīṯ* follow.

> [from Ibn ʿAbbās] Gabriel recited to me one *ḥarf*, whereupon I repeated it and I asked for more and he gave me more until it reached seven *aḥruf*.

> [from Abī ibn Kaʿb] The Prophet was at the pool of the Banī Ġafar and Gabriel came to him and said, "Verily God commands that you recite the Qurʾan to your community in a single *ḥarf*." And he said, "I ask God's forgiveness, but that is not possible for my community"; whereupon he came to him a

> second time and said, "Verily God commands that you recite to your community in two *ḥarfs* [Muhammad repeats his reply, and each time Gabriel comes back with permission to recite another *ḥarf* until the number reaches seven].
>
> [from Abī ibn Kaʿb] The Prophet encountered Gabriel and said, "Oh Gabriel, verily I have called to my community illiterates, among them the weak, the aged, the youth, the slave woman, and the man who has never read a book." He said, "Oh Muhammad, verily the Qur'an was revealed in seven *aḥruf*."
>
> [from Abī ibn Kaʿb] I was in the mosque when a man came in to pray and he recited a reading that seemed unacceptable to me. Then another man came in and he was reciting the same way. And when prayers were over we went into the Prophet and I said, "Verily this man recited what I must deny, and another came in and recited the same way." The Prophet commanded them to recite and they did. And the Prophet deemed their reciting good, and . . . said to me, "Oh, Abī, I was told to recite the Qur'an in a single *ḥarf*, and I asked that he make it easy for my community, and he replied, 'Recite it in two *ḥarfs*,' and I asked that he make it easy for my community, and he replied, 'Recite it in three *aḥruf*,' and I asked that he make it easy for my community, and he replied the third time, 'Recite it in seven *aḥruf*.' "[2]

The definition of the term *aḥruf* has been the subject of much scholarly discussion and is included in general works on the Qur'an. Al-Qurṭubī says there are thirty-five different opinions regarding the definition, and he mentions five of them (al-Qurṭubī 1968: 1/42ff.). Among the most commonly accepted interpretations are the following. 1. The *aḥruf* are the dialects of all the Arabic tribes. The Qur'anic verse "Verily we have made it an Arabic Qur'an" (Qur. 43/3; i.e., not just a *Qurayšī* Qur'an) is cited to support this view. 2. The *aḥruf* are the seven aspects in which the reciting of the Qur'an differs. These aspects govern differences in noun gender and number, verbal tense and mood, inflection, adding or dropping of words, differences in word order, substitution, and what are called dialectal differences, such as the pronunciation of /ā/, assimilation, and pharyngealization.

Whatever the precise definition of *aḥruf*, all of the *ḥadīṯ* on the subject indicate the following principles: all variants are of equal status in terms of their truth and rightness and all variation is the word of God as revealed to Muhammad, with no human intervention involved. The principal justification given for the existence of the seven *aḥruf* was to make it easy for speakers of different dialects and abilities to understand and learn the Qur'an.

The relationship of the canonical variant readings, the *qirā'āt*, to the *aḥruf* is also the subject of much discussion in Islamic works, and there are differing opinions. However, most scholars agree that the seven *aḥruf* do not refer to the seven canonical readings, although they are the basis for them. The *qirā'āt* are drawn from the phonetic material of the *aḥruf*, and identified with particular reciters whose readings became well known and widely transmitted. The readings that can be secondarily traced to the reciter are called the *riwāyāt*. Thus the prevailing reading in Egypt is called *ḥafṣ ʿan ʿĀṣim*, or the *riwāyah* of *Hafṣ*, as it comes from the *qirā'ah* of ʿAṣim. In addition, from each *riwāyah* are derived several *ṭuruq*, from which are derived further *ṭuruq*. The number of actual variants, therefore, exceeds the seven of the *qirā'āt*.[3]

The main criteria of canonical acceptability for the *qirā'āt* are that the reading be based on the ʿUṯmanī text, that it be consonant with the rules of the Arabic language, and that it demonstrate a verifiable chain of transmission.

Notes

Introduction

1. See Eickelman 1978: 485–516.

2. Lois al-Faruqi is an exception in that she correlates prosody and melody in recitation (1978), as well as elucidating some of the terminology and attitudes surrounding Qur'anic recitation (1979).

3. Although many scholars do refer to the special quality of the Qur'an, few have followed up its concrete implications. William Graham (1982), for example, focuses on the oral aspect of the Qur'an, but the discussion is in terms of textual rather than contextual meaning. Richard Martin is one scholar engaged in such an enterprise. He proposes that "the Qur'anic text in both its literary and oral forms constitutes a speech act situation involving a speaker and addressee(s), and that we must attempt to discover the rules that govern the various cultural contexts in which such communication takes place" (1982: 364).

4. I refer to a recitation tradition which is exclusively male. Although this study deals with Qur'anic recitation in general in Egypt, the focus is on the tradition of professional male reciters which is known and imitated all over the Islamic world as characteristically Egyptian. The professional female reciter participates in another tradition, in which musicality is largely unconscious and in which artistry does not figure in the expectations of her female audience (and which men dismiss as "having no art"). Thus, the presence of the audience can be attributed more to the particular occasion than to her particular talent as a reciter. There is little interaction between listeners and reciter, and her intent more closely resembles the devotional intent of a more private recitation context. In fact, in keeping with traditional Muslim ideals the professional female reciter is in no sense a public figure. She is neither broadcast over the media nor featured as a personality, nor is she recorded by the public or by commercial companies. Although some women were known for their recitation and were broadcast to the general public in the 1930s and 1940s, they were also known as singers (the most famous being Umm Kalṯūm). One explanation given me for stopping the practice of broadcasting women reciters is that

"a woman's voice makes one think of things other than Allah." However, in Indonesia and Malaysia, where Qur'anic recitation has been greatly influenced by the Egyptian male tradition, women reciters do become public figures.

5. *Ṣalāt* is usually translated as "ritual prayer." Perhaps a more informative term would be "worship-liturgy." See Wensinck 1961: 493–95, for a comprehensive description of the verbal and gestural material of the *ṣalāt*.

6. *Murattal* is also used to render a specific Qur'anic text which has the force of invocation or prayer by virtue of its traditional use. Such usage includes binding a wedding contract, concluding a public performance of recitation, blessing a newborn baby, and so forth. Some of these involve corporate recitation, for which the *murattal* style is more suitable.

7. The Institute is one of many in Egypt affiliated with al-Azhar University (founded in 962 A.D.). It provides training for religious scholars and teachers as well as offering a more general religious education to secondary school boys. Many professional reciters have studied at these institutes.

8. The *maqām* principle comprises the melodic system of Arabic music. A *maqām* is not a scale so much as a group of pitches which manifest characteristic melodic patterns and some hierarchy of pitch organization. There may be some association of specific *maqāmāt* with moods or even astrological signs, but these connections are no longer strongly present for most listeners or performers.

9. To the rites-of-passage and ceremonial types of ritual Gilsenan (1973: 182) adds the liturgical. The fourth context of recitation I have in mind fits none of these categories; in fact, I would hesitate to give it the status of ritual. Its organizing principle is not so much an order of events, a code of behavior, but rather the recognition of the independent status of Qur'anic recitation as an art form.

10. The men sit in the presence of the reciter while the women are out of sight, in an adjoining building, in a special annex, or in the far corner of the tent. This is true of all public recitations, whatever the occasion.

1. The Text: The Qur'an

1. It is generally held that either this or the following, "Oh thou wrapped in a mantle, arise and warn" (*yā ayyuha l-muḍaṭṭir qum fa nḍir*, Qur. 74/1–2), is the first of the revelations. English interpretations of the Qur'an are drawn, with slight modifications, from the edition of 'Abdullah Yūsuf 'Abdullah Yūsuf 'Alī (1946).

2. See Appendix B for accounts of this and interpretations of the term *aḥruf*.

3. Readers unfamiliar with Arabic many be confused by the interchange of the terms "reading" and "reciting" with regard to the Qur'an. Both translate the verb *qara'a* and its derivatives, and the term "reading" should be understood here as an oral rendering of the written text.

4. For example, *raḥmat* for both *raḥmah* and *raḥmāt*

5. See Labīb al-Saʿīd's statement justifying his project to record all the Qur'an in the *murattal* style, to make a standard and authoritative oral equivalent of the ʿUṯmānī text: "Only through oral tradition can the Qur'an's essential character as something recited, something orally delivered, be preserved" (Weiss, Berger, and Rauf 1975: 56).

6. Since most of the material in these pages is covered comprehensively elsewhere, I do not think it is necessary to duplicate it in detail. I have, therefore, presented only the minimum description to serve as a basis for conveying something of the effect of the sound of the Qur'anic text. I refer the reader to Blachère 1959; Naṣr 1966; and Watt 1970.

7. Or what Adūnīs, in *al-Ṯābit wa l-Mutaḥawwil* (1974) calls "stasis."

8. In Ṣaqr (1976: 19) we read: "And in that regard some who have memorized the Qur'an say, 'Were it not for the *mutašābihāt* in the Qur'an youths would sing it,' i.e., it would certainly be the easiest of things to memorize." Šayx Muḥammad al-Ṭablāwī quoted the following variant: "Were it not for the *mutašābihāt* even girls could memorize it" (*law lā l-mutašābihāt lataḥfaḏuhā l-banāt*). The study of the *mutašabihāt* in the Qur'anic disciplines concerns, properly speaking, identification and elucidation of the more obscure passages.

9. I discuss the latter in chapter 2. There are many elements in the phonetic system of Qur'anic Arabic which set it apart from any known spoken Arabic, just as there are orthographic conventions which set Qur'anic Arabic apart from the written language. But whereas the orthographic conventions may represent a stage in the development of the writing system or an attempt to accommodate certain variations in the text, the phonetic system is considered to be the sound of God's utterance.

10. Al-Saʿīd (1967: 324) and Salīm (1939: 245). For a comprehensive list of these elements, see al-Suyūṭī (1910: 1/83–105) and various *iʿjāz* works.

11. This system of quantitative syllabic notation can be employed here and in the following examples as the durations of long and short vowels correspond fairly consistently to a 2:1 (-:⏑) ratio. However, this is not always the case. See the section on durations (*madd*) in chapter 2.

12. See al-Saʿīd (1967: 324–25) and al-Suyūṭī (1910: 1/96–105) for a list of some of these lines.

2. *Tajwīd*

1. Thus, in Islam, there can be no history of the development of *tajwīd*, except in terms of its scholarly codification. Mūsā b. ʿUbayd Allāhibn Xaqān al-Baġdādī (d. 936 A.D.) is credited as the first to write down the science of *tajwīd* (al-Daʿʿās 1964: 9).

2. For a discussion of the term *tartīl*, and further references to its association with *tajwīd*, see chapter 4.

3. Pretzl (1933–34) deals with *tajwīd* as it is treated in a specific text and gives further references to other texts. Boubakeur (1968) conveys the

material of *tajwīd* briefly and concisely, but also relies on translations of the Arabic terms.

4. I should perhaps make it clear that I do not question Semaan's right to investigate the raison d'être of *tajwīd*, and to pursue its historical development. But I believe a valid treatment of *tajwīd* must take into account its attributed significance or else miss the point, because that significance is what ultimately and dynamically shapes both attitude and sound. Moreover, even in references of more "phonetic interest" to the author, he seems content to transfer definitions from the Arabic without further explanation—for example, *qalqalah* (see my definition, above) is produced "with 'strong' sound" (p. 66). It is significant that ben Cheneb and Semaan cite the same classic *tajwīd* works in their bibliographies: I suspect that neither has knowledge of its practical application to sound.

5. Cantineau (Cantineau and Barbès, 1942–47) introduces his article as follows: "Si les règles théoriques de la lecture coranique sont maintenant assez bien connues, grace à l'examen de divers traités de tajwid et à l'étude des principes qui en découlent . . . la façon dont ces règles sont appliquées dans la pratique, ainsi que le rhythme et la psalmodie qui accompagnent la récitation coranique ont été jusqu'ici assez négligées" (p. 66).

6. The ordering of the phonemes is the same as that of Sibawayhī; however it differs from Xalīl ibn Aḥmad's phonetic ordering of lexemes in his *Kitāb al-ʿAyn* in that the glottal stop, and not the *ʿayn*, is given the most anterior position.

7. Further application of *tajwīd* to recitation can be found in chapter 5.

8. A phrase transcribed in terms of nasality and durations would look like this:

1. *la ʾil lam ṯa(n) taẖu laṉarjumannakum wala*
yamassannakum minnā ʿaḏābun ʿalīm (Qur. 36/38)
2. *yā ʾayyuha llaḏīna ʾāmanū lā yasxạṛ*
qawmum̱ mi(n) qawmin ʿasā ʾay yakūna
xạyṛạm minhum wa lā nisāʾum min nisāʾin
ʿasā ʾay yakunna xạyṛạm minhunn (Qur. 49/11)

9. See transcriptions of Bergsträsser (1932–33: 114), *waqad-jaaʾa-hum* instead of *wa qadə* (p. 40); *falaʾ uqsimubilhunnas* instead of *falaʾuqə simu*; *bimağnun* instead of *bimagənun*; and so forth; and Cantineau (Cantineau and Barbès 1942–47: 95), *burug, hariq, tağrī* instead of *burūqə, harīqə*, and *tagərī*, and so forth.

I have not heard the recitation which is described in the Bergsträsser article, so I cannot say with certainty that the reciter did in fact execute a *qalqalah* which does not show up in the transcription. However, the melodic line seemed to indicate two syllables where only one is noted, and it seems a good example of how *tajwīd* can affect the melodic line:

wa la qad(ə) nağ ğay nā (p. 118)
wal la ḍī na mi(n) qab(ə) li him (p. 119)

10. Durations are fixed only in relation to one another. Thus a one-beat

syllable takes half the time of a two-beat syllable. The tempo varies according to the style of recitation (*mujawwad* is slower) and the individual reciter.

11. These are listed in al-Ḥuṣarī (1967: 16ff.).

12. The signs in the written text which guide the reader according to the rules of pause, extension, elision, and so forth, are by no means a complete notation system for recitation. These presume a thorough knowledge of the rules and serve only as a reminder.

13. See al-Ušmūnī (1889: 1/6) and al-Ḥuṣarī (1967: 11) for examples of the pause which clarifies and/or affects meaning. See chapter 7 for a discussion of how the reciter uses pause to enhance the dramatic effect of the text.

3. The *Samāʿ* Polemic

1. The earliest recordings date only from the 1930s.

2. The *Ḥadīṯ* are, briefly, words of God uttered by the Prophet Muhammad and not part of the Qurʾan, Muhammad's own statements, and others' observations of the Prophet's behavior. This body of material specifies or elaborates on the material of the Qurʾan. The common English translation is "tradition."

3. This disapproval was strong enough and widespread enough that al-Hujwīrī, in the eleventh century, could state: "Their chief argument for the objectionableness of music is the fact that the Muslim community, both now and in past times, is generally agreed in regarding it [*samāʿ*] with disapproval" (al-Hujwīrī/Nicholson 1976: 411).

4. The thesis is by Suhayr ʿAbd al-ʿAḏim Muḥammad. The magazine *al-Iḏāʿah wa l-Tilifizyūn* includes the weekly media programming and has wide circulation. The anonymous report appeared in the June 17, 1978, issue of the magazine (46–47).

5. Anonymous: *al-Kawākib*, 1613, June 29, 1982, and Ġunaym ʿAbduh, *al-Kawākib*, 1614, July 7, 1982.

6. In Buṭrus 1968: 97–105. I have translated the terms *mūsīqā* and *ġinaʾ* together as "music." *Mūsīqā* denotes either theoretical music or instrumental music, as opposed to *ġināʾ*, which denotes either practical music or singing.

7. In Taymūr 1963: 12–20.

8. Because the debate cannot be finally resolved, the status of music has varied throughout the Islamic world. That it thus tends to respond to the ideology of a regime, as well as social, economic, and political factors, may be illustrated by comparing its status in Iran under the shah, when it flourished, to its status after the revolution, when some music traditions were banned and others officially restricted.

9. The authoritative sources are elsewhere (Roychoudhury 1957) classified as Qurʾan, *Ḥadīṯ*, the four orthodox Caliphs, Companions of the

Prophet, Jurisprudence (*Fiqh*), and Legal pronouncements [*Fatāwā*] of the religious scholars.

10. Those committed to music as art—that is, professional musicians—have not, in general, participated in the polemic. Certainly aware of the disapproval directed toward them, and certainly able to articulate their position, they seem to have been supremely confident of the effect of their talents and felt under no obligation to justify themselves. The following story is told of a singer who lived in the early days of Islam (ca. 634–726):

> Ibn Surayj was sitting, and Ata' and Ibn Jurayj passed by. He swore by divorce that he would sing to them on the condition that if they forbade him to sing after having listened to him he would forsake it [singing]. So they agreed, and he sang to them. . . . and Ibn Jurayj swooned, and Ata' got up and danced.
>
> (al-Isfahānī 1927: 1/31)

11. It is the same tradition carried on by the Sufis, and in fact, many attribute the development and preservation of this music up to modern times to its importance in Sufi ritual, pointing to the number of master musicians who learned their art in the Sufi context (see El Mahdī 1972). See also Naṣr 1971: 171–79. Naṣr says: "The traditional music of Persia with its gnostic and Sufi character must be preserved in all of its authenticity. . . . Obviously the best way to preserve this music is to protect and maintain the Sufi tradition which has brought it into existence" (Naṣr 1971: 178).

12. This multivolume work is a celebration of Arabic musical and poetical life from pre-Islamic times up to the tenth century and is a major source for the history of Arabic music. The book contains biographical information on poets and singers, samples of the texts they rendered, and modal and rhythmic indications of actual performance practice (unfortunately, not recoverable). References in this work are to the edition published by Dār al-Kutub al-Miṣriyyah, Cairo (vols. 1–16). These volumes date from 1927 (vol. 1) to 1967 (vol. 16). The publishing of this edition was continued by al-Hay'ah al-Miṣriyyah al-ʿĀmmah li l-Ta'līf wa l-Našr, Cairo (vols. 17–23). This publishing house changed its name to al-Hay'ah al-Miṣriyyah li l-Kitāb, which name appears on volumes 18–23. These volumes date from 1970 (vol. 18) to 1974 (vol. 23). Volumes 2–23 are collocated with the Bulāq edition of this work.

13. For example, al-Isfahānī (1927–74: 9/293) reports that Caliph al-Wāṭiq bi-Allāh composed some 100 songs, and he gives the texts and performance indications of some of these.

14. The four Islamic schools of law (Šāfiʿī, Māliki, Ḥanafī, and Ḥanbalī), while not proscribing music directly, made their disapproval of it evident by proscribing the use of certain instruments, the testimony of musicians in court, and so forth. At the same time, there are a number of stories in the *samāʿ* literature which testify to an enjoyment of music on the part of the founders of these schools.

15. Farmer (1973: 34) defines the *šāhīn* as a fife and refers to "its plaintive sound." Elsewhere, he classifies it as a member of the woodwind family (1973: 210). I do not know what his sources for these definitions are and have not been able to find a definition in any Arabic works.

16. Farmer 1965: 1073.

17. The many examples of the relationship between Arabic poetry and music should be brought together in a comprehensive study. It is impossible to deal with the subject adequately here. For a significant aspect of this topic, the influence of music on the development of the *gazal* genre of poetry, see Ḥusayn 1959: vol. 1.

18. See Ibn ʿAbd Rabbih 1968: 6/53, 80; and al-Isfahānī 1927–74: 11/8–9.

19. Touma 1975b: 12–13. See also al-Isfahānī 1927–74: 1/284, 314–15; Ibn ʿAbd Rābbih 1968: 6/57; and al-Asad 1969.

20. Two modern interpretations adhere to this traditional view: "yet this, too, was probably not directed against poetry as such, but simply against the poet who in the eyes of the Prophet was the incarnation of pagan ideals, and who, moreover, was pouring out satires and invective against him" (Farmer 1973: 23). Also, "Poetry and other arts are not in themselves evil, but may on the contrary be used in the service of religion and righteousness. But there is a danger that they may be prostituted for base purposes. If they are insincere ("they say what they do not"), or are divorced from actual life or its goodness or its serious purpose, they may become instruments of evil or futility. They then wander about without any set purpose, and seek the depths (valleys) of human folly rather than the heights of divine light" (ʿAlī 1946: 923). This is ʿAlī's commentary on the verse quoted above.

21. Al-Šāfʿī (767–820), the founder of the Šāfʿī school of Islamic law.

22. For further reference, see al-Qušayrī 1959: 166; al-Sarrāj al-Tūsī 1960: 348.

23. The reference is from Macdonald 1901: 244, footnote 1. The edition of the *Tanbīh* to which Macdonald refers is edited by Juynboll.

24. See Roychoudhury 1957: 58–64, for a more detailed exposition of the interpretation of these verses.

25. This is a reference to the Qurʾanic verse "What is the life of this world but amusement and play?" (Qur. 29/64, and 6/32). ʿAlī comments: "Play and amusement are for preparing our minds for the serious things of life" (ʿAlī 1946: 297).

26. This interpretation is given on the authority of Ibn ʿAbbās (d. ca. 688) and Mujāhid (d. ca. 720) (al-Nuwayrī 1925: 4/133; and al-Dunyā/Robson 1938: 467). Lane (1872: 4/1423) cites several lexicographical sources for this sense. See also Roychoudhury 1957: 59.

27. Ibn Abī l-Dunyā cites Mujāhid's interpretation that what is meant here by *ṣawt* is the *mizmār* (al-Dunyā/Robson 1938: 53). Lane (1867: 3/1251) translates *mizmār* as "musical reed or pipe," but also "flute." We

cannot be certain that the reed instrument called *mizmār* in use in the Middle East today is the same instrument.

ʿAlī (1946: 713) has the following commentary on the verse: "Evil has many snares for mankind. The one that is put in the foreground is the voice, the seductive personal appeal, that 'makes the worse appear the better part.'"

28. Al-Qušayrī 1959: 167; al-Sarrāj al-Ṭūsī 1960: 338; al-Ġazālī n.d.: 8/1125; Majd al-Dīn/Robson 1938: 148; Ibn ʿAbd Rabbih 1968: 6/4; al-Saʿīd 1970: 10; and al-Qurṭubī 1968: 1/14.

29. Al-Ġazālī n.d.: 8/1125; al-Qušayrī 1959: 167; al-Sarrāj al-Ṭūsī 1960: 344. Perhaps the existence of one extreme presumes its opposite, and the "beautiful voice" is considered pleasing.

30. See also al-Sarrāj al-Ṭūsī 1960: 345. Lexicographical sources (as cited in Lane 1865: 2/408) give as the sense of Ḥ B R, "to beautify or adorn," one source (Tāj al-ʿArūs) adding, "with respect to the voice reciting."

31. See note 27.

32. Al-Qušayrī 1959: 167; in al-Dunyā/Robson 1938: 51, this statement is attributed to al-Ḥasan al-Baṣrī (d. 728).

33. Al-Ġazālī n.d.: 8/1125; al-Qušayrī 1959: 168; al-Sarrāj al-Ṭūsī 1960: 338; al-Ixtiyār 1953: 17; al-Makkī 1961: 1/26; Ibn ʿAbd Rabbih 1968: 6/4; and so forth.

34. Al-Ġazālī n.d.: 8/1136–37. Variants: Majd al-Dīn/Robson 1938: 132; al-Qušayrī 1959: 166–67; al-Ixtiyār 1953: 12; al-Sarrāj al-Ṭūsī 1960: 345; and so forth.

35. Al-Ġazālī n.d.: 8/1151; al-Dunyā/Robson 1938: 46.

36. Al-Qušayrī 1959: 167; al-Sarrāj al-Ṭūsī 1960: 340; al-Ḥujwīrī/Nicholson 1976: 400.

37. Al-Qušayrī 1959: 167; al-Sarrāj al-Ṭūsī 1960: 340; al-Ḥujwīrī/Nicholson 1976: 399–400; al-Ġazālī n.d.: 8/1132.

38. They are so characterized by Farmer 1942, al-Dunyā/Robson 1938, and Roychoudhury 1957: 46, although the latter admits a group which says that music is conditionally unacceptable; in fact his basic conclusion rests on the conditionality of acceptance or rejection of music. Although the authors preface their respective translations with an overview and introduction to the *samāʿ* polemic, in the case of Farmer it is extremely brief, and in the case of Robson, although carefully detailed, it tends to be more a summary of the evidence than a presentation of the overall issues and structure.

39. Again, the authoritative evidence is such that the position of *samāʿ* cannot be a matter of law, but only of suggestion or persuasion. Caliph Hārūn al-Rašīd, asking about singing, said to al-Zuhrī, "I hear Mālik ibn Anas [founder of the Māliki school of Islamic law] forbids it." Al-Zuhrī responded, saying, "And has Mālik the power to forbid or permit? By Allah that did not belong to your cousin Muhammad [the Prophet] save that it was revealed from his Lord, so who gave this power to Mālik?" (Ibn ʿAbd

Rabbih 1968: 17, 18; see also Majd al-Dīn's comment in Majd al-Dīn/Robson 1938: 18).

40. Naṣr 1966: 176; see also al-Sarrāj al-Ṭūsī 1960: 343.

41. See, specifically, al-Qušayrī 1959: 166, 168, 169–70; al-Ġazālī n.d.: 8/1183; al-Sarrāj al-Ṭūsī 1960: 349, for ranking of listeners, and 358–67, for detail on three stages of listening; Roychoudhury 1957: 85, 93, 96–97, for quotes from Sufi texts. The various Sufi orders have defined codes of proper response to *samā*ʿ which vary in degree of restraint. The religious "establishment" has long looked askance on the more frenzied rituals. To the outsider, especially one concerned with rank and dignity, these rituals may confirm a suspicion that music excites the animal passions, stripping people of dignity. Michael Gilsenan (1973) describes how the Ḥāmidīyya Šādhiliyyah order in Egypt has consciously set itself apart from the "excesses" of other orders in Egypt in an attempt to gain mainstream respectability.

42. A number of *ḥadīṯ* quoted in the *samā*ʿ literature relate that the Prophet allowed his wife, ʿĀʾišah, to observe the singing and dancing of the Abyssinians in the mosque, even supporting her when she grew weary (e.g., al-Ġazālī n.d.: 8/1135–38).

43. Farmer (1973: 211) defines this drum as "hour-glass-shaped." See also Roychoudhury 1957: 88.

44. Al-Nawawī, *Minhaj al-Ṭālibīn*, quoted in al-Dunyā/Robson 1938: 3.

45. This view is documented by many anecdotes in the works of early Arab grammarians, and in the Arab literature (e.g., Sibawayhī and al-Jāḥiḍ). See also chapter 5 in this work for how this affects Qurʾanic recitation.

46. See also al-Sarrāj al-Ṭūsī 1960: 346–47, 356–57.

47. Ibn ʿAbd Rabbih 1968: 6/9; al-Ḥujwīrī/Nicholson 1976: 398; al-Ġazālī n.d.: 8/1128, 44. A modern defender of *samā*ʿ states that "singing is [ultimately] words." If these are blameless, then the singing is blameless. And he responds to opponents who make use of the term *lağw*, saying that if the text be shameless or obscene, then *that* is *lağw*, *al-Kawākib*, 1614, July 7, 1982, Ġunaym ʿAbduh—interview with Dr. Muḥammad Jalāl.

48. Al-Makkī 1961: 1/118. See also al-Sarrāj al-Ṭūsī 1960: 352–55.

49. For example, al-Ġazālī n.d.: 8/1169–71; al-Sarrāj al-Ṭūsī 1960: 354–55.

50. Al-Qušayrī 1959: 184; al-Ġazālī n.d.: 8/1176; al-Sarrāj al-Ṭūsī 1960: 356.

51. See al-Bāqillānī 1935 and al-Suyūṭī 1910 in particular.

52. That the Qurʾan is not poetry has been authoritatively established. Early association of the Qurʾan with the rhymed sayings of the soothsayers and the poets was enough of a threat to its uniqueness to warrant the following verses:

It is not the word of a poet.

(Qur. 69/41, ʿAlī 1946)

We have not instructed him [Muhammad] in poetry, nor is it meet for him. This is no less than a message and a Qur'an making things clear.
(Qur. 36/69, ʿAlī 1946)

4. The Ideal Recitation of the Qur'an

1. Al-Zarkašī 1957: 1/455; al-Ḥuṣarī 1966: 33; ʿUṯmān 1969: 15.

2. Naṣr 1930: 246; al-Ḥuṣarī 1966: 24; al-Qurṭubī 1968: 1/28; ʿUṯmān 1969: 13.

3. Al-Zarkašī 1957: 1/456; ʿUṯmān 1969: 6.

4. For an excellent analysis of the ramifications of the "memorizing-learning" equation of Islamic education, and a convincing demonstration of its flexibility, I refer the reader to Eickelman 1978: 485–546. See also Labīb al-Saʿīd (1967: 353–66) for a more traditional but informative treatment of the importance of *hifḍ* to Qur'anic learning in Egypt.

5. Al-Ḥuṣarī 1966: 24–25; ʿUṯmān 1969: 15; and others.

6. Al-Ḥuṣarī 1966: 24; ʿUtmān 1969: 13; al-Qurṭubī 1968: 1/28; al-Suyūṭī 1910: 1/105; Naṣr 1930: 246.

7. Al-Suyūṭī 1910: 1/109; Naṣr 1930: 246.

8. Al-Ḥuṣarī 1966: 24, 26, 36–37; ʿUṯmān 1969: 13; Naṣr 1930: 245–46.

9. *Ḥadīṯ* cited in al-Makkī 1961: 97; al-Sarrāj al-Ṭūsī 1960: 353.

10. Al-Makkī 1961: 97; Naṣr 1930: 240. See also al-Suyūṭī (1910: 1/108), where *tartīl* is substituted for *tadabbur*.

11. *Xatm* also denotes a completed memorization of the whole text, for example: "I completed the *xatm*," that is, "I finished memorizing the whole Qur'an."

12. Al-Suyūṭī 1910: 1/106; Ibn Saʿd 1960: 376; al-Zarkašī 1957: 1/471.

13. Al-Zarkašī 1957: 1/461–63; al-Makkī 1961: 128; al-Suyūṭī 1910: 1/108–110.

14. It was explained to me by one of the members of the committee that some of the candidates were weak in *hifḍ* because they had been given a year to prepare for another audition, but the period of time had extended to three years, so they lost what they had prepared. Although these reciters should know the whole text, they tend to forget it because they recite only certain parts of it regularly. The committee member did not condone this, but admitted the reality of the practice.

15. Al-Zarkašī 1957: 1/461; al-Qurṭubī 1968: 1/28.

16. Al-Makkī 1961: 124, 125, 127; al-Zarkašī 1957: 1/464; Ibn al-Ḥājj 1929: 51; Naṣr 1930: 238; al-Suyūṭī 1910: 1/108.

17. Al-Makkī 1961: 124ff.; al-Zarkašī 1957: 1/463–64; Naṣr 1930: 238ff.; al-Suyūṭī 1910: 1/108.

18. Al-Makkī 1961: 124. For variants, see Ibn al-Ḥājj 1929: 51; al-Suyūṭī 1910: 1/109; Naṣr 1930: 238.

19. Al-Zarkašī 1957: 1/463–64; al-Suyūṭī 1910: 1/109; Naṣr 1930: 239.

20. Al-Ḥuṣarī 1966: 44–47; al-Makkī 1961: 124, 128.

21. Al-Makkī 1961: 125; Naṣr 1930: 239; al-Suyūṭī 1910: 1/109, quoting al-Nawawī.

22. Al-Makkī 1961: 124; Naṣr 1930: 238.

23. See al-Zarkašī 1957: 1/363, 364; al-Makkī 1961: 124.

24. *Niyyah* (plural *niyyāt*). In Islam, any religious act must be preceded with conscious intent, to prevent the automatic and empty gesture.

25. *Ḥadīṯ*, in Ibn al-Ḥājj 1929: 51; al-Jawziyyah 1970: 1/166; al-Nuwayrī 1925: 139; al-Suyūṭī 1910: 1/109; al-Zarkašī 1957: 1/464; Ibn al-Manḏūr 1966: 373. The version in al-Qušayrī (1959: 167) is without the term *yajharu*, but al-Anṣārī explains in the margin of the text that *yataġannā* means *yajharu*.

26. In regard to the *ḥadīṯ* cited above—"God does not listen . . ."—he says that if the Prophet had meant *ṭarab* by his use of the term *taġannī*, he would have added, "and he enchants musically with it" (*wa yuṭribu bihi*) instead of "and he raises his voice in it" (*wa yajharu bihi*), for *jahr* means "to hear oneself and those who follow along" (al-Qurṭubī 1968: 1/15).

27. Šayx Muḥammad al-Ṭablāwī pointed out to me another aspect of the importance of the professional reciter's understanding of the text in terms of choosing a text appropriate to the occasion. He related that he once attended a conference in Kairouan, Tunisia. Two heads of state, H. Bourguiba and M. Qaḏḏāfī, as well as a number of delegates from all over the Middle East were present. The participants gathered together to celebrate the final night of the Prophet's birthday feast. Each of the delegates was to recite ten lines or so, and the first to recite was a Sudanese. He began with the verse "And if God visits thee with affliction none can remove it but He" (Qur. 6/17). Šayx al-Ṭablāwī said, "And it was as if you had brought a stick and given me a whack! It is a Qur'anic verse, all right, but the meaning! God!" He went on to say how inappropriate the text was for an occasion which called for hope and good tidings.

28. The term is ʿAbd al-Wahhāb Ḥamūdah's (1977: 25–28).

29. Al-Saʿīd 1967: 343, footnote 3. Zakariyā Aḥmad was justifying his plan to compose music for the Qur'an with the aim of "evoking the meanings and fixing the tunes in *tartīl*" so as to avoid just such a situation.

30. Compare this to a statement in Ibn ʿAbd Rabbih (1968: 6/32) regarding the best kind of singer: "He sings to everyone as if he were created from the heart of each man."

31. For example, al-Jawziyyah 1970: 1/166; al-Makkī 1961: 126, 128; Ibn Xaldūn n.d.: 426; Anonymous 1974: 29; al-Qamḥāwī 1972–73: 85; and so forth.

32. *Zayyin* and *ḥassin* are used interchangeably, as are their verbal nouns, *tazyīn* and *taḥsīn* (see below).

33. Most sources explain that *aḏina* in the context of these *ḥadīṯ* means *istamaʿa*, "to listen." See al-Nuwayrī 1925: 139 (footnote); al-Ḥuṣarī 1966: 101; al-Qušayrī 1959: 167 (margin); al-Saʿīd 1967: 311 (foot-

note); and others. I only mention this because the consensus of this interpretation has escaped the notice of several scholars, Arab and Western, writing recently on Qur'anic recitation, and they have translated *aḏina* as "to permit."

34. Al-Ḥuṣarī 1966: 21, 44–47; ʿUṯmān 1969: 8; al-Makkī 1961: 126; al-Suyūṭī 1910: 1/111; al-Jawziyyah 1970: 1/167.

35. Al-Qurṭubī 1968: 1/11–12; al-Jawziyyah 1970: 1/165.

36. Al-Sarrāj al-Ṭūsī 1960: 339; al-Qušayrī 1959: 168.

37. Al-Jawziyyah 1970: 1/167; al-Ibšīhī 1888: 2/130–31; al-Saʿīd 1970: 40; and others.

38. Roychoudhury (1957: 92) translates the *ḥadīṯ "zayyinū l-qur'ān bi aṣwātikum"* as "Beautify the Qur'an with melody." This is not the general interpretation of *aṣwāt* in this context.

39. Al-Suyūṭī 1910: 1/101; Ibn al-Jazarī 1908: 4.

40. The term used by one of my informants to denote melodic reciters was *al-qurrā' fi l-aṣwāt*. See also Ibn ʿAbd Rabbih 1968: 6/25; al-Isfahānī 1927–74: throughout; al-Jawziyyah 1970: 1/166; and others.

41. Naṣr 1930: 235–36; see also ʿUṯmān 1969: 9.

42. *Istiʿāḏah* and *basmalah* denote the two formulae with which the reciter begins recitation of the Qur'an.

43. In some contexts *qirā'ah* seems to specify oral (or melodic) rendering of the Qur'an as opposed to that of any other text. See Ibn Xaldūn n.d.: 427, and two stories in Ibn ʿAbd Rabbih (1940–68: 6/14, 23) in which a man who is arrested for rendering a song in the mosque with *tarannum* or *taġannī* (see below) is released when a witness testifies that it was, in fact, *qirā'ah*.

44. See above, and note 13 in this chapter.

45. The preference for improvised melody in Qur'anic recitation is explained in chapter 7.

46. Al-Suyūṭī 1910: 1/109; Ibn Xaldūn n.d.: 425–26.

47. The reference here is to a *ḥadīṯ* widely quoted in differing contexts. The relevant part of the *ḥadīṯ* is "There will come after me a people who will trill the Qur'an . . . and their reciting will go no further than their throats . . ." The full text of the *ḥadīṯ* is in chapter 7 and in al-Qurṭubī 1968: 1/17; al-Jawziyyah 1970: 1/168; Naṣr 1930: 25; al-Saʿīd 1967: 309; and others.

48. Ibn al-Aʿrābī makes the same point about finding acceptable substitutions when he writes that the Prophet desired that the Arabs' passion for singing the caravan song would be replaced by a passion for the Qur'an, cited in Ibn al-Manḏūr 1966: 373–74; see al-Qurṭubī 1968: 1/18, for variant.

49. The sense of "to chant" cited in Wehr (1961: 686) and Lane (1863–93: 6/2303) can, I believe, be traced to the term's association with the Qur'an and poetry, as well as with the earlier and so-called simpler stages of pre-Islamic singing. But it must denote a rather more ornamented melodic

mode than is commonly understood by "chant." In most contexts, to be understood as simple "chanting," it would have to be specified. See below, and the association of the term with *tarannum*.

50. I do not hesitate to translate *taġanna bi* as "sing" here because I do not think the meaning of the term would be such a debatable subject if "chant" were the intended meaning.

51. A partial list: al-Jawziyyah 1970: 1/165–69; Ibn al-Manḍūr 1966: 373; al-Qušayrī 1959: 167; al-Sarrāj al-Ṭūsī 1960: 338; al-Qāṣih 1934: 6; Ibn al-Ḥājj 1929: 51; al-Nuwayrī 1925: 139; al-Qurṭubī 1968: 1/12–15; and others.

52. Again, if *ġinā'* were simply a synonym for *našīd* there would be no call to explain the statement.

53. For example, another favorite *ḥadīṯ* quoted in support of melodic recitation is "Embellish the Qur'an with your voices." Al-Qurṭubī says that many *ḥadīṯ* authorities have shown that what is meant is the reverse, that is, "Embellish your voices with the Qur'an," according to the pattern "I brought the watering trough to my horse." Furthermore, two *ḥadīṯ* support this interpretation: on the authority of Abū Hurayrah, "Embellish your voices with the Qur'an," and on the authority of ʿUmar, "Beautify your voices with the Qur'an" (cited in al-Qurṭubī 1968: 11).

54. Al-Qurṭubī 1968: 1/15; al-Jawziyyah 1970: 1/166, 167.

55. Al-Qurṭubī 1968: 1/14; al-Jawziyyah 1970: 1/166.

56. Al-Fīrūzabādī 1913: 3/28; Lane 1863–93: 3/1039.

57. As for the statement "*tarjīʿ* in recitation is the reiteration of phonemes [syllables?] as in the recitation of the Christians" (al-Qurṭubī 1968: 1/17; Ibn al-Ḥājj 1929: 54), it contains a clue to the meaning of *tarjīʿ*, but is beyond the scope of this research.

58. Al-Suyūṭī 1910: 1/107; al-Sarrāj al-Ṭūsī 1960: 338; al-Qāri' 1948: 23; al-Qurṭubī 1968: 1/16; Ibn Saʿd 1960: 376; and others.

59. Anonymous 1974: 29; al-Sarrāj al-Ṭūsī 1960: 338.

60. Al-Qurṭubī 1968: 1/16, quoted in Ibn al-Ḥājj 1929: 53, without attribution.

61. Al-ʿAllāf 1963: 2; al-Ixtiyār 1953: 9; see also Ibn Xaldūn n.d.: 427.

62. I do not understand Farmer's translation of *tarjīʿ* as a "refrain of a song" (1942: 7, footnote 2; see also Farmer 1965: 2/1073). There is some sort of repetition involved in *tarjīʿ*, but it seems rather to be the reiteration of smaller units of sound to produce trilling or quavering. There is, of course, repetition of the *šahādah* mentioned above, and the pairing of *taqṭīʿ* (scansion) with *tarjīʿ* ("repeated poetical feet" with "repeated musical phrase," Farmer 1942: 7) to indicate the repetition of longer units, but the word "refrain" specifically denotes a recurring phrase which punctuates new material, and it seems unlikely that his meaning would be applied to the recitation of the Qur'an.

63. See al-Saʿīd 1967: 312, footnote 3. The pairing of *tarjīʿ* and *taḥnīn* here adds another dimension to the meaning of *tarjīʿ*: not only does *ḥanna* express the sound of the bow, and the creaking of the mast, but also the

(plaintive) sound of the wind, and the sound of the lute which stirs emotion (Lane 1863–93: 652–53).

64. Al-Fīrūzabādī 1913: 4/122–23; Lane 1863–93: 3/1166.

65. Al-Jawziyyah 1970: 1/166; Lane 1863–93: 3/1166; al-Fīrūzabādī 1913: 4/12, 13, in margin.

66. Al-ʿAllāf 1963: 3; Ibn Xaldūn n.d. (probably the source): 427.

67. Kāmil 1973: 11; Ibn Xaldūn n.d.: 427.

68. For example, in a poem by ʿAbdah ibn al-Ṭabīb (al-Mufaḍḍal 1921: 293), we read: "*tuḏrī ḥawāšīyahu jaydāʾu ānisatun fī ṣawtihā li-samāʿi al-šarbi tartīlu.*" But notice that one of the commentators, al-Marzūqī (footnote), explains the term in reference to Qurʾanic usage.

69. See Lane 1863–93: 3/1028.

70. Variant: "like poetry recited with *tartīl*" in Ibn al-Ḥājj 1929: 54. See also Ibn al-Jazarī (1908: 6). He cites Xalīl ibn Aḥmad and al-Asmaʿī.

71. ʿUṯmān 1969: 19; Ibn al-Jazarī 1908: 6.

72. *Ḥadīṯ*, on the authority of Zayd ibn Ṯābit, in al-Qāriʾ 1948: 23; al-Suyūṭī 1910: 1/101; Naṣr 1930: 15; Ismāʿīl 1978*b*: 49.

73. This is said to be ʿAlī's response when asked about the meaning of the verse, Qur. 73/4, al-Qāriʾ 1948: 22; Ibn al-Jazarī 1908: 36; ʿUṯmān 1969: 18; Ismāʿīl 1978*b*: 151.

74. This is the report of Umm Salmah and is widely quoted in the context of explanations of *tartīl*, for example, al-Suyūṭī 1910: 1/107; Ibn Saʿd 1960: 376; al-Qurṭubī 1968: 1/17; Naṣr 1930: 16; Ismāʿīl 1978*b*: 49.

75. Naṣr 1930: 17 (attributed to al-Ġazālī). See also al-Suyūṭī 1910: 1/108. Related to this is the more specific use of the term *tartīl* to denote the medium of the three tempi in which the Qurʾan is recited. For this, and the relation of *tartīl* to *taḥqīq*, see chapter 2.

76. Al-Suyūṭī 1910: 1/108; al-Ḥuṣarī 1966: 58. See also al-Zarkašī 1957: 1/455, 449–50. For a different interpretation of this phrase, see Semaan 1968: 32, footnote 4.

77. Those who claim it is better to read more of the Qurʾan quickly than less with *tartīl* base their view on the *ḥadīṯ* (from Ibn Masʿūd) "Whosoever recites a single syllable of the Qurʾan gains a merit," and others have said "every syllable is worth ten merits," cited by Ismāʿīl 1978*b*: 50.

78. Again, a reference to the *ḥadīṯ* mentioned in note 47. Al-Qāriʾ (1948: 22) adds: "The people whose reciting goes no further than their throats are those who do not contemplate it or act according to it."

79. Al-Zarkašī 1957: 1/450; al-Suyūṭī 1910: 1/108.

80. Al-Qurṭubī (1968: 1/12) interprets this to mean that he was reciting too fast. For variants without the term *tartīl*, see al-Makkī 1961: 126; al-Jawziyyah 1970: 1/166.

81. Šayx ʿAlī Ḥajjāj al-Suwaysī seemed to be specifying the enunciation and articulatory aspect of *tartīl* in his usage: "When Rifʿat recited, everyone stopped to listen because of the beauty of the reciting and the art and the *tartīl*, and the ordering of the verses and the melody."

82. Al-Qāriʾ 1948: 22; see also al-Daʿʿās 1964: 17.

83. An exception would be the more scholarly reciter's statement that before he learned the rules of *tajwīd* theoretically, he memorized the Qur'an and recited with a practical knowledge of the rules: "*jawwadt il-qur'ān tajwīdan 'amaliyyan*" (al-Ḥuṣarī).

84. Ibn al-Jazarī, 1934: 9. The context of this reference is: "The recommendation to *tajwīd* is an obligation. Whoever does not recite the Qur'an with *tajwīd* [*jawwad*] is a sinner because God revealed it with *tajwīd* and thus it reached us from Him."

85. See, for example, the definition in al-Sa'īd (1967: 320), which equates *tartīl* with "lowering the voice and *taḥzīn* in reciting."

86. See also Ibn al-Hājj 1929: 51.

87. Farmer 1952: 63. He is translating from Ibn Qutaybah 1960: 533.

88. Al-Suyūṭī 1910: 1/109; variants in al-Ġazālī n.d.: 3/502; al-Sa'īd 1967: 319.

89. Al-Suyūṭī 1910: 1/109; other variants of the above in al-Ġazālī n.d.: 3/502; Ibn al-Ḥājj 1929: 55; Naṣr 1930: 241; al-Sa'īd 1967: 320. Ibn Ḥujjah al-Ḥamāwī (1888: 1/84) adds to this *ḥadīṯ*: ". . . and sing it, for he is not one of us who does not sing the Qur'an."

90. Al-Ġazālī n.d.: 3/502; Naṣr 1930: 241; al-Sa'īd 1967: 320.

91. Al-Ġazālī n.d.: 3/502; al-Sa'īd 1967: 320–21.

92. Ibn Qutaybah 1960: 533. See also al-Sa'īd 1967: 321.

93. Al-Sa'īd 1970: 108. The reference is to Abū Bakr.

94. The context of these examples is the debate over the meaning of *taġannā bi* in the *ḥadīṯ* cited above.

95. Al-Qāri' 1948: 23; see also Ismā'īl 1978*b*: 327.

96. This is a devotional ritual involving the repeating of the name of God and certain fixed phrases accompanied by gestures and breathing patterns, and, sometimes, music and dance.

97. For example, al-Makkī 1961: 126; al-Sarrāj 1960: 365; al-Jawziyyah 1970: 1/166; al-Ġazālī n.d.: 8/1169ff., and others.

98. Ibn al-Jazarī 1908: 4; Naṣr 1930: 19.

99. See also al-Ġazālī n.d.: 3/502: "Indeed the path of feigning weeping brings *ḥuzn* to the heart."

100. See also al-Zarkašī 1957: 1/450–51; al-Sa'īd 1970: 95–96.

101. Al-Makkī 1961: 99. See also al-Makkī 1961: 106; al-Sarrāj al-Ṭūsī 1960: 353; al-Qurṭubī 1968: 1/10.

102. Al-Suyūṭī 1910: 1/109; other variants in al-Makkī 1961: 99; Naṣr 1930: 241.

5. The Sound of Qur'anic Recitation

1. For example, physiological and psychological studies of the effects of sound.

2. The notation is intended to serve as a quick reference to specific aspects of the sound mentioned in this chapter. It is not intended as a visual

translation of the sound. Obviously, there is no tradition of notating Qur'anic recitation within the culture.

3. Not all Muslims, by any means, have mastered these rules, but the sound of their reciting is still characterized by the elements of the *murattal* style, such as the restricted pitch range, quick tempo, and so forth. The most obvious deviation from the sound of the *murattal* style is in the rhythm: the particular lilt of the correct rhythm is sometimes missing.

4. Al-Saʿīd's book, *Al-Jamʿ al-Ṣawtī l-Awwal li l-Qur'ān 'aw al-Muṣḥaf al-Murattal* (1967), is basically an account of the history and justification of this project.

5. This passage is basically from *The Recited Koran* (Weiss, Berger, and Rauf 1975: 69), an English version of al-Saʿīd 1967 (see note 4). It is not so much a translation of al-Saʿīd's text as a shorter version, since it does not include all of the original material, and the order of some material is changed. Moreover, many passages are not literal translations, but summaries. In the quoted passages the phrases followed by transliteration into Arabic are my own translations from the original text, al-Saʿīd 1967: 103.

6. Al-Saʿīd 1967: 105, 107, 349.

7. Al-Saʿīd 1967: 108; Weiss, Berger, and Rauf 1975: 81.

8. A few reciters, such as Š Muḥammad Salāmah and Š Muḥammad Ṣiddīq al-Minšāwī, have made the short duration of the final long vowel before pause a mark of personal style.

9. Compare Touma's description of the pause in secular music: "After one or more phrases there usually comes a short pause of one to four seconds which puts the listener in a state of tension, for he does not know what is going to happen after the pause. At a concert of secular music an Arab audience will release the tension during short pauses by uttering words of praise or loud shouts . . ." (Touma 1976: 35).

10. Initially there was controversy over the amplification and broadcast of Qur'anic recitation. On one hand, it was intended to reach a wider audience, and on the other, there was a risk that it would reach into lavatories, bars, and other places unsuitable to the Qur'an. One reciter, Šayx Muḥammad Salāmah, consistently refused to become a radio reciter on the grounds that the studio environment itself was unsuitable.

11. But the *rīfī* reciters do have their own following. Voice quality, breath control, and the virtuosic use of the high register all contribute to their popularity.

12. Explanation of this varies: it fits the voice, there are more openings to other *maqāmāt*, it is easiest to do, and so forth.

13. In fact, the majority of reciters return to a transposed *bayātī*. It is extremely difficult to keep the starting pitch in mind through dozens of transpositions and modulations, and the reciter is not helped by any accompanying drone pitch. In transcribing a number of recitations, I was interested to see that the widely acclaimed melodic skill and musical sense

of Šayx Muḥammad Rifʿat was borne out by his being the only reciter to return to the original *bayātī* pitches.

14. Frequency and initial and final position define the key pitches of a *maqām*.

15. That is, *Ḥafṣ ʿan ʿĀṣim*. The ʿUtmānī text is the basis for all the *qirāʾāt*; in Egypt the printed text is vocalized and given the diacritical marks according to *qirāʾat Ḥafṣ ʿan ʿAṣim*.

16. The sudden silences that punctuate *qirāʾat Ḥamzah* make it a particularly dramatic sound, and I have seen this exploited by gesture on the part of the performer. One reciter, for instance, emphasized his silence with the pronounced, even showy, gesture of dropping his hands from the sides of his head, then swinging them back into place as he prepared to break the silence with the glottal stop.

6. Maintaining the Ideal Recitation of the Qurʾan

1. *Kuttāb* (plural *katātīb*) is the traditional primary school. Children from the age of four are sent here to learn (memorize) the Qurʾan and learn their alphabet. The Azhari institute may be a primary or secondary school under the supervision of al-Azhar University/Mosque. Once exclusively Islamic, the University and the institute under its jurisdiction now combine religious study with subjects such as geography, health, and drawing. See the entry "al-Azhar" in the *Shorter Encyclopedia of Islam* (Vollers 1961: 50–52), and ʿAwf 1970. For more on the traditional Islamic education, see Eickelman 1978.

Maqraʾah (plural *maqārīʾ*) is the public recitation class administered by the Ministry of Religious Endowments. For some history of the *maqraʾah* in Egypt, see al-Saʿīd 1970.

2. See such articles as "Someone from the *katātīb* Always Triumphs" (Ḥāšim 1977: 14), and "Two Boys from a Small Village Triumph with the Gold Medal in the World Competition for the Blessed Qurʾan" (Ibrāhīm 1979: 6).

3. *Adāʾ* here means "reciting according to the rules of *tajwīd*."

4. The above material and what follows was obtained from an interview with the director of the Mudīriyyah, Dr. Muḥsin al-Širbīnī, as well as my own attendance at some of the events and classes covered.

5. Most of the personnel of the Ministry are trained religious scholars.

6. Muḥsin al-Širbīnī. Jomier says it is the standard text for the Friday prayer (Jomier 1952: 13).

7. For example, Šayx al-Ḥuṣarī at the Ḥusayn mosque, Šayx al-Šaʿšāʿī at the Sayyidah Zaynab; Šayx Muṣṭafā Ismāʿīl was at the al-Azhar mosque until his death in December, 1978, and was replaced by Šayx al-Ṭablāwī.

8. As listed in the weekly program schedule for August, 1979, they are Idāʿat al-Qurʾān al-Karīm (Broadcast of the Holy Qurʾan), al-Šaʿb (the People), al-Barnāmaj al-Ṭānī (the Second Program), al-Šabāb (Youth), al-Barnāmaj al-ʿAmm (the General Program), al-Mūsīqā (Music), al-Sūdān

(Sudan), Ṣawt al-ʿArab (Voice of the Arabs), Filisṭīn (Palestine), al-Šarq al-Awsaṭ (the Middle East), and al-Iskandariyyah (Alexandria).

9. Dr. Kāmil al-Būhī. See chapter 5 for more on this project.

10. Mr. ʿAbd al-Xāliq ʿAbd al-Wahhāb was the controller of programs in 1978.

11. The role of the critical listening session, the *nadwah* (see chapter 7), is comparable, but unlike the *nadwah*, by its selection and regulation the Radio defines the body of material considered acceptable and provides a model.

12. One of the religious scholars (who also evaluates candidates in the children's competition and in the Friday prayer auditions) is respected for his knowledge of music, having taught the subject in an earlier stage of his career. However, he would not be considered a professional musician.

13. The highest rank, eighty-six to ninety percent, receives a half-hour of prime-time exposure every two weeks. The lowest rank, sixty-one to seventy percent, is restricted to fifteen minutes a week on the smaller or less prestigious stations.

14. Such an official project would be the joint production of Sono Cairo, the Ministry of Religious Endowments, and the National Broadcasting and Television Corporation. They have issued recordings of the complete Qurʾan in both styles by the four top-ranking reciters.

7. Overlap and Separation: The Dynamics of Perception and Response

1. For example, Farmer 1952, 1954, and 1957; Shiloah 1968; Anderson 1971; and others.

2. One scholar, H. H. Touma, distinguishes between the "religious singing style of the Qurʾan" and that of art song, "even though the same musical phenomena underlie both singing styles and the same musical structure is used in both." He correctly attributes the uniqueness of recitation "that can be confused with no other song style, whether secular or religious" to its basis of *tajwīd*, but still designates Qurʾanic recitation as "a form of religious music" (Touma 1975*a*: 89, 90).

3. Talbi 1958: 185. It is Talbi's contention that early Arab music was characterized by improvisation and that precomposition was a feature of foreign influence. He equates the former to "simple" and "natural," and the latter to "complex" and "artificial." This distinction becomes important in defining the limits of melodic recitation (see chapter 4).

4. Ibn Qutaybah 1935: 232. See also Ibn al-Manḍūr 1966: 19/374; al-Saʿīd 1967: 321; and others.

5. The complete passage of Ibn Qutaybah is as follows:

> The first who recited with tunes was ʿUbayd Allāh ibn Abī Bakrah, and his reciting was emotionally affecting [*ḥazanan*] . . . and his grandson, ʿUbayd Allāh ibn ʿUmar ibn ʿUbayd Allāh, inherited that [way of reciting] from him. And it is of him that it is said, the [style of] reciting of

Ibn ʿUmar. And al-Ibādī took from him, and Saʿīd al-ʿAllāf and his brother took from al-Ibādī the [style of] reciting of Ibn ʿUmar. And Hārūn al-Rašīd [the caliph] liked the reciting of Saʿīd al-ʿAllāf and showed him favor and granted him reward, and he was known as the Reciter of the Prince of the Believers.

6. Ibn ʿAbd Rabbih 1968: 6/53; see also Talbi 1958: 186–89, for more detail and other references. Talbi mentions a man known as al-Qāriʾ (the reciter) who introduced song tunes into recitation, and refers the reader to the Bulāq edition of *Kitāb al-Aġānī*. However, I could not trace these references. I did find mention of al-Qāriʾ in Ibn Qutaybah 1935: 232. Talbi bases much of his material on an eleventh-century manuscript ("The Book of Novelty and Heresy") by al-Turtūsi, the chapter on heretical innovations in Qurʾanic recitation in particular.

7. In the sources, I found earlier reports of this type of recitation, for example, Ibn al-Ḥājj 1929: 51, 53–54.

8. Although the reciter may be specifically referred to as *qāriʾ*, by virtue of his religious training and authority he shares the respectful title *šayx* with religious scholars. Likewise, the scholar and reciter share the traditional dress. This is a caftan, sashed at the waist, over which is worn the *kakūla*, a loose robe, open down the front. The headgear, which distinguishes the *šayx* in particular, is a fez, around the base of which is wrapped a white scarf.

9. Šayx Rašād Mašʿal is a good example of this professional overlap. He is a member of the Arabic Music Ensemble (Firqat al-Mūsīqa l-ʿArabiyyah), a professional group of singers and instrumentalists under the direction of M. Nuywayrah dedicated to the revival of the "art" music heritage of Egypt. I first met Šayx Rašād at a rehearsal of the Religious Singing Ensemble (Firqat al-Inšād al-Dīniyyah), a subgroup of the above. Šayx Rašād is also a professional reciter, and on another occasion he opened a concert of Arabic music with Qurʾanic recitation.

10. The starting salary for a college graduate in the civil service was LE 24 a month in 1978.

11. I do not quite know how to classify the man who was introduced to me at a public recitation with the words, "he is deaf, but very enthusiastic!"

12. There was also some description of the reciter's surroundings, and the rumor that the *šayx* was a skilled pianist and performer of Beethoven has been traced to the interviewer's pointing out the presence of a piano in the house!

13. Al-Najmī 1968: 178. Šayx Rifʿat responded by asking that the title be dropped.

14. Like the three Cairo newspapers, *al-Jumhūriyyah*, *Akbār al-Yawm*, and *al-Ahrām*, the radio stations are unofficially typed by the audience their programming caters to. In the case of the newspapers, it is, roughly, lowbrow, middlebrow, and highbrow, respectively. The radio station Iḏāʿat

al-Šaᶜb is considered to have a less educated, less sophisticated audience than al-Barnāmaj al-ᶜĀmm, and only the highest-ranking of the Radio reciters are featured on al-Barnāmaj al-ᶜĀmm. The religious station, Iḏāᶜat al-Qur'ān al-Karīm, probably has the most specialized audience (except for its recitation programs), but, as it features all of its reciters regularly in its programming, a recitation on this station does not carry the same prestige.

15. Another aspect of studio recording to which the reciters object is the time limit imposed on the recitation. See Ali Jihad Racy 1977 for how music was changed by the recording industry. Racy concludes that one of the effects of commercialized recording was "the abandonment of improvisation in favor of precomposition. This is shown most clearly by the gradual disappearance of the highly improvised soloistic *qasida*" (1977: 250). Singers did make adjustments, but more and more pieces with a time limit to fit onto a phonodisc were commissioned. Since improvisation is the basis of Qur'anic recitation (see above), reciters are not so free to adapt their art to the demands of the recording industry. In practice, the reciter is given two minutes' warning before the end by the sound engineer, and, in that time, he must work his way back to *maqām bayātī* from wherever he is.

16. The responsibility for not giving the sources of these comments is mine. None of my informants placed any conditions on talking to me, but I would rather not expose them to possible criticism.

17. Some of the copies of these recitations are made with the desired repetitions spliced in so that one does not have to interrupt the flow by stopping the machine!

18. It is difficult to understand Talbi's conclusion (1958: 90) that the inspiration and excesses of melodic recitation have not lasted, that there is no longer any link with music. He says, "En définitive l'éxperience fut sterile et on ne peut affirmer que le tagwid actuel, timoré, et sans prétention musicale réelle comme l'a prouvé une enquête récente, lui doive quelque chose." The reference is to Cantineau and Barbès 1942–47, but Talbi was writing in 1958, when some of the most musical of the Egyptian reciters, such as Šayx Muṣṭafā Ismāᶜīl and Šayx Kāmil Yūsuf al-Bahtīmī, had already established their reputations.

19. Actually, everyone waits to hear *ṣabā*, period. It is a favorite *maqām*, and according to several informants, the one which best expresses the Egyptian spirit. It seems to evoke feelings of yearning, a haunting sadness.

20. Whether or not a recognizable Arabic *maqām* is rendered or merely hinted at is not important. Pacholczyk, in his study of one man's reciting, concludes that "there is no preestablished intermodal scale out of which the modal pitches are selected. The lack of such a scale indicates that each piece is constructed upon a scale built up especially for this piece and has a unique intervallic pattern" (1971: 130). But listeners and reciters alike do recognize the sound in terms of the pre-established *maqāmāt*.

21. This statement reflects the association of systematic training with a

notation system imported from the West. Although this was not always the case, it is a prevailing attitude in the music institutes and conservatories today.

22. "Good voice" denotes both vocal technique and voice quality. See chapter 4.

23. See chapter 4, note 47, for the same *ḥadīṯ* in the context of a different discussion.

24. Al-Saʿīd reports a number of accounts of al-Šāfiʿī's disapproval in terms of the inviolability of *tajwīd* (1970: 44, footnote 3).

25. See al-Ġazālī's discussion of the superiority of listening to song or Qur'ān. He bases part of the argument (n.d. 8/1174–75) on the effectiveness of playing with meter and rhythm, something not allowed in Qur'ānic recitation.

26. Naṣr 1930: 19. The complete list of such practices begins on page 18.

27. Al-Suyūtī 1910: 1/83–105; Ḥamūdah 1977: 25–28; Abū l-ʿAynayn 1974: 24–25; al-Saʿīd 1967: 324–30; and others.

28. Articles such as "Aṯar al-Qur'ān al-Karīm fī l-Mūsīqā ʿArabiyyah" (the Influence of the Qur'an on Arabic Music) by Salīm (1939: 5–8), reprinted in the same journal (1977: 23–27), represent an attempt to link the two definitions and, at the same time, establish the Qur'an as the source of musical principles, thus both guaranteeing the primacy of the Qur'an and mitigating any un-Islamic aspects of *al-mūsīqā*. This view was also expressed by Šayx al-Ruzayqī, who explained that after he had been reciting some time, he became convinced that music study was necessary to develop his talent, so he enrolled in the Music Institute: "Not that the Qur'an is tied to music, rather, the opposite." He went on to explain that musical durations which he expressed in terms of Western notation—that is, quarter notes, half notes, and so forth—are equal to the durations set out in the rules of *tajwīd*. Thus, a whole note (four beats) is equal to a *madd munfaṣil* (see chapter 2).

29. See also Al-Suyūṭī 1910: 1/109; Ibn al-Ḥājj 1929; al-Jawziyyah 1970: 1/167.

30. In Egypt today, when many reciters do learn the art of music and apply its melodic system, the *maqāmāt*, to their reciting, the style characterized as "natural" (*ṭabīʿī*) is that which is more closely related to the speech-bound style, *murattal*, in its tempo and momentum.

31. See al-Jawziyyah 1970: 1/165; al-Saʿīd 1970: 43—"and all novelty is heresy"; al-Saʿīd 1967: 474; and Talbi 1958. Talbi's article is on a chapter about melodic recitation which is part of a larger work entitled "The Book of Novelty and Heresy."

32. The exception is in the *qaflah*, the melodic cadence. Reciters often quote from each other's cadences: these are marks of personal style. However, the *qaflah* is built on one, at most two, syllables, so it is not a question of imposing one rhythmic pattern on another.

33. See al-Saʿīd 1967: 330–44; and Weiss, Berger, and Rauf 1975: 114–15.

34. Compare to Šayx Muḥammad al-Tablāwī's description of what is imitated in the learning process: "I would travel to other towns to listen, and would take from other reciters, would steal something. I mean, was I born with this? No. Was Muṣṭafā Ismāʿīl? No. Others? No. Everyone makes his own—taking from here and there, here a melodic cadence, there an ascent."

35. The reputations of some recitations are such that certain *suwar* have become associated with certain reciters and are regarded as their domain. The feeling is that few prominent reciters would invite comparison with Šayx Rifʿat by reciting *suwar al-Raḥmān, Yūsuf,* or *Maryam,* although Šayx al-Suwaysī, as the best imitator of Rifʿat, is "allowed" to recite *sūrat Maryam.* One prominent reciter, whose recitation of *sūrat al-Qiyāmah* was broadcast for the Friday prayer, was criticized for even attempting this text, and it was noted that "he couldn't keep it up" and had to end ten minutes early. The famous rendition of this *sūrah* is by Šayx al-Bahtīmī (also by his mentor Šayx Muḥammad Salāmah). It is not just a question of unfavorable comparison, however: it may be that the familiarity with the particular rendition is such that it is difficult to avoid imitation. Some members of the Reciters' Committee (Lajnat al-Qurrāʾ) agreed that it would have been better if a certain candidate had chosen to do another part of the text, as his own style would have shown better. The text in question was associated with another reciter.

36. See also al-Ġazālī n.d., 8/1174–75.

37. The cemeteries seem to be a place for aberration of Qurʾanic reciting. See also al-Qurṭubī 1968: 1/16. I heard a number of practices in the cemeteries of Cairo unacceptable to the recitation tradition, such as the simultaneous reciting of different parts of the text. Moreover, those who earn money reciting in the cemeteries are considered the most ignorant of reciters.

38. See al-Ġazālī n.d.: 8/1174; and al-Saʿīd 1967: 338ff., regarding use of instrumentation in recitation.

39. Al-Jawziyyah 1970: 1/165; al-Qurṭubī 1968: 1/10–11; Ibn al-Ḥājj 1929: 51. Again, this is not a new issue: we read in early texts (thirteenth and fourteenth centuries) of those who depend on crafted songs (*aṣwāt maṣūġah*) in recitation in order to attract listeners (al-Sarrāj al-Ṭūsī 1960: 357), and that the Day of Judgment will come when people take up the Qurʾan not because they are the best reciters or the most worthy souls, but only to sing for entertainment (al-Jawziyyah 1970: 1/168). The various lists of unacceptable practices in recitation found in the sources are prefaced by such statements as "Know that the reciters of our day have introduced many things, unacceptable because they exceed the limit or fall short of it, and that is done by means of melodies for the sake of directing people's attention to listen to them and pay heed to their melodies" (Naṣr 1930: 18).

Appendix B. The Seven *Aḥruf* and the *Qirā'āt*

1. For a bibliography of Western works and Arabic sources on the *qirā'āt*, see Paret 1979: 127–29.

2. For more examples and more complex texts, see al-Qurṭubī 1968: 1/41ff., and al-Ḥuṣarī 1966: 62–66.

3. Some have added to the seven three and then four more, making a total of fourteen *qirā'āt*.

Selected Bibliography

ʿAbduh, Ġunaym

1982 "Al Ḥalāl wal-Ḥarām fī l-fann." *al-Kawākib*, vol. 1614 (July 7).

Abū l-ʿAynayn, Kāmil

1974 "Al-Mūsīqā fī l-Qurʾān al-Karīm." *al-Majallah al-Mūsīqiyyah*, no. 1 (January), 24–25.

Adūnīs

1974 *Al-Ṯābit wa l-Mutaḥawwil*. Vol. 1. Beirut: Dār al-ʿAwdah.

ʿAlī, ʿAbdullah Yūsuf (trans. and commentator)

1946 *The Holy Qurʿān* (2nd edition). Washington, D.C. (?): Khalil al-Rawaf.

al-ʿAllāf, ʿAbd al-Karīm

1963/1382 A.H. *Al-Ṭarab ʿind al-ʿArab*. Baghdad: al-Maktabah al-Ahliyyah.

Anderson, Lois A.

1971 "The Interrelation of African and Arab Musics: Some Preliminary Considerations." In *Essays on Music and History in Africa*, edited by Klaus P. Wachsmann (Evanston: Northwestern University Press), 143–69.

Anonymous

1948 "Al-Taġannī bi l-Qurʾān wa Ḥukm al-Šarʿ fīh." *Majallat al-Mūsīqā wa l-Masraḥ*, no. 22 (December). Reprint 1974. In *al-Majallah al-Mūsīqiyyah*, no. 10 (October), 28–29.

Anonymous

1978 "Awwal Risālat Dukturāh ʿan: al-Mūsīqā: Ḥalāl am Ḥarām?" *al-Iḏāʿah wa l-Tilivizyūn*, no. 2257 (June 17), 46–47.

Anonymous

1979 "Hāʾulā . . . Yanšurūna l-fann wa Yaṣnaʿūna Nujūmahu." *al-Kawākib*, vol. 15 (June 19), 61–62.

Anonymous

1982 "Tartīl al-Qurʾān . . . hal huwa Ṭarab?" *al-Kawākib*, vol. 1613 (June 29).

Arberry, Arthur J. (trans.)

1955 *The Koran Interpreted*. New York: Macmillan.

al-Asad, Nāṣir al-Dīn

1969 *Al-Qiyan wa l-Ġinā' fī l-ʿAṣr al-Jāhilī*. Cairo: Dār al-Maʿārif.

ʿAwf, Aḥmad Muḥammad

1970 *Al-Azhar fī Alf ʿĀm*. Cairo: Majmaʿ al-Buḥūṯ al-Islamiyyah.

Baily, John

1977 "Music and Religion in Herat." Unpublished paper delivered at the 12th conference of the International Musicological Society. Berkeley, California.

al-Bāqillānī, Abū Bakr Muḥammad ibn al-Ṭayyib

1935 *Iʿjāz al-Qur'ān*. Cairo: n.p.

al-Bāqūrī, Aḥmad Ḥasan

1959 *Aṭar al-Qur'ān al-Karīm fī l-Luġah al-ʿArabiyyah*. Cairo: Dār al-Maʿārif.

al-Baʿṭī, Aḥmad and Munīr ʿAbd al-Bārī (eds.)

1978 "Niqābah li Qurrā' al-Qur'ān al-Karīm . . . li Māḏā?" *al-Ahrām* (April 21), 11.

Beeston, AFL

1974 "Parallelism in Arabic Prose." *Journal of Arabic Literature*, vol. 5, 134–46.

ben Cheneb, Muḥammad

1961 "Tadjwid." In the *Shorter Encyclopedia of Islam*, edited by H. A. R. Gibb and J. H. Kramers (Leiden: E. J. Brill), 557–58.

Bergsträsser, Gotthelf

1926 "Die Koranlesung des Hasan von Basra." *Islamica*, vol. 2, 11–57.

1932–33 "Die Koranlesung in Kairo." *Der Islam*, vols. 20, 21, 1–42 and 110–40.

Bergsträsser, Gotthelf and Otto Pretzl

1938 *Die Geschichte des Korantexts*. Vol. 3 of Theodor Nöldeke, *Geschichte des Qorans*. Leipzig: T. Weicher.

Biesterfeldt, Hans Heinrich

1976 "Notes on Abū Zayd al-Balkhi's Medico-Ethical Treatise, 'Maṣāliḥ al-Abdān wa l-Anfus.'" In *Actes du 8me Congrès de l'UEAT*, Aix en Provence, 29–33.

Blachère, Regis

1959 *Introduction au Coran* (2nd edition). Paris: Besson et Chantemerle.

Boubakeur, Si Hamza

1968 "Psalmodie coranique." In *Encyclopédie de musiques sacrées*, edited by Jacques Porte (Paris: Editions Labergerie), vol. 1, 388–403.

Burton, John W.

1977 *The Collection of the Qur'an*. Cambridge: Cambridge University Press.

Buṭrus, Fikrī

1968 *Al-Mūsīqā wa l-Ġinā' Munḏu Bad' al-Alīqah li l-'Ān*. Alexandria, Egypt: Issued by the author.

Cantineau, Jean and Leo Barbès
1942–47 "La récitation coranique à Damas et à Alger." *Annales de l'Institut des Etudes Orientales*, vol. 6, 66–107.
al-Daʿʿās, ʿIzzat ʿUbayd
1964/1384 A.H. *Fann al-Tajwīd*. Aleppo: Maktabat Rabīʿ.
al-Dānī, ʿAmr ʿUṯmān ibn Saʿīd
1930 *Kitāb al-Taʿsīr fī l-Qirāʾāt al-Sabʿ*. Vol. 2 of *Islamica*, edited by O. Pretzl.
n.d. *Al-Mufradāt al-Sabʿ*. Cairo: Maktabat al-Qurʾān.
D'Erlanger, Baron Rodolphe
1930–59 *La musique arabe*, vols. 1–6. Paris: Paul Geuthner.
Diyāb, Sāmī
1977 "Qirāʾat al-Qurʾān—Bayna l-Talḥin wa l-Tartīl." *al-Ahrām* (March 25), 11.
al-Dunyā, Ibn Abī
1938 See Robson, James 1938
Eickelman, Dale F.
1978 "The Art of Memory: Islamic Education and Its Social Reproduction." *Comparative Studies in Society and History*, vol. 20, no. 4 (October), 485–516.
Farmer, Henry George
1942 *Music: The Priceless Jewel, From the Kitab al-ʿIqd al-Farid of Ibn ʿAbd Rabbihi (d. 940)*. Bearsden, Scotland: Issued by the author.
1952 "The Religious Music of Islam." *Journal of the Royal Asiatic Society*, vol. 62, 60–65.
1954 "Muhammedan Music." In *Grove's Dictionary of Music*, edited by Eric Blum (5th ed.; London: Macmillan), vol. 5, 817–18.
1957 "The Music of Islam." In *The New Oxford History of Music*, vol. 1, *Ancient and Oriental Music*, edited by Egon Wellesq (Oxford: Oxford University Press), 228–54.
1965 "Ghināʾ." In the *Encyclopedia of Islam*, edited by B. Lewis, Ch. Pellat, and J. Schacht (2nd ed.; Leiden: E. J. Brill), vol. 2, 1072–75.
1973 *A History of Arabic Music to the Thirteenth Century*. London: Luzac. (Reprint of 1929 edition.)
al-Faruqi, Lois Ibsen/Lamyāʾ
1978 "Musical Accentuation in Qiraʾah or Qurʾanic Chant." Unpublished paper delivered at 108th annual meeting of the American Oriental Society, Toronto, Canada.
1979 "Tartīl al-Qurʾān al-Karīm." In *Islamic Perspective: Studies in Honor of Sayyid Abūl Aʿlā Mawdūdī*, edited by Khurshid Ahmad and Zafar Ishaq Ansari (Leicester, United Kingdom: Islamic Foundation), 105–19.
al-Fīrūzabādī
1913/1344 A.H. *Al-Qāmūs al-Muḥīṭ*. Vol. 4. Cairo: al-Maṭbaʿah al-Ḥusayniyyah al-Miṣriyyah.

Gätje, Helmut
1976 *The Qur'an and Its Exegesis*. Berkeley and Los Angeles: University of California Press.
al-Ġazālī, Abū Ḥāmid
n.d. *Iḥyā ʿUlūm al-Dīn*. Vols. 3 and 8. Cairo: Dār al-Šaʿb.
Geertz, Clifford
1976 "Art as a Cultural System." *Modern Language Notes*, vol. 91, 1473–99.
Gilsenan, Michael
1973 *Saint and Sufi in Modern Egypt: An Essay in the Sociology of Religion*. Oxford: Oxford University Press.
Goldziher, Ignacz
1920 *Die Richtungen der Islamischen Koranauslegung*. Leiden: E. J. Brill.
Graham, William A.
1982 "Qur'an as Spoken Word: An Islamic Contribution to the Understanding of Scripture." In *Islam and the History of Religions: Perspectives on the Study of a Religious Tradition*, edited by Richard C. Martin (University of Arizona Press, forthcoming).
Ḥamūdah, ʿAbd al-Wahhāb
1977 "Mūsīqā l-Qur'ān." *al-Majallah al-Mūsīqiyyah*, no. 46 (October–November), 25–28.
Ḥāšim, Aḥmad
1977 "Wāḥid Min al-Katātīb Yafūzu Dā'iman." *al-Ahrām* (November 11), 14.
Hodgson, M. G. S.
1974 *The Venture of Islam*. Vol. 1. Chicago and London: University of Chicago Press.
al-Ḥujwīrī, ʿAlī ibn ʿUṯmān
1976 *The Kashf al-Mahjub*. Translated by Reynold A. Nicholson. Lahore: Islamic Book Foundation. (Reprint of 1911 edition.)
al-Ḥuṣarī, Maḥmūd Xalīl
1966 *Maʿa l-Qur'ān al-Karīm*. Cairo: al-Majlis al-Aʿlā li l-Šu'ūn al-Islāmiyyah.
1967 *Maʿālim al-Ihtidā' ilā-Maʿrifat al-Wuqūf wa l-Ibtidā'*. Cairo: al-Majlis al-Aʿlā li l-Šu'ūn al-Islāmiyyah.
Ḥusayn, Ṭaha
1959 *Ḥadīṯ al-Arbiʿā': al-Ġinā' wa Nahḍat al-Ġazal*. Vol. 1. Cairo: Dār al-Maʿārif.
Husseini, H.
1979 "Iraqi Music in a C. Sc. Thesis." *Baghdad Observer*, vol. 7, no. 3402 (April 14).
Ibn ʿAbd Rabbih
1940–68 *Kitāb al-ʿIqd al-Farīd*. Vol. 6. Cairo: Lajnat al-Ta'līf wa l-Tarjamah wa l-Našr.

Ibn al-Aṭyab
1948/1367 A.H. *Al-Furqān*. Cairo: al-Maktabah al-Miṣriyyah.
Ibn al-Ḥājj
1929 *Al-Madxal*. Vol. 1. Cairo: al-Maṭbaʿah al-Miṣriyyah bi l-Azhar.
Ibn Ḥujjah al-Ḥamāwī
1888/1314 A.H. "Kitāb Ṯamarāt al-ʾAwrāq." In the margin of *Kitāb al-Mustaṭraf fī Kull Fann al-Mustaḏraf* by al-Ibsīhī (n.p.).
Ibn al-Jazarī
1908/1326 A.H. *Al-Tamhīd fī ʿIlm al-Tajwīd*. Cairo: ʿAlī Ḥasan al-Farrā.
n.d. *Al-Durrah al-Muḏiyyah fī l-Qirāʾāt al-Ṯalāṯ al-Mutammimah li l-ʿAšar*. Cairo: Muḥammad Sulaymān Ṣāliḥ.
1932 *Ġāyat al-Nihāyah fī Ṭabaqāt al-Qurrāʾ*. Vol. 1. Edited by G. Bergsträsser. Cairo: Maktabat al-Anjī. Reprint (n.d.) Baghdad: Maktabat al-Muṯannā.
1934/1353 A.H. *Matn al-Jazariyyah fī fann al-Tajwīd*. Cairo: al-Maktabah al-Tujāriyyah al-Kubrā.
1937/1350 A.H. *Munjid al-Muqriʾīn wa Muršid al-Ṭālibīn*. Cairo: Maktabat al-Quds.
Ibn Jinnī
1966–69/1386–89 A.H. *al-Muḥtasab*. Vols. 1 and 2. Edited by ʿAlī l-Najdī Nāṣif, ʿAbd al-Ḥalīm al-Najjār, ʿAbd al-Fattāḥ Ismāʿīl Šalabī. Cairo: al-Majlis al-Aʿlā li l-Buḥūṯ al-Islāmiyyah.
Ibn al-Manḏūr
1966 *Lisān al-ʿArab*. Vol. 19, 372–74. Cairo: Dār al-Miṣriyyah li l-Taʾlīf wa l-Tarjamah.
Ibn Qutaybah
1935 *Al-Maʿārif*. Edited by Muḥammad Ismāʿīl ʿAbd Allāh al-Ṣawt. Cairo: n.p.
1960 *Al-Maʿārif*. Cairo: Dār al-Kutub.
Ibn Saʿd, Muḥammad
1960 *Al-Ṭabaqāt al-Kubrā*. Vol. 1. Beirut: Dār Ṣādir.
Ibn Xaldūn
n.d. *Al-Muqaddimah*. Cairo: al-Maktabah al-Tujāriyyah al-Kubrā.
1958 *The Muqaddimah: An Introduction to History*. Translated by Franz Rosenthal. Vol. 2. New York: Pantheon Books.
Ibrāhīm, Ismāʿīl (ed.)
1979 "Ṭiflān Min Qaryah Ṣaġīrah Yaḥfūḏān bi l-Jāʾizah al-Ḏahabiyyah fī Musābaqah ʿĀlamiyyah li l-Qurʾān al-Karīm wa l-Suʾāl: Māḏā baʿd al-Jāʾizah?" *al-Ahrām* (August 27), 6.
al-Ibšīhī, Aḥmad
1888/1314 A.H. *Al-Mustaṭraf fī Kull Fann Mustaḏraf*. Cairo: n.p.
al-Isfahānī, Abū l-Faraj
1927–74 *Kitāb al-Aġānī*. 23 vols. Cairo: Dār al-Kutub al-Miṣriyyah (vols. 1–16), al-Hayʾah al-Miṣriyyah al-ʿĀmmah li l-Taʾlīf wa

l-Našr (vols. 17–23), al-Hay'ah al-Miṣriyyah li l-Kitāb (vols. 18–23).

Ismā'īl, Ša'bān Muḥammad
1978 *Ma'a l-Qur'ān al-Karīm*. Cairo: Dār al-Ittiḥād al-'Arabī li l-Ṭibā'ah.

al-Ixtiyār, Nasīb
1953 *Ma'ālim al-Mūsīqā l-'Arabiyyah*. Beirut: al-Maktabah al-'Aṣriyyah.

Jansen, J. J. G.
1974 *The Interpretation of the Koran in Modern Egypt*. Leiden: E. J. Brill.

al-Jawziyyah, Ibn Qayyim Muḥammad ibn Abī Bakr
1970 *Zād al-Ma'ād*. Vol. 1. Cairo: n.p.

Jeffrey, Arthur
1937 *Materials for the History of the Text of the Qur'an*. Leiden: E. J. Brill.

Jomier, Jacques
1952 "La place du Coran dans la vie quotidienne en Egypte." *Revue de l'Institut des Belles Lettres Arabes*, no. 58, 131–67.

Kafāfī, Muḥammad 'Abd al-Salām
1972 *Fī 'Ulūm al-Qur'ān: Dirāsāt wa Muḥāḍarāt*. Beirut: Dār al-Nahḍah al-'Arabiyyah.

Kahle, Paul
1949 "The Arabic Readers of the Koran." *Journal of Near East Studies*, vol. 8, 65–71.

Kāmil, Maḥmūd
1973 *Taḏawwuq al-Mūsīqā l-'Arabiyyah*. Cairo: Muḥammad al-Amīn.

Lane, Edward
1863–93 *Madd al-Qamus: An Arabic-English Lexicon*. 8 vols. London: Williams and Norgate. Reprint 1968. Beirut: Librairie du Liban.

Macdonald, Duncan B. (trans.)
1901 "Emotional Religion in Islam as Affected by Music and Singing: Being a Translation of a Book of the Ihya 'Ulum ad-Din of al-Ghazzali with Analysis, Annotation and Appendices." *Asiatic Journal*, 1–28, 192–252, 705–748.

El Mahdi, Salah
1972 *La musique arabe*. Paris: n.p.

Majd al-Dīn
1938 See Robson, James 1938.

al-Makkī, Abū Ṭālib Muḥammad ibn 'Alī
1961 *Qūt al-Qulūb fī Mu'āmalāt al-Maḥbūb*. Vol. 1. Cairo: Muṣṭafā l-Bābī l-Ḥalabī.

Martin, Richard C.
1982 "Understanding the Qur'an in Text and Context." *History of Religions*, vol. 21, no. 4, 361–84.

al-Mufaḍḍal
1921 *Diwān Al-Mufaḍḍaliyyāt*. Edited by Charles James Lyall. Oxford: Clarendon Press.
Muḥaysin, Muḥammad Sālim
1970/1390 A.H. *Muršid al-Murīd ilā ʿIlm al-Tajwīd*. Cairo: Maktabat al-Kulliyyāt al-Azhariyyah.
al-Najmī, Kamāl
1968 *Aṣwāt wa Aġānī ʿArabiyyah*. Cairo: Dār al-Hilāl.
Naṣr, Muḥammad Makkī
1930/1349 A.H. *Nihāyat al-Qawl al-Mufīd fī ʿIlm al-Tajwīd*. Cairo: Maṭbaʿat Muṣṭafā l-Bābī l-Ḥalabī wa Awlādih.
Naṣr, Seyyid Hossein
1966 *Ideals and Realities of Islam*. London: George Allen and Unwin.
1971 "The Influence of Sufism on Traditional Persian Music." *Islamic Culture*, no. 45, 171–79.
al-Nawawī
1971 *Fatāwā l-Imām al-Nawawī al-Musammā bi l-Masāʾil al-Manṣūrah*. Edited by Šayx ʿAlāʾ al-Dīn ibn al-ʿAṭṭār. Aleppo: n.p.
Nöldeke, Theodor
1909 *Geschichte des Qorans*. Vols. 1 and 2. Edited by Friederich Schwally. Leipzig: T. Weicher. Reprint 1970. Hildesheim, N.Y.: G. Ohm. (See also Bergsträsser, 1938.)
al-Nuwayrī, Šihāb al-Dīn
1925 *Nihāyat al-Arab fī Funūn al-Adab*. Vol. 4. Cairo: Dār al-Kutub al-Miṣriyyah.
Pacholczyk, Jozef
1971 "Regulative Principles in the Koran Chant of *Shaikh* ʿAbdu'l-Bāsiṭ ʿAbdu'ṣ-Ṣamad." Ph.D. dissertation, 1970, University of California, Los Angeles. Ann Arbor, Michigan: University Microfilms.
Paret, R.
1979 "Ḳirāʾa, Reading." In *Encylopedia of Islam*, edited by C. E. Bosworth, E. van Donzel, B. Lewis, and Ch. Pellat (Leiden: E. J. Brill), vol. 5, fasc. 79–80, 81–82, 127–29.
Pretzl, Otto
1933–34 "Die Wissenschaft der Koranlesung." *Islamica*, vol. 6, 1–47, 230–46, 290–331. (See also al-Danī 1930.)
al-Qāḍi, ʿAbd al-Fattāḥ
n.d. *Al-Qirāʾāt al-Šaḏḏah wa Tawjīhihā Min Luġāt al-ʿArab*. Cairo: Dār Iḥyāʾ al-Kutub al-ʿArabiyyah.
n.d. *Al-Wāfī fī Šarḥ al-Šaṭibiyyah fī l-Qirāʾāt al-Sabʿ*. Cairo: Maktabat wa Maṭbāʿat ʿAbd al-Raḥmān Muḥammad li Našr al-Qurʾān al-Karīm wa Kutub al-Islamiyyah.
1973/1393 A.H. *Al-Qirāʾāt fī Naḏr al-Mustašriqīn wa l-Mulḥidīn*. Cairo: Majmaʿ al-Buḥūṯ al-Islamiyyah.

Qamḥāwī, Muḥammad al-Ṣādiq
1972–73/1392 A.H. *Al-Burhān fī Tajwīd al-Qur'ān wa Risālah fī Faḍā'il al-Qur'ān*. Kuwait: Dār al-Qur'ān al-Karīm.
al-Qāri', ʿAlī ibn Sulṭān Muḥammad
1948 *Al-Minaḥ al-Fikriyyah: Šarḥ al-Muqaddimah al-Jazariyyah*. Cairo: Maktabat wa Maṭbāʿat Muṣṭafā l-Bābī al-Ḥalabī wa Awlādih.
al-Qāṣiḥ
1934/1352 A.H. *Sirāj al-Qāri' al-Mubtadā wa Taḏkār al-Muqri' al-Muntahā*. Cairo: al-Maktabah al-Tujāriyyah al-Kubrā.
Qureshi, Regula
1969 "Tarannum: The Chanting of Urdu Poetry." *Ethnomusicology*, vol. 13, no. 3, 425–68.
al-Qurṭubī
1968 *Al-Jāmiʿ li-Aḥkām al-Qur'ān*. Vol. 1. Cairo: Dār al-Kātib al-ʿArabī li l-Ṭibāʿah wa l-Nāšr.
al-Qušayrī
1959 *Al-Risālah al-Qušayriyyah fī ʿIlm al-Taṣawwuf*. Vol. 1. Cairo: Muṣṭafā l-Bābī l-Ḥalabī wa Awlādih.
Racy, Ali Jihad
1977 "Musical Change and Commercial Recording in Egypt, 1904–1932." Ph.D. dissertation, 1977, University of Illinois at Urbana-Champaign. Ann Arbor, Michigan: University Microfilms.
Razack, Sayed Ismail A. and Ahmad el-Sharqawi (eds.)
1966 *Voice from Heaven: Al-Qari Shaikh Abdul Basit Abdus Samud*. Cairo: n.p.
Robson, James (ed. and trans.)
1938 *Tracts on Listening to Music—Being Dhamm al-Malahi by Ibn Abi l-Dunya and Bawariq al-Ilmaʿ by Majd al-Din al-Tusi al-Ghazali*. London: Royal Asiatic Society.
Rosenthal, Franz
1958 See Ibn Xaldūn n.d.
Roychoudhury, M. L.
1957 "Music in Islam." *Journal of the Asiatic Society, Letters*, vol. 23, no. 2, 43–103.
al-Safāqisī, Sayyidī ʿAlī l-Nūrī
1934/1352 A.H. "Kitāb Ġayṯ al-Nafʿ fī l-Qirā'āt al-Sabʿ." In the margin of *Sirāj al-Qāri' al-Mubtadā* by al-Qāṣiḥ. Cairo: al-Maktabah al-Tujāriyyah al-Kubrā.
al-Saʿīd, Labīb
1967/1387 A.H. *Al-Jamʿ al-Ṣawtī l-Awwal li l-Qurʿān al-Karīm aw al-Muṣḥaf al-Murattal*. Cairo: Dār al-Kātib al-ʿArabī li l-Ṭibāʿah wa l-Našr.
1970 *Al-Taġannī bi l-Qur'ān*. Cairo: al-Maktabah al-Taqāfiyyah.
1976/1397 A.H. *Al-Maqāri' wa l-Qurrā*. Cairo: Maṭbaʿat al-Saʿādah.

Salīm, Ḥasan Ṭanṭāwī
1939 "Aṯar al-Qur'ān al-Karīm fī l-Mūsīqā l-ʿArabiyyah." *al-Majallah al-Mūsīqiyyah*, no. 80, 245–48. Reprint 1977. *al-Majallah al-Mūsīqiyyah*, no. 42, 23–27.
Sāmī, Maḥmūd
1979 "Awwalu Niqābah li Qurrā' al-Qur'ān al-Karīm." *al-Ahrām* (April 27), 13.
Ṣaqr, ʿAbd al-Badīʿ
1976/1396 A.H. *Al-Tajwīd wa ʿUlūm al-Qur'ān* (6th edition). Cairo: Maktabat Wahbah.
al-Sarrāj al-Ṭūsī, Abū Naṣr
1960/1370 A.H. *Kitāb al-Lumaʿ*. Edited by ʿAbd al-Ḥalīm Maḥmūd and ʿAbd al-Bāqī Surūr. Cairo: Dār al-Kutub al-Ḥadīṯ.
Semaan, Khalil
1962 "Tajwid as a Source in Phonetic Research." *Wiener Zeitschrift für die Kunde des Morganlandes*, vol. 58, 112–20.
1968 *Linguistics in the Middle Ages: Phonetic Studies in Early Islam*. Leiden: E. J. Brill.
Shiloah, Amnon
1968 "L'Islam et la musique." In *Encyclopédie des musiques sacrées*, edited by Jacques Porte (Paris: Editions Labergerie), Vol. 1, 146–69.
al-Suyūṭī, Jalāl al-Dīn
1910 *Al-Itqān fī ʿUlūm al-Dīn*. Vol. 1. Cairo: Maṭbaʿat Ḥijāzī.
Talbi, M.
1958 "La Qirā'a bi-l-alḥān." *Arabica*, vol. 5, no. 2 (May), 183–90.
Taymūr, Aḥmad
1963 *Al-Mūsīqā wa Ġinā' ʿinda l-ʿArab*. Cairo: n.p.
Touma, Habib Hassan
1975*a* "Die Koranrezitation: Eine Form der Religiosen Musik der Araber." *Bessler-Archiv*, Neue Folge, vol. 23, 87–133.
1975*b* *Die Musik der Araber*. Wilhelmshaven: Heinrichschafen's Verlag.
1976 "Relations between Aesthetics and Improvisation in Arab Music." *World of Music*, vol. 18, no. 2, 33–36.
Tufayl, S. Muḥammad
1974 *The Qur'an Reader*. Trinidad: Ladies Islamic Association.
al-Ušmūnī, Aḥmad ibn Muḥammad
1889/1308 A.H. *Manār al-Hudā*. Vol. 1. Cairo: al-Maṭbaʿah al-Ḫayriyyah.
ʿUṯmān, ʿĀmir ibn al-Saʿīd
1969/1389 A.H. *Kayfa Yutlā l-Qur'ān* (as dictated to Dr. Ḥusnī Hijāzī). Cairo: n.p.
Vollers, K.
1961 "Al-Azhar." In the *Shorter Encyclopedia of Islam*, edited by H. A. R. Gibb and J. H. Kramers (Leiden: E. J. Brill), 50–52.

Wansbrough, John
1977 *Qur'anic Studies: Sources and Methods of Scriptural Interpretation*. Oxford: Oxford University Press.

Watt, Montgomery W.
1970 *Bell's Introduction to the Qur'an*. Edinburgh: Edinburgh University Press.

Wehr, Hans
1961 *A Dictionary of Modern Written Arabic*. Edited by J. Milton Cowan. Ithaca, N.Y.: Spoken Language Services.

Weiss, Bernard, Morroe Berger, and M. A. Rauf (trans. and adapters)
1975 *The Recited Koran: A History of the First Recorded Version/Labib as-Sa'id*. Princeton, N.J.: Darwin Press.

Wensinck, A. J.
1961 "Ṣalāt." In the *Shorter Encyclopedia of Islam*, edited by H. A. R. Gibb and J. H. Kramers (Leiden: E. J. Brill), 493–95.

Xašabah, Ġaṭṭās 'Abd al-Mālik
1975 "Al-Qurrā' wa l-Muġannun . . . wa Haqq al-Adā' al-'Alānī." *al-Majallah al-Mūsīqiyyah*, no. 17 (May), 11–12.

al-Zarkašī, Muḥammad ibn 'Abd Allāh
1957 *Al-Burhān fī 'Ulūm al-Qur'ān*. Vol. 1. Edited by Muḥammad Abū l-Faḍl Ibrāhīm. Cairo: Dār Iḥyā' al-Kutub al-'Arabiyyah.

Index

www.ingramcontent.com/pod-product-compliance
Ingram Content Group UK Ltd.
Pitfield, Milton Keynes, MK11 3LW, UK
UKHW032029240225
455518UK00001B/94

9 781477 306208